Higher Education in Turmoil

The Changing World of Internationalization

GLOBAL PERSPECTIVES ON HIGHER EDUCATION

Volume 2

Higher education worldwide is in a period of transition, affected by globalization, the advent of mass access, changing relationships between the university and the state, and the new technologies, among others. *Global Perspectives on Higher Education* provides cogent analysis and comparative perspectives on these and other central issues affecting postsecondary education worldwide.

Series Editor:

Philip G. Altbach
Center for International Higher Education, Boston College

Editorial Board:

Manuel Gil Antón, *Autonomous Metropolitan University of Mexico, Tlalpan, Mexico*
Molly Lee, *UNESCO Bangkok, Thailand*
Damtew Teferra, *Journal of Higher Education in Africa, Boston College, USA*

This series is co-published with the Center for International Higher Education at Boston College.

Higher Education in Turmoil

The Changing World of Internationalization

Jane Knight
*Ontario Institute for Studies in Education,
University of Toronto,
Canada*

SENSE PUBLISHERS
ROTTERDAM / TAIPEI

A C.I.P. record for this book is available from the Library of Congress.

ISBN: 978-90-8790-520-0 (paperback)
ISBN: 978-90-8790-521-7 (hardback)
ISBN: 978-90-8790-522-4 (e-book)

Published by: Sense Publishers,
P.O. Box 21858, 3001 AW
3001 AW Rotterdam
Rotterdam, The Netherlands
http://www.sensepublishers.com

Printed on acid-free paper

All Rights Reserved © 2008 Sense Publishers

No part of this work may be reproduced, stored in a retrieval system, or transmitted in any form or by any means, electronic, mechanical, photocopying, microfilming, recording or otherwise, without written permission from the Publisher, with the exception of any material supplied specifically for the purpose of being entered and executed on a computer system, for exclusive use by the purchaser of the work.

TABLE OF CONTENTS

Abbreviations... vii

Introduction... ix

1. The Internationalization of Higher Education in the 21st Century: New Realities and Complexities..1

2. An Internationalization Model: Meaning, Rationales, Approaches, and Strategies...19

3. Monitoring the Quality and Progress of Internationalization.....................39

4. An Internationalization Quality Review Process at the Institutional Level..63

5. Borderless, Offshore, Transnational, and Crossborder Education: Are They Different?..81

6. Crossborder Education: Programs and Providers on the Move..................97

7. Higher Education Crossing Borders: Quality Assurance and Accreditation Issues...123

8. Financial Aspects and Implications of Commercial Crossborder Education..137

9. Higher Education in a Trade Environment: An Analysis of the General Agreement on Trade in Services (GATS)..149

10. The Impact of GATS on Higher Education Policy and Practice...............171

11. Internationalization around the World: The Results of a Global Survey on the International Dimension of Higher Education............................187

Index..229

ABBREVIATIONS

AAU. African Association of Universities
ACA. Academic Co-operation Association
ACE. American Council on Education
ACU. Association of Commonwealth Universities
ADEA. Association for the Development of Education in Africa
APEC. Asia Pacific Economic Council
APQN. Asia Pacific Quality Network
AU. African Union
AUCC. Association of Universities and Colleges of Canada
CERI. Center for Education, Research, and Innovation
CHEA. Council for Higher Education Accreditation
CHEPS. Center for Higher Education Policy Studies
CPC. Central Product Classification
EU-ASEAN. Association of South East Asian Nations
EU. European Union
GATE. Global Alliance for Transnational Education
GATS. General Agreement on Trade in Services
GATT. General Agreement on Trade and Tariffs
GEI. Global Education Index
GUNI. Global University Network for Innovation
HDI. Human Development Index
HEIs. higher education institutions
IAU. International Association of Universities
ICT. information and communication technology
IDP. International Development Program
IMHE. Institutional Management of Higher Education
ISO. International Standards Association
MFN. Most Favored Nation
NAFTA. North American Free Trade Association
NIIT. National Indian Institute of Technology
NT. National Treatment
NUAs. national-level university associations
OAU. Organization of African Unity
OBHE. Observatory for Borderless Higher Education
OECD. Organization for Economic Cooperation and Development
RMIT University. Formerly Royal Melbourne Institute of Technology
RUAs. regional-level university associations
SAUVCA. South Africa University Vice Chancellors Assocation
TRIPS. Trade Related Aspects of Intellectual Property Rights
UKCOSA. United Kingdom Council for Overseas Student Affairs
UMAP. University Mobility Program of Asia Pacific

UNCTAD. United Nations Conference for Trade and Development
UNDP. United Nations Development Program
UNESCO. United Nations Educational Scientific and Cultural Organization
WTO. World Trade Organization.

INTRODUCTION

Internationalization is one of the major forces impacting and shaping higher education as it evolves to meet the challenges of the 21st century. Overall, the picture of internationalization that is emerging is one of complexity, diversity, and differentiation. The internationalization of higher education is a process in rapid evolution—both as actor and as reactor to the new realities of globalization and to the rather turbulent times facing higher education.

The purpose of this book is to highlight new developments and trends related to the international dimension of higher education during this period of turmoil and change. The first two chapters examine the growth in the importance and scope of internationalization, identify macro trends, and examine emerging issues. The conceptual framework for internationalization presented in these chapters is designed to aid in analyzing the diversity of (and shifts in) rationales, approaches, policies, and strategies that must be considered and weighed during the process of integrating an international, intercultural, and global dimension into higher education's major functions and delivery modes at both the institutional and national levels.

Internationalization is not an end in itself but rather is a means to an end. While internationalization's purposes and anticipated benefits differ from institution to institution and from country to country, the overall expectation is widely shared that internationalization will contribute to the quality and relevance of higher education in a more interconnected and interdependent world. This expectation means that the internationalization process itself needs to be reviewed and evaluated. Chapters 3 and 4 focus on systems and tools for monitoring the quality and progress of implementing an internationalization plan or strategy at the institutional level.

The international dimension is understood to include its manifestations both "at home" and "abroad." The growing demand for higher (or further) education in many countries has led to a major expansion in academic mobility and an unprecedented interest in crossborder education. While the number of students who study abroad is growing every year, so is the number of traditional higher education institutions and new providers who are delivering their academic programs internationally. It is no longer just the students who are moving; so are programs and providers. The growing phenomenon of delivering education to students in their home countries through franchising, twinning, distance education, or branch campuses receives in-depth exploration in Chapters 5, 6, 7, and 8. First, the similarities and differences among the concepts of "borderless," "transnational," "offshore," and "crossborder" education are examined. "Crossborder education" is the term of choice in this book, given the central role that national and regional jurisdiction boundaries play in providing and regulating higher education. The growth in new types of providers, delivery, and partnership arrangements may signal progress and innovation in crossborder education; but such proliferation also creates much misunderstanding and confusion. An analytical framework is offered and examined to clarify various types of crossborder providers and modes of program delivery. Individual chapters are also dedicated to examining two controversial and key aspects of crossborder education: quality assurance/accreditation (Chapter 7) and financial implications (Chapter 8).

The General Agreement on Trade in Services (GATS) has been an important wake-up call for higher education. While academic mobility has been an aspect of higher education for centuries, it is only now in the beginning of the 21st century that an international trade law treats higher education as a tradable commodity subject to a multilateral set of trade rules. Two chapters address the considerations and issues posed by GATS. Chapter 9 provides a basic introduction to the principles, purposes, and elements of the trade agreement, while Chapter 10 spells out the implications of those elements for higher education. GATS is still in the negotiating phase, and its potential impact on higher education—including new opportunities, benefits, and risks—are still at the conceptual level, exactly the reason why higher education policymakers and practitioners should become involved at this stage.

The final chapter reports on the results of the worldwide survey on internationalization carried out in 2005 by the International Association of Universities. This is the largest survey of its kind to date, unique in scope and findings, and designed to be replicated at regular intervals to track trends over time. It polled the opinions of leaders in higher education institutions and national university associations in 95 countries. The findings paint a fascinating—and sometimes counterintuitive—picture of higher education's international dimension during this decade of turmoil and turbulence. The findings are presented in terms of differences and similarities among the six regions of the world and between developed and developing countries. It is not possible to present all the findings of the survey, so this chapter gives priority to the following aspects of internationalization: importance, rationales at institutional and national levels, benefits and risks, future growth areas, implementation of an internationalization strategy at the institutional level, geographical priorities for internationalization activities over the next few years, and emerging issues that require more attention. Grateful appreciation is extended to the International Association of Universities for permission to include these results in this book.

The growing interest in the international dimension and delivery of higher education is accompanied by an increase in the number of terms used to describe the changes. Even though one objective of this publication is to examine the meaning of key terms in the world of internationalization, it is important to be clear at the outset how different terms and concepts are used. The following list arranges the most frequently used terms hierarchically—from generic concepts such as "globalization" and the "internationalization of higher education" to very specific terms such as "trade of commercial education services."

As this volume uses the term, *globalization* is the process that is increasing the flow of people, culture, ideas, values, knowledge, technology, and economy across borders, resulting in a more interconnected and interdependent world. Globalization affects each country in different ways and can have positive and/or negative consequences, according to a nation's specific history, traditions, culture, priorities, and resources. Education is one of the sectors impacted by globalization.

INTRODUCTION

The internationalization of higher education is also a process, albeit different from globalization. Internationalization of higher education is the process of integrating an international, intercultural, and global dimension into the purpose, functions (teaching, research, and service), and delivery of higher education at the institutional and national levels.

Internationalization strategies can include international cooperation and development projects; institutional agreements and networks; the international/intercultural dimension of the teaching/learning process, curriculum, and research; campus-based extracurricular clubs and activities; the mobility of academics through exchange, field work, sabbaticals, and consultancy work; the recruitment of international students; student exchange programs and semesters abroad; joint/double degree programs; twinning partnerships; branch campuses, etc. The international dimension of higher education includes both campus-based activities and cross-border initiatives.

Crossborder education refers to the movement of people, knowledge, programs, providers, curriculum, etc. across national or regional jurisdictional borders. Crossborder education is a subset of internationalization and can be part of development cooperation projects, academic exchange programs, and commercial initiatives.

Trade of education services is a term used primarily by the trade sector. It focuses on crossborder education initiatives that are commercial in nature and are usually intended to be for profit, although this is not always the case.

Acknowledgements

Hans de Wit and Philip Altbach have been close and important colleagues during my journey of studying the international dimensions of higher education. To them I extend a deep gratitude for their inspiration, partnership, and support.

The chapters in this book are edited, expanded, and updated versions of previously published papers. Grateful appreciation is extended to the different organizations and publishers for their permission to include them in this book. Special thanks go to Lavina Fielding Anderson who completed the editing of the manuscript with professionalism, collegiality, and an endless supply of patience.

The final manuscript was prepared during the period of my visiting professorship at the Research Institute of Higher Education of Hiroshima University and my participation in the 2007–2008 Fulbright New Century Scholars Program. I wish to acknowledge the interest and support of both institutions in bringing this publication to fruition and to thank them and my colleagues at the Comparative International Development Education Centre at the Ontario Institute for Studies in Education of the University of Toronto, Canada.

CHAPTER ONE

THE INTERNATIONALIZATION OF HIGHER EDUCATION IN THE 21ST CENTURY:

New Realities and Complexities

Internationalization is changing the world of higher education, and globalization is changing the world of internationalization. Key drivers for this transformation are the development of advanced communication and technological services, the dominance of the knowledge society, increased international labor mobility, more emphasis on the market economy and the trade liberalization, increased levels of private investment and decreased public support for education, and lifelong learning. As the 21st century progresses, the international dimension of postsecondary education is becoming increasingly important and at the same time, more and more complex.

Internationalization is a term that is being used more and more to discuss the international dimension of higher education and, more widely, postsecondary eduation. Because it means different things to different people, it appears in the literature in a variety of ways. While it is encouraging to see increased attention to and use of "internationalization," there is a great deal of confusion about what it means. For some people, it means a series of international activities such as academic mobility for students and teachers; international linkages, partnerships, and projects; new international academic programs and research initiatives. For others it means delivering education to other countries using a variety of face-to-face and distance techniques and such new types of arrangements as branch campuses or franchises. To many, it means including an international, intercultural, and/or global dimension in the curriculum and teaching learning process. Still others see international development projects or, alternatively, the increasing emphasis on trade in higher education as internationalization. Finally, there is frequent confusion about the relationship of internationalization to globalization. Is internationalization the same as globalization? If so, why, how, and to what end? If not, then how is it different or what is the relationship between these two dynamic processes? Thus, "internationalization" is interpreted and used in different ways, in different countries, and by different stakeholders.

In addition to questions about what, exactly, the term means, other important questions are being raised about internationalization: What is the purpose of internationalization? What are the benefits and risks? What values undergird it? Who are the main actors, stakeholders, and beneficiaries? What are the positive consequences, the unintended results, and the negative implications? How are institutions responding to the competing interests in the domain of internationalization? What are the policy and funding implications of increased emphasis on internationalization both at the national and institutional level? How are governments and NGOs addressing the issue and moving forward? Is internationalization a response to or a stimulant for globalization? What role does internationalization play in the brain drain, homogenization/hybridization of culture, and international labor mobility?

Clearly, these issues and questions are an important part of the changes in the international dimension of higher education during this transition period marked by turmoil, competition, and anxiety. Addressing them squarely is critical in making sense of the internationalization process and in making it benefit higher education.

THE EVOLUTION OF INTERNATIONAL EDUCATION TERMINOLOGY

"Internationalization" is not a new term nor is the debate over its definition new. "Internationalization" has been used for years in political science and governmental relations, but its popularity in the education sector has really soared only since the early 1980s. Prior to this time, "international education" and "international cooperation" were favored terms—and still are in some countries. In the 1990s, the discussion centered on differentiating "international education" from such overlapping terms as "comparative education," "global education," and "multi-cultural education." But today, the relationships and nuances of meaning among "crossborder," "transnational," "borderless," and "international" modes of education are causing confusion. Table 1.1 provides a longitudinal view of the evolution of terms related to the international dimension of higher education.

Table 1.1. Evolution of international education terminology

New Terms (Since 1990s)	Existing Terms	Traditional Terms
Generic Terms		
Globalization	Internationalization	International education
Borderless education	Multicultural education	International development
Crossborder education	Intercultural education	cooperation
Transnational education	Global education	Comparative education
Virtual education	Distance education	Correspondence
Iinternationalization "abroad"	Offshore/overseas education	education
Internationalization "at home"		
Specific Elements		
Education providers	International students	Foreign students
Corporate universities	Study abroad	Student exchange
Liberalization of educational	Institution agreements	Development projects
services	Partnership projects	Cultural agreements
Networks	Area studies	Language study
Virtual universities	Double/joint degrees	
Branch campus		
Twinning and franchise		
programs		
Global Education Index		

Source: Knight (2005).

During the 1960s, the most commonly used terms were "international cooperation," "international relations," and "international education," usually defined in terms of such activities as development projects, foreign students, and international academic and cultural agreements. In the mid-1980s, "internationalization" was likewise defined by such activities as study abroad, language studies, institutional agreements, and area studies. During the first decade of the 21st century, however, less emphasis has been given to development activities and more to academic mobility which includes students, research, programs, and providers moving across borders (Marginson & Sawir, 2005). Also characterizing this stage has been a greater orientation toward commercial and market-driven activities. A third defining characteristic has been substantial growth in international academic networks and partnerships based on mutual benefits and collaboration—in other words, for-profit and nonprofit aspects of the internationalization of education.

The international dimension is a key factor, shaping and challenging the higher education sector in countries all over the world. Since the 1990s, it has become a formidable force for change, perhaps *the* central feature of the higher education sector. Landmarks of this changing horizon include:
- The development of new international networks and consortia
- The growing numbers of students, professors, and researchers participating in academic mobility schemes
- The increase in the number of courses, programs, and qualifications that focus on comparative and international themes
- More emphasis on developing international/intercultural and global competencies
- Stronger interest in international themes and collaborative research
- A growing number of crossborder delivery of academic programs
- An increase in campus-based extracurricular activities with an international or multicultural component
- The impetus given to recruiting foreign students
- The rise in the number of joint or double degrees
- The expansion in partnerships, franchises, offshore satellite campuses
- The establishment of new national, regional, and international organizations focused on international education
- New regional and national-level government policies and programs supporting academic mobility and other internationalization initiatives.

Clearly, the international dimension of higher education has been steadily increasing in importance, scope, and complexity. Could anyone have anticipated the creative uses of information and communication technologies (ICT) by which international "click" institutions are extending, complementing, and in some cases competing with traditional "brick" institutions? Who would have predicted the current rate and state of massification, privatization, corporatization, and commercialization of crossborder higher education? The diversity of actors, providers, and recently interested stakeholders are bringing new waves of innovation, influence, and competition to the provision of international higher education and the policies governing it. In short, the world of higher education is changing and the world in which higher education plays a significant role is in turmoil and undergoing a significant transformation.

NEW REALITIES AND CHALLENGES OF TODAY'S ENVIRONMENT

It is impossible to look at the international dimension of higher education in the first decade of the 21st century without considering the realities of the environment in which higher education is operating (Innis & Hellsten, 2004). Changes and challenges are springing up as the changing environment of globalization impacts education but also as internationalization itself becomes an agent of change. Most of these challenges group themselves in eight areas: globalization, regionalization, information and communication technologies, new providers, alternate funding sources, borderless issues, lifelong learning, and the growth in the numbers and diversity of actors.

Globalization

Globalization is probably the most pervasive and powerful feature of the changing environment. As a phenomenon, it dominates the minds of policymakers, academics, and professionals/practitioners no matter what their sector or discipline. Education is no exception (Stromquist, 2007). The role of education—particularly postsecondary education—as both agent and reactor to globalization is a critical area of debate and study. The discussion on its nature, causes, elements, consequences, and future implications for education is prolific, rather controversial, and very important (Altbach, 2006; Breton & Lambert, 2003; Enders & Fulton, 2002; Marginson, 2001; Scott, 2000). This volume purposely adopts a neutral definition of "globalization," also positioning it as a key environmental factor with multiple effects, both positive and negative, on education.

It is important to note that the discussion does not center on the "globalization of education" per se. Rather, it is presented as a phenomenon that impacts internationalization. In fact, substantial efforts have been made during this past decade (Knight & de Wit, 1999) to maintain the focus on the "internationalization of education" and to avoid using the term "globalization of education." This approach has had mixed results, but some success has been achieved in ensuring that these two terms are not seen as synonyms and are not used interchangeably.

Globalization is not usually seen as a neutral concept. Laden with implications of political, social, and economic turmoil, it engenders strong reactions, both supportive and critical of its process and impact (Odin & Mancias, 2004). This volume's working definition of globalization is the flow of people, culture, ideas, values, knowledge, technology, and economy across borders resulting in a more interconnected and interdependent world. This definition acknowledges that globalization is a multifaceted process that can impact countries in vastly different ways—economically, culturally, politically, and technologically. But it does not take an ideological stance on whether this impact has positive and/or negative consequences. A key aspect of this definition is that it refers to borders of countries and infers worldwide scope and movement; thus, it is decidedly different from "internationalization," which emphasizes relations between and among nations.

Key elements of globalization include: (a) the knowledge society, (b) information and communication technologies, (c) the market economy, (d) trade liberalization, and (e) changes in governance structures. It remains a matter of debate whether these factors are causes or effects of globalization (in many cases they are almost certainly both); but this discussion treats them as critical elements of globalization that have a major impact on the education sector.

Table 1.2 describes each of these five elements of globalization, noting some of their more important implications for higher education in general and for the international dimension in particular. This table presents highlights only, not the full analysis. Its purpose is to illustrate several of the major environmental changes that are shaping the responses and actions of internationalization to globalization. It is important to note that they relate to all aspects of internationalization—curriculum and teaching, student and academic mobility, the crossborder delivery of education programs, international development projects, the study of foreign languages, commercial trade, staff development, etc. Although the table is arranged in three columns, they should not be read as aligned. Globalization is not a linear process. The five elements of globalization listed in Column 1 have implications for many aspects of higher education and, in turn, for the international dimension.

Regionalization

An unexpected result of globalization is the growing importance of regions. Forecasts that the nation-state would erode under globalization's impact have so far proved too pessimistic. Instead, regional needs and networks have developed a new importance. Examples are such regional-based trade blocs as the North American Free Trade Association (NAFTA), Asia Pacific Economic Council (APEC), and European Union (EU). The development of regional-based organizations, consortia, and alliances are further illustrations of the regionalization trend. Higher education has seen the development of new regional-based mobility programs—for example, the University Mobility Program of Asia Pacific (UMAP), which focuses on student mobility schemes among member institutions. New regionwide quality assurance agencies have been developed in all regions of the world.

Building on the success of ERASMUS, the first student mobility program sponsored by the European Commission, interregional mobility programs have now developed, of which EU-ASEAN and EU-Latin America are examples. International education organizations are operating now in Europe, Asia Pacific, and North America, while new organizations are even now being formed in Latin America and Africa.

South-to-South cooperation and networks are increasing. Regional hubs are being developed as several Asian countries—including Singapore, Japan, Malaysia, and India—are establishing themselves as a regional education centers to capitalize on the growing demand for higher education from Asian countries and the desire to increase their competitiveness in research and technology. Increased economic,

Table 1.2. The implications of five elements of globalization for the internationalization of higher education

Element of Globalization	Impact on Higher Education	Implications for the International Dimension of Higher Education
Knowledge Society Increasing importance is attached to the production and use of knowledge as a wealth creator for nations.	A growing emphasis on continuing education, life-long learning, and continual professional development; creates a greater unmet demand for post-secondary education. The need to develop new skills and knowledge results in new types of programs and qualifications. Universities' role in research and knowledge production alters, becomes more commercialized.	New types of private and public providers deliver education and training programs across borders—e.g., private media companies, networks of public/private institutions, corporate universities, multinational companies. Programs become more responsive to market demand. Specialized training programs are developed for niche markets and professional development and distributed worldwide. The international mobility of students, academics, education/training programs, research, providers, and projects increases. Mobility is both physical and virtual.
ICTS – Information and Communication Technologies New developments in information and communication technologies and systems.	New delivery methods are used for domestic and cross-border education, especially online and satellite-based forms.	Innovative international delivery methods are used, including e-learning, franchises. Satellite campuses require more attention to accreditation of programs/providers, more recognition of qualifications.
Market Economy Growth in the number and influence of market-based economies around the world.	The commercialization and commodification of higher education and training at domestic and international levels increases.	New concerns emerge about the appropriateness of curriculum and teaching materials in different cultures/countries. New potential develops for homogenization and hybridization.
Trade Liberalization New international and regional trade agreements develop to decrease barriers to trade.	Import and export of educational services and products increases as barriers are removed	The emphasis increases on the commercially oriented export and import of education programs; international development projects continue to diminish in importance.
Governance The creation of new international and regional governance structures and systems.	The role of national-level education actors both government and non-government is changing. New regulatory and policy frameworks are being considered at all levels.	Consideration is given to new international/regional frameworks to complement national and regional policies and practices, especially in quality assurance, accreditation, credit transfer, recognition of qualifications, and student mobility.

Source: Knight (2006; updated 2008).

science, and technology competitiveness between and among countries is forcing neighboring nations to increase their collaboration on a regional or subregional basis.

Cooperation within Europe is probably the best known and, to some degree, the most successful case of regional collaboration, especially in the higher education sector. Europe's Bologna Process is the most striking example of major region-wide reform. Now with a very strong external dimension, it is actively engaged in making European higher education more attractive and more competitive with that of the United States in terms of their international dimension and cooperation. It is interesting to see that, while the Europeanization process remains active, there is concurrently an increasing emphasis on exporting to the rest of the world their higher education reform measures and programs. Europeanization has been part of the deliberate, planned agenda motivated by the political and economic objectives of the European Union. Africanization, on the other hand, is often seen in the context of preserving indigenous knowledge and is frequently seen as an antidote to the homogenizing effects of Westernization. Regionalization can therefore used in different ways and for different purposes.

Much of the discussion on regionalism has been in the context of regionalization versus internationalization. But the "versus" approach is neither productive nor helpful in exploring this theme. The key issue which requires further analysis is how to achieve the most appropriate balance of interests and needs among local, national, regional, and international levels. When one juxtaposes the interdependence among nations needed to solve some of the global challenges against individual nations' growing technological and scientific competitiveness, the importance of finding the optimal balance among national, regional, and international levels comes into clearer focus. The process of internationalization emphasizes the concept of the nation-state and encourages relationships and exchanges between and among countries, either bilaterally or multilaterally. It is important that internationalization not be seen as a process that jeopardizes local, national, or regional needs and priorities.

Information and Communication Technologies

The international mobility of information has exploded. It is an important complement to the mobility of students and teachers but does not and should not replace the mobility of people. The new information and communication technologies are enabling a far larger percent of students to have international contacts and access to information.

Distance and time are no longer barriers. Opportunities for distance and cross-border delivery of educational programs are growing rapidly through the use of the new technologies. The excitement generated by new ways to internationalize the curriculum, the learning process, and scholarly activities is tangible. However, unbridled enthusiasm can be as problematic as the cynicism of sceptics. Careful thought and attention need to be focused on why, when, and how the new information and communication technologies enhance higher education and the international dimension. The key challenge is to determine how these emerging technologies can be used to enhance the learning process, extend its benefits, and bring international expertise together to solve shared problems in new and creative ways.

Vigilance is needed over the increased use of English for information sharing and communication purposes and as a teaching language for international delivery. A worrisome issue is the loss of national languages as the medium of instruction in many smaller, non-English-speaking countries, especially in Europe. Furthermore, many of the electronic data sources and information are available in English only. As a steadily increasing amount of information becomes available in English, the risk that English-speaking students will not see the necessity or advantage of learning other languages intensifies. Learning a language is an introduction to learning about another culture, another way of thinking, another perspective on the world, or at least a deeper understanding of how other cultures perceive the world. An appreciation of different ways of knowing and thinking about the world combined with heightened intercultural communication skills are important attributes for graduates of colleges and universities.

New Providers

Given the increase in demand for higher education, the rise of new providers, new delivery methods, and new types of programs is predictable. New types of higher education providers are active in delivering education programs both domestically and internationally. They include media companies such as Pearson (UK) and Thomson (Canada); multinational companies such as Apollo (USA), Informatics (Singapore), and Aptech (India); corporate universities, such as those run by Motorola and Toyota; and networks of professional associations and organizations (Knight, 2005).

Generally, these new commercial providers are mainly occupied with teaching/ training or providing services and do not focus on research per se. They can complement, cooperate, or compete with public and private higher education institutions (HEIs), whose mandate is traditionally the trinity of teaching, research, and service. Because many of the new providers focus on delivering education across borders, they must be included as actors in the internationalization scene.

DIVERSIFICATION OF FUNDING SOURCES

It would be a major oversight if funding and support for higher education were not acknowledged as a key new challenge for internationalization. Driving this development is the growing demand for further postsecondary education opportunities, which often outstrips the ability of national governments to provide public funding adequate to meet this need. At the global level, some indications suggest that the rate of funding is rising more rapidly from private investment than from public funding (Levy, 2003). Among the results of this trend are the diversification, privatization, and commercialization of higher education and research and their funding sources.

The necessity is growing for institutions—both public and private—to seek alternative sources of income. Among the most common are funding from social foundations, sponsorship from the private corporate sector, income from the commercialization of research findings, and revenue from fee-based education for domestic and international students as well as from other types of crossborder education delivery. In fact, generating income from importing and exporting education programs is expected to increase at a significant rate in the next decade (Larsen, Morris & Martin, 2002). Thus, trade in higher education services is becoming increasingly competitive, and the presence of new commercial providers will likely have a significant impact on public and private nonprofit higher education institutions.

Borderless Issues

Issues such as the degradation of the environment, population growth, security, global warming, immigration, terrorism, human rights, and health epidemics are not necessarily confined by the borders of one country or region. As problems without borders, they require international collaboration and cooperation to find policies and strategies that will mitigate negative effects and lead to positive solutions.

Multilateral government agencies, international nongovernmental organizations, national governments, the private sector and also the higher education sector all have a role to play at national and international levels in addressing these trends. The role that higher education plays in researching, teaching about, and analyzing these areas needs to be given greater attention and prominence in public policy debates.

Lifelong Learning

A contemporary trend in higher education is increased recognition for the concept of lifelong learning as a benefit, not only for individuals but also for the collective good of a country. This trend constitutes a gradual but profound societal shift and will have a major impact on higher education providers. A strong emphasis on learning motivates individuals toward continuous learning and helps to equip them with the skills and knowledge to be contributing citizens at the local, national, and international levels. Closely related to this trend is the emergence of information and communication technologies which empower learners of all ages to access global resources via books, CD-ROMs, or the internet, increasing their international awareness and exposure.

Growth in Number and Diversity of Actors

For several reasons, it is important to examine the different levels and types of actors involved in promoting, providing, and regulating the international dimension of higher education. First is the fact that internationalization now encompasses a vast array of programs and activities that have brought new actors into play. Second, these activities and issues have implications for policies and regulations at the international, regional, and domestic levels. Third, the lines or boundaries separating these different levels are becoming increasingly blurred and porous.

Table 1.3 provides a schema for organizing and addressing the growth in the number and diversity of stakeholders with interests in the international dimension of higher education. It illustrates that the actors include many different types: not only the educational institutions and providers themselves but also government departments and agencies; nongovernmental and semi-governmental organizations, private and public foundations; and conventions and treaties. The categories of actors can be further analyzed by considering the nature of their mission—e.g., policy-making, regulating, funding, programming, advocacy, and networking. It is important to note that actors often occupy more than one role and that these categories are therefore not mutually exclusive (Jaramillo & Knight, 2005).

The activities of these actors are diverse and include for example, student mobility, research and development, curriculum, scholarships, and quality assurance. The analysis becomes more complex when considering the levels of the actors: national, bilateral, subregional, regional, interregional and international are considered. It is also important to note that, in many circumstances all levels of actors can be involved or influence the development and implementation of policy, programs, and regulation of international higher education.

Table 1.3. Actors and their roles in the internationalization of higher education

Type of Actor	Level/Scope	Role	Typical Activities
Government departments or agencies	National	Policymaking	Scholarships
Non- (or semi-)governmental organizations	Bilateral	Regulating	Academic mobility
Professional associations or special interest groups	Subregional	Advocacy	Research
Foundations	Regional	Funding	Curriculum
Educational institutions and providers	Interregional	Programming	Quality assurance
	International	Networking	Science and technology
		Disseminating information	

Source: Knight (2004).

Table 1.4 gives examples that illustrate the growing number and diversity of actors who are increasing global connectivity and who are involved in promoting, providing, and making policy related to the international dimension of higher education. It also reinforces the reality that issues such as quality assurance, accreditation, qualification recognition, student exchange, new international or cross-border providers, brain drain, commercialization, and trade of education—to name but a few issues—are no longer the sole purview of national level actors.

It is clear from the diversity of actors influencing the international dimension of higher education that we must examine how national-level policies, programs, and providers relate to bilateral, regional, and international level actors and policies.

Table 1.4. Examples of actors involved in the internationalization of higher education

	National	Bilateral	Subregional, Regional, Interregional	International
Government Departments or Agencies	**National Ministries**	**International Development Agencies**	**Intergovernmental Organizations**	**Intergovernmental Organizations**
	For example: Education Culture Science and technology Foreign affairs Immigration Trade Industry Economic Development	For example: JAICA (Japan) USAID (USA) SIDA (Sweden) CIDA (Canada)	For example: European Commission Asian Development Bank IOHE African Union	For example: UNESCO World Bank, UNDP, OECD, WTO, UNICEF
Non (or Semi-) Governmental Organizations	**Professional or Service Organizations**	**International Cooperation Organizations**	**University Associations**	**University Associations**
	For example: University associations Quality assurance and accreditation agencies Granting councils Scholarship organizations Science councils Export agencies Student groups	For example: DAAD British Council, NUFFIC	For example: African Association of Universities European University Association (EUA) **Quality Assurance and Accreditation Agencies** For example: Asia Pacific Network for Quality Assurance	For example: International Association of Universities Association of Commonwealth Universities (ACU) Association of Francophone Universities (AUF)
Foundations	Private and public foundations (e.g., Ford, Aga Khan, Japan, Carnegie) supporting activities such as student/professor mobility, scholarships, research/ publications, science, conferences/workshops			
Treaty/ Convention		Cultural, Academic, Political, Economic, Trade Agreements	UNESCO regional conventions on recognition qualifications Regional and subregional trade agreements	GATS
Education Providers	– Public nonprofit HEIs, Public for-profit HEIs – Private nonprofit HEIs, Private for-profit HEIs – Corporate universities (e.g., Motorola) – Commercial companies (e.g., Aptech, Apollo, Sylvan, Informatics) – Networks (e.g., Universitas 21) – Media/publishing companies (Pearson, Thomson) – Private virtual universities (Jones International University)			

Source: Knight (2004).

CHAPTER ONE

EMERGING TRENDS, ISSUES, AND QUESTIONS

This chapter approaches the issues impacting internationalization in light of the new realities and turbulent environment of the 21st century's first decade. An important element of that discussion is identifying and examining the terminology used in the discourses involving the study of higher education. The literature shows that some adjectives occur again and again: "complex," "multifaceted," "diverse," "controversial," "changing," and "challenging." They paint a picture of internationalization as a phenomenon that is evolving on many fronts, both in impacting and in being impacted in a more globalized world. This evolutionary process reveals a number of macro trends (Knight, 2006b) that impact higher education both domestically and internationally:
- The movement to a knowledge-based society and economy
- New developments in ICTs
- A stronger sense of regionalism (trade, economic, cultural, political)
- Greater mobility of people, capital, ideas, knowledge, and technology
- More trade liberalization through bilateral and multilateral trade agreements
- Increased emphasis on market economy
- Shifts in the locus of governance from national to subregional, regional, and international levels.

These macro trends have important implications for the international dimension of higher education including:
- An increased demand for postsecondary education, especially lifelong learning and professional training
- A greater diversity of education providers including nongovernment/social foundations, commercial companies, private for-profit institutions, for-profit entities of public institutions and, more negatively, "degree mills"
- Innovations in distance/online delivery and crossborder provision of higher education
- New types of awards and qualifications being offered
- Additional and new levels (or types) of quality assurance and accreditation
- Rates of private investment in higher education increasing more rapidly than public investment
- New forms of administrative/academic partnerships among different types of providers
- Changing forms and purposes of strategic alliances
- Increased brain drain/gain including physical and virtual forms
- New forms of intra- and interregional higher education programs, especially mobility initiatives
- More international-level competition and innovation in a market-based approach to education
- A shift from development aid to partnership exchange to commercial trade in education.

These changes and new scenarios introduce a number of issues that are central to the study of the international dimension of higher education. These issues are sketched below and analyzed in greater detail in subsequent chapters.

Cultural Diversity. The impact of new forms and types of international academic mobility on the recognition and promotion of indigenous and diverse cultures is a subject that evokes strong positions and sentiments. Many believe that modern information and communication technologies and the movement of people, ideas, and culture across national boundaries are presenting new opportunities to promote one's culture to other countries and are also presenting further chances for the fusion and hybridization of culture. Undergirding their position is the assumption that this flow of culture across borders is not new at all; only the speed has been accelerated.

Others see both the movement and the speed as alarming. They contend that these same forces are eroding national cultural identities and that, instead of creating new, hybrid cultures, native cultures are being homogenized—by which, in most cases, they mean Westernized.

Because education has traditionally been seen as a vehicle of acculturation, these arguments focus on the specifics of curriculum content, language of instruction (particularly the increase in English) and the teaching/learning process in international education. Both perspectives have strengths to their arguments.

The commercialization of higher education. The General Agreement on Trade in Services (GATS) has been a wake-up call for higher education around the world. Higher education has traditionally been seen as a "public good" and a "social responsibility." But with the advent of this new international trade agreement, higher education has become a tradable commodity or, more precisely in GATS terms, an internationally tradable service. Many see GATS as presenting new opportunities and benefits while others see it as introducing new risks.

At the heart of the debate for many educators is the impact of increased commercial crossborder education on the purpose, role, and values of higher education. The growth in new commercial and private providers, the commodification of education, and the prospect of new trade policy frameworks are catalysts for stimulating serious reflection on the role, social commitment, and funding of public higher education institutions in society. The trinity of teaching/learning, research, and service to society has traditionally guided the evolution of universities and their contribution to the social, cultural, human, scientific, and economic development of a nation. Is the combination of these roles still valid, or can they be disaggregated and rendered by different providers?

Such traditionally fundamental values as academic freedom, collegiality, and institutional autonomy are being closely examined. Is education still considered to be a public good or a social responsibility in the sense of contributing to the development of society and/or is it being perceived as a private good for individuals' consumption and benefit? Some believe that these traditional values and roles are even more relevant and important in today's environment; others suggest that globalization underscores the need to shift away from these longstanding values. And still others argue that, if higher education is to fulfill its role as a "public good," then it will need to move away from its traditional public funding sources in favor of more market-based approaches. The commercialization and commodification of higher education on an international basis are important catalysts, demanding a rigorous review of the values fundamental to higher education and a nation's perception of how education meets national priorities and needs.

The internationalization of academic relations. Many public and private nonprofit institutions have a wider interest in the international dimension of education, than the delivery of education across national jurisdictional boundaries. Higher education institutions are actively expanding the international dimension of their research, teaching, and service functions. This different approach is a necessity given the increasing interdependency of nations who hope to address such global issues as climate change, crime, terrorism, and health through collaborative research and scholarly activity. The international and intercultural aspects of curriculum and the teaching/learning process are important for their contribution to the quality and relevancy of higher education.

One of the leading rationales at the institutional level for internationalization is preparing graduates to be internationally knowledgeable and interculturally skilled, able to live and work in more culturally diverse communities both at home and abroad. An important question to ask is how an increased emphasis on the commodification and new trade regulations will affect the nature and priority given to academic, social, cultural, and political rationales of nonprofit international education activities.

Student access. The increasing numbers of secondary school graduates coupled with demographic changes, lifelong learning, and changing human resource needs created by the knowledge economy are accelerating the demand for postsecondary education. Does international education help countries satisfy this growing demand for further education? Many would answer yes and see increased access for students as a strong motivation for all forms of education that are moving between countries. But movement alone does not answer thorny questions about the equity of access and whether it will be available only to those who can afford it (Van der Wende, 2003).

Quality assurance of crossborder education. The increase in crossborder education by institutions and new private commercial providers has introduced a new challenge (and gap) in the field of quality assurance. Historically, national quality assurance agencies, with some notable exceptions, have generally not focused on assessing the quality of imported and exported programs. The question now facing this sector is how to deal with the increase in crossborder education by traditional HEIs and by the new private commercial providers who are not normally part of nationally based, quality assurance schemes.

New developments in accreditation. The increased awareness of the need for quality assurance and/or accreditation has led to several new developments in accreditation, some of which are assisting in the tasks of recognizing both domestic and international qualifications, but some of which are only hindering and complicating matters. It is important to acknowledge the efforts of many countries to establish criteria and procedures for systems of quality-assurance recognition and for approving bona fide accreditors. At the same time, it is necessary to recognize the increase in self-appointed and rather self-serving accreditors, as well as accreditation mills that simply sell "bogus" accreditation labels.

Market forces are making the profile and reputation of an institution/provider and their courses more and more important. Major investments are being made in marketing and branding campaigns to achieve name recognition and increase enrollments. Possessing some type of accreditation is part of the campaign and assures prospective students that the programs/awards have high standing. The desire for accreditation status is leading to a commercialization of quality assurance/accreditation, as programs and providers strive to gain as many "accreditation" stars as possible as a way of increasing their market competitiveness and perceived international legitimacy. The challenge is how to distinguish between bona fide and rogue accreditors, especially when neither the crossborder provider nor the accreditor is nationally based or recognized as part of a national higher education system.

Such rogue accreditors should not be confused with networks of institutions and new organizations that, though self-appointed, engage in accreditation of their members. These are positive developments in terms of trying to improve the quality of the academic offer. However, this departure from traditional accreditation methods opens the door to concerns that they are not totally objective in their assessments and may be more interested in generating income than in improving quality. While this concern can apply to both crossborder and domestic providers, it is particularly worrisome in the case of crossborder providers, who often fail to give adequate attention to national policy objectives and cultural orientation.

Recognition of qualifications. Increased academic mobility gives new prominence to the issue of credential recognition in international education policy. The credibility of higher education programs and their qualifications is extremely important for students, their employers, the public at large, and of course for the academic community itself. It is critical that the qualifications awarded by crossborder providers are legitimate and will be recognized for employment or further studies both at home and abroad. This major challenge facing the national and international higher education sector cannot be avoided as new crossborder providers and programs multiply.

Brain drain/gain. Brain power, meaning the skills and abilities of a qualified person, is an increasingly important issue for many countries because of the growing mobility of professional/skilled workers. The increase in the crossborder movement of scholars, experts, and teachers/professors is due in part to the increasing competitiveness for human capital in the knowledge economy. Not only is there a trend for higher education personnel to move from country to country, but they are also attracted to the corporate sector where benefits can heavily outweigh those in the education sector. A country's higher education sector can be affected either negatively (if it is experiencing a net brain drain as trained personnel move out) or positively (if trained personnel are moving in). There are also direct links between foreign student recruitment/mobility and the recruiting country's needs for skilled labor in the form of immigrants. Thus, the complex and increasingly interrelated dynamics between national policies for international education, migration policies, and nation building/human capacity building efforts are areas demanding serious consideration by education policymakers.

QUESTIONS FOR ACADEMIC LEADERS AND POLICYMAKERS

These emerging issues and trends raise questions in terms of institutional-, national-, and regional-level policies and programs that need to be put into place. The chapters that follow will discuss their impact on internationalization policies, programs, and strategies:

1. How does internationalization deal with the intersection of international and intercultural? Is internationalization a vehicle for increased understanding and appreciation of cultural diversity and fusion or is it an agent of cultural homogenization? How do the curriculum, teaching/learning process, research, extracurricular activities, and academic mobility contribute to intercultural understanding and cultural hybridization/homogenization?
2. Is there a subtle but discernible shift away from the social and cultural rationales toward the economic and commercial interests of internationalization? What are the implications for higher education policy in general: funding, access, quality, role in society, research, curriculum, and regulatory frameworks?
3. How is internationalization contributing to brain drain or brain gain? What mechanisms can help enhance the benefits of increased academic and professsional mobility and the diaspora but mitigate the negative impact of imbalances caused when talent is flowing out of countries?
4. What are the connections between academic mobility, labor mobility, and temporary or permanent immigration? Are targeted recruitment campaigns for international students and professors linked to migration patterns?
5. As education/training programs move across borders, what are the implications for quality assurance and the accreditation of programs and providers? What role do institutions, national quality assurance, and accreditation agencies play in monitoring incoming and outgoing programs? Is there a need for regional or international mechanisms to augment national/institutional efforts to monitor the increased crossborder delivery?
6. The emergence of new, private-sector, for-profit companies brings new actors to the world of internationalization. How will these new providers of education programs and services collaborate, compete, complement, or change the work of traditional public and private postsecondary institutions in the internationalization of teaching/learning, research, and service?
7. The complexities involved in working in the field of internationalization require additional sets of knowledge, attitudes, skills, and understandings about the international/intercultural/global dimension of higher education. How are these competencies developed and recognized for academics, administrators,

and policy-makers working in the field of the internationalization of higher education?
8. What are the implications of increased academic mobility for recognizing academic and professional credentials? What is the relationship between recognizing credentials and the trend toward the validation of competencies? What is the role of the existing regional UNESCO conventions on credential recognition?
9. The international dimension of higher education is gaining a higher profile in such policy arenas outside education as immigration, trade and commerce, culture, and economic development. How can the education sector work collaboratively with these sectors at the national/regional level to ensure that the internationalization process is understood and that it contributes to human, social, cultural, scientific, and economic development?
10. In concrete terms, how does internationalization facilitate regional integration and conversely, how does regional integration impact internationalization?

Looking ahead, it is important to reflect on what will be seen as the major accomplishments of internationalization during the first two decades of the 21st century. Are we taking a long-term perspective on the implications and consequences of internationalization, or are we merely reacting to contemporary issues and opportunities? Wise and thoughtful planning at this stage will deflect many problems that could otherwise drain energy and mire progress over decades to come.

Note: This chapter is based on and updated from J. Knight (2004, 2005, 2006a, 2006b) and Knight and de Wit (1999) as cited in the Related References.

RELATED REFERENCES

Altbach, P. (2006). Globalization and the university: Realities in an unequal world. In P. Altbach & J. Forest (Eds.), *International handbook of higher education* (pp. 121–140). Dordrecht, Netherlands: Springer Academic Publishers.
Breton, G., & Lambert, M. (Eds.). (2003). *Universities and globalization: Private linkages, public trust.* Paris: UNESCO/Université Laval/Economica.
Enders, J., & Fulton, O. (2002). *Higher education in a globalizing world: International trends and mutual observations.* Dordrecht, Netherlands: Kluwer.
Innes, P., & Hellsten, M. (2004). *Internationalizing higher education: Critical perspectives for critical times.* London: Routledge.
Jaramillo, I. C., & Knight, J. (2005). Key actors and programs: Increasing connectivity in the region. In H. de Wit, I. C. Jaramillo, J. Gacel-Avila, & J. Knight (Eds.), *Higher education in Latin America: The international dimension* (pp. 301–340). Washington, DC: World Bank.
Knight, J. (2004, September). *Internationalization issues, actors and questions: A comparative regional Internationalization analysis.* Paper prepared for the Institutional Management of Higher Education/Organization for Economic Cooperation and Development. Conference, Paris. Organization for Economic Cooperation and Development.
Knight, J. (2005). *Borderless, offshore, transnational and crossborder education: Definition and data dilemmas.* Report for Observatory for Borderless Higher Education. London: OBHE.
Knight, J. (2006a). *Higher education crossing borders: A guide to the implications of GATS for cross-border education.* Paris: Commonwealth of Learning/UNESCO.

CHAPTER ONE

Knight, J. (2006b). *Internationalization of higher education: New directions, new challenges.* 2005 International Association of Universities Global Survey Report. Paris: International Association of Universities.

Knight, J., & de Wit, H. (Eds.). (1999). *Quality and internationalization in higher education.* Paper prepared for the Institutional Management of Higher Education/Organization for Economic Co-operation and Development. Conference, Paris.

Levy, D. (2003). *Expanding higher education capacity through private growth: Contributions and challenges.* London: Observatory on Borderless Higher Education.

Larsen, K., Morris, R., & Martin, J. (2002). *Trade in educational services: Trends and emerging issues.* Draft of chapter. Paris: Organization for Economic Cooperation and Development.

Marginson, S. (Ed.). (2001). *Globalization and higher education: Views from the South.* Papers from the Society for Research into Higher Education Conference, Capetown, South Africa.

Marginson, S., & Sawir, E. (2005). Interrogating global flows in higher education. *Globalization, Societies, and Education, 3*(3), 281–309.

Odin, J., & Mancias, P. (Eds.). (2004). *Globalization and higher education.* Honolulu, HI: University of Hawaii Press.

Scott, P. (2000, Spring). Globalisation and higher education: Challenges for the 21st century. *Journal of Studies in International Education, 4*(1), 3–10.

Stromquist, N. (2007). Internationalization as a response to globalization: Radical shifts in university environments. *Higher Education, 53*(1), 81–105.

Wende, M. (2003). Globalization and access to higher education. *Journal of Studies in International Education, 7*(2), 193–206.

CHAPTER TWO

AN INTERNATIONALIZATION MODEL:

Meaning, Rationales, Approaches, and Strategies

Internationalization is one of the major forces impacting and shaping higher education as it changes to meet the challenges of the 21st century. As discussed in Chapter 1, the picture of internationalization that is emerging is one of complexity, diversity, and differentiation especially in light of the diversity of new providers and the growth of commercial crossborder education. The internationalization of higher education is a process that is evolving as both actor and reactor to the new realities and rather turbulent times facing higher education.

The purpose of this chapter is to develop a framework or model to understand the very complex subject and process of internationalization. It is important to have a solid grounding in the conceptual aspects of internationalization before proceeding on to the remaining chapters in the book. The major aspects of the model which are examined include the meaning, rationales, approaches, and strategies of internationalization. A model of internationalization needs to address both the institutional level and national/sector level. The national/sector level has an important influence on the international dimension of higher education through policy, funding, programs and regulatory frameworks. Yet it is usually at the level of individual institutions that the real process of internationalization is taking place. Therefore, this analysis and conceptual model of internationalization uses both a bottom-up (institutional) approach and a top-down (national/sector) approach, examining the dynamic relationship between these two levels.

THE MEANING OF INTERNATIONALIZATION

"Internationalization" is not a new term. It has been used for centuries in political science and governmental relations, but its popularity in the education sector has really soared only since the early 1980s. Prior to this time, international education and international cooperation were the favored terms, and still are in some countries. In the 1990s, the discussion on using the term "international education" centered on differentiating it from terms like "comparative education," "global education," and "multicultural education." Now, in the first decade of the 21st century, related terms are emerging, which include "transnational education," "borderless education," "offshore education," and "crossborder education," as well as "transnationalization," "multinationalization," and "regionalization." It is interesting to note that these descriptors relate to the concept of borders and differ substantially from the previous key concept of culture.

The purpose of trying to develop a clear and somewhat comprehensive definition for internationalization is to help clarify the confusion and misunderstanding which currently exist. While it is true (and appropriate) that there will likely never be a true universal definition, it is important that common understandings govern discussions, analyses, and increased attention and support from policymakers and academic leaders.

Evolution of the Concept

In the late 1980s, "internationalization" was commonly defined at the institutional level and in terms of a set of activities. The definition proposed by Arum and Van de Water (1992) is a good example of this approach. They proposed that internationalization refers to "the multiple activities, programs and services that fall within international studies, international educational exchange and technical cooperation" (p. 202). By the mid-1990s, a process or organizational approach was introduced by Knight (1994) to illustrate that internationalization was a process that needed to be integrated and sustainable at the institutional level. By this definition, internationalization was seen as the "process of integrating an international and intercultural dimension into the teaching, research and service functions of the institution" (p. 7).

Van der Wende (1997) correctly pointed out that an institutional-based definition has limitations and therefore proposed a broader definition suggesting that internationalization is "any systematic effort aimed at making higher education responsive to the requirements and challenges related to the globalization of societies, economy and labor markets" (p. 18). While this definition includes important elements, it only positions the international dimension in terms of the external environment—specifically globalization—and therefore, does not contextualize internationalization in terms of the education sector itself.

De Wit (2002) concludes:

> As the international dimension of higher education gains more attention and recognition, people tend to use it in the way that best suits their purpose. While one can understand this happening, it is not helpful for internationalization to become a catchall phrase for everything and anything international. A more focused definition is necessary if it is to be understood and treated with the importance that it deserves. Even if there is not agreement on a precise definition, internationalization needs to have parameters if it is to be assessed and to advance higher education. This is why the use of a working definition in combination with a conceptual framework for internationalization of higher education is relevant (p. 114).

Updated Working Definition

It is interesting to look at the way in which definitions can shape policy and also how practice can influence definitions and policy. Given the changes in the rationales, the providers, the stakeholders, and the activities of internationalization, it is important to revisit the question of definition and ensure that the meaning reflects the realities of today and is also able to guide and be relevant to new developments. It is increasingly clear that internationalization needs to be understood both at the national/sector level and also the institutional level. Therefore, a new definition is here proposed that acknowledges both levels and also acknowledges the relationship and integrity between them.

The challenging part of developing a definition is the need for it to be generic enough to apply to many different countries, cultures, and education systems. This is no easy task. While it is not necessarily the intention to develop a universal definition, it is imperative that it be appropriate for use in a broad range of contexts and for comparative purposes across countries and regions of the world. With this in mind, it is therefore important to ensure that a definition does not specify the rationales, benefits, outcomes, actors, activities, and stakeholders of internationalization as they vary enormously across nations and also from institution to institution. What is critical is that the international dimension relates to all aspects of education and the role that it plays in society. This volume proposes the following working definition: Internationalization at the national/sector/institutional levels is the process of integrating an international, intercultural or global dimension into the purpose, functions or delivery of higher education at the institutional and national levels.

This definition is intentionally neutral. Many would argue that the process of internationalization should be described in terms of promoting cooperation and solidarity among nations, improving the quality and relevance of higher education, or contributing to the advancement of research for international issues. While these are noble intentions—and internationalization can certainly contribute to these goals—a definition needs to be objective enough that it can be used to describe a phenomenon which is, in fact, universal but which has different purposes and outcomes, depending on the actor or stakeholder and the national or institutional context.

EXPLANATION OF KEY CONCEPTS

Given the varying conceptions of international higher education and the level of turmoil in this sector, it is important to explain that specific terms and concepts have been carefully chosen for the proposed working definition of internationalization articulated above.

The term *process* is deliberately used to convey that internationalization is an ongoing and continuing effort and to note that there is an evolutionary or developmental quality to the concept. Process is often thought of in terms of a tri-part model to education: input, process, and output. The concepts of input and output were deliberately not used even though, in today's environment, there is increased emphasis on accountability and outcomes. If internationalization is defined in terms of inputs, outputs, or benefits, it becomes less generic as it must reflect the particular priorities of a country, institution, or group of stakeholders.

The notion of *integration* is specifically used to denote the process of embedding the international and intercultural dimension into policies and programs to ensure sustainability and centrality to the mission and values of the institution or system.

International, intercultural, and global are three terms intentionally used as a triad, as together they reflect the breadth of internationalization. *International* carries the sense of relationships between and among nations, cultures, or countries. However, internationalization is also about relating to the diversity of cultures that exist within countries, communities, institutions, and classrooms so *intercultural* seems the best term for addressing aspects of cultural diversity. Finally, *global* is included to provide the sense of worldwide scope. These three terms complement each other and together give richness both in breadth and depth to the process of internationalization.

The concepts of purpose, function, and delivery have also been carefully chosen. *Purpose* refers to the overall role that higher education has for a country/region or more specifically the mission of an institution. *Function* refers to the primary elements or tasks that characterize a national higher education system and also an individual institution. Usually these include teaching/training, research, scholarly activities, and service to the society at large. *Delivery* is a narrower concept and refers to the offering of education courses and programs either domestically or in other countries. It includes delivery by traditional higher education institutions, but it also includes new providers such as companies who are more interested in the global delivery of their programs than perhaps the international/intercultural dimension of the curriculum, research, and service.

As already mentioned, one of the previous definitions that has been widely used described internationalization as the "process of integrating an international or intercultural dimension into the teaching, research and service functions of the institution." This definition does not conflict with the proposed working definition. In fact the opposite is true. The definitions are very complementary. First, the new definition attempts to address the realities of today's context where the national/sector level is extremely important and therefore must be covered in a definition. Second, a growing number and diversity of education providers have very different interests and approaches to the international, intercultural, and global dimensions. Therefore, the more generic terms of "purpose," "function," and "delivery" are used instead of the specific functional terms of "teaching," "research," and "service." By using these three more general terms, the proposed definition can be relevant for the sector/national level, the institutional level, and the variety of providers—public, private, for-profit, nonprofit, local, and/or international—in the broad field of higher education.

TWO STREAMS: INTERNATIONALIZATION "AT HOME" AND "ABROAD"

An interesting development in the conceptualization of internationalization in the last five years has been the introduction of the term "internationalization at home" or (another way of expressing the same notion) "internal internationalization." It appears that there is a growing need to differentiate between internationalization which is campus-based (or at home) and internationalization which focuses more on international education abroad or crossborder education. Two different streams or pillars of internationalization seem to be emerging.

The first is "internationalization at home," a term developed to bring attention to those aspects of internationalization which would happen on a home campus. They include the intercultural and international dimension in the teaching-learning process and research, extracurricular activities, and relationships with local cultural and ethnic community groups, as well as the integration of foreign students and scholars into campus life and activities. The emergence of this concept can perhaps be seen as a way to counteract the increased emphasis on academic mobility whether it is people, programs, providers, or projects moving across borders.

A more detailed look at internationalization "at home" includes a diversity of activities such as the following:

Curriculum and programs. New programs with international themes; the infusion of international, cultural, global, or comparative dimensions into existing courses; foreign language study; area or regional studies; and joint or double degrees.

Teaching/learning processes. The active involvement of international students, returned study-abroad students, and cultural diversity in the classroom in teaching/learning processes; virtual student mobility for joint courses and research projects; the use of international scholars and teachers and local international/intercultural experts; and the integration of international materials, intercultural case studies, role plays, and reference materials.

Extra-curricular activities. Student clubs and associations; international and intercultural campus events; liaison with community-based cultural and ethnic groups; and peer support groups and programs.

Liaison with local cultural/ethnic groups. The involvement of students in local cultural and ethnic organizations through internships, placements, and applied research; and the involvement of representatives from local cultural and ethnic groups in teaching/learning activities, research initiatives, and extracurricular events and projects.

Research and scholarly activity. Area and theme centers; joint research projects; international conferences and seminars; published articles and papers; international research agreements; research exchange programs; international research partners in academic and other sectors; and the integration of visiting researchers and scholars into academic activities on campus.

This elaboration is perhaps broader than the original concept of internationalization "at home" (Nilsson, 2003) which put more focus on the intercultural aspects of the teaching/learning process and the curriculum.

At the same time that "internationalization at home" has been introduced, so has the term "crossborder education." Of course, "crossborder education" is not necessarily a new term but the use of the term "crossborder" is causing some confusion and concern. The word is starting to be used as a synonym for "internationalization" and thereby neglects the "at home" components. But it is frequently being used to describe commercial trade in education. Of course, both interpretations are too narrow, and this is why it is important to have further analysis and clarity on the two streams of internationalization.

CHAPTER TWO

A more detailed look at internationalization "at home" includes a diversity of activities such as the following:

Movement of people. Such movement includes students in award-based programs changing location through semester/year abroad, internship or research programs, or full program abroad; and the movement of professors/scholars and experts for purposes of teaching and research, technical assistance and consulting, sabbaticals and professional development.

Delivery of programs. The program/course moves to the student (not vice versa); models of delivery include franchising, twinning, double/joint degree, and articulation; delivery includes educational or training programs offered through a linkage or partnership arrangement between international/foreign and domestic institutions/providers on an exchange (nonprofit) or commercial (for-profit) basis.

Mobility of providers. The institution/provider moves to have a physical or virtual presence in the receiving country; the foreign or international provider has academic responsibility for the program and awards a foreign degree (The provider may or may not have an academic or financial partner in the receiving country.); and examples are branch campuses, stand-alone foreign institutions, and some franchise models.

International projects. Such projects include a wide diversity of non-award-based activities such as joint curriculum development, research, benchmarking, technical assistance, e-learning platforms, professional development, and other capacity building initiatives; projects and services could be undertaken as part of development aid projects, academic linkages, and commercial contracts.

It is important to emphasize that the four categories included in crossborder education are implemented through the three primary and yet very different modes of internationalization: (a) development assistance projects; (b) exchanges, linkages, and mutually beneficial initiatives (nonprofit internationalization), and (c) commercial and market-driven ventures (usually for-profit in design and purpose).

The links between the two streams are important; and more attention and research are needed to study the nature and implications of their connections. It is important to point out that these two streams should be seen as closely linked, interdependent rather than independent. Internationalization "abroad" has significant implications for internationalization "at home" and vice versa.

CHANGING RATIONALES AT INSTITUTIONAL AND NATIONAL LEVELS

The necessity of having clear, articulated rationales for internationalization cannot be overstated. Rationales are the driving force why a country, sector, or institution wants to address and invest in internationalization. Rationales are reflected in the policies and programs that are developed and eventually implemented.

Rationales dictate the kind of benefits or expected outcomes those involved expect from internationalization efforts. Without a clear set of rationales, accompanied by a set of objectives or policy statements, a plan, and a monitoring/evaluation system, the process of internationalization is often an ad hoc, reactive, and fragmented response to the overwhelming number of new international opportunities available.

Traditionally, the rationales for internationalization have been presented in four groups: social/cultural, political, academic, and economic (Knight & de Wit, 1999). The first column in Table 2.1 presents the four categories of existing rationales as updated by de Wit (2002). They are still relevant, but an unmistakable blurring of rationales has occurred across categories, accompanied by less clarity on what constitutes, for example, a political or economic rationale. Neither do the four categories of rationales distinguish between national and institutional levels of rationales, which is becoming increasingly important. Therefore, the third column presents a new approach to analyzing rationales of emerging importance at both the national and institutional levels. This list of rationales guides the analysis of why internationalization is important to systems and institutions of higher education around the world.

Table 2.1. Rationales driving internationalization

Rationales	Existing Rationales	Of Emerging Importance
Social/cultural	National cultural identity Intercultural understanding Citizenship development Social and community development	**National level** Human resources development Strategic alliances Income generation/commercial trade Nation building/institution building Social/cultural development and mutual understanding
Political	Foreign policy National security Technical assistance Peace and mutual understanding National identity Regional identity	**Institutional Level** International branding and profile
Economic	Economic growth and competitiveness Labor market Financial incentives	Quality enhancement/international standards Income generation Student and staff development Strategic alliances
Academic	Extension of academic horizon Institution building Profile and status Enhancement of quality International academic standards International dimension to research and teaching	Knowledge production

Source: Knight (2005).

CHAPTER TWO

NATIONAL-LEVEL RATIONALES

The rationales that appear to be driving the internationalization of higher education at the national or sector level are the following:

Human Resources Development: Brain Power

Demographic shifts, the knowledge economy, the mobility of the labor force, and increased trade in services are driving nations to place more importance on developing and recruiting highly qualified people/brain power through international education initiatives. There are signs of heightened pressure to recruit the brightest of students and scholars from other countries to increase scientific, technological, and economic competitiveness. Changes in recruitment strategies, incentives, and immigration policies are examples of efforts to attract and retain students and academics with the potential for enhancing the human capital of a country. Similarly, more attention is being paid to enhancing the international dimension of teaching and research so that domestic students and academics can be better equipped to contribute to their countries' effectiveness and competitiveness on the international stage. Finally, increasing recognition is being given to the need to deepen intercultural understanding and skills for personal, professional, and citizenship development. It is also worth noting that the growing importance attached to "brain power" is directly related to the increasing interest in and concern regarding brain gain/drain and the issue of migration.

Strategic Alliances

Strategic alliances can be seen both as a driving rationale and as an instrument of internationalization. This discussion looks at strategic alliances as rationales, whether they are entered into for academic, economic, political, or social/cultural purposes. The international mobility of students and academics, as well as collaborative research and education initiatives, are being seen as productive ways to develop closer geo-political ties and economic relationships. There has been a definite shift from alliances for cultural purposes to those for economic reasons. This is especially true at the regional level where countries are trying to achieve stronger economic and political integration with neighbors through increasing their international education activities on a regional basis. The development of strategic alliances through the internationalization of higher education is therefore seen as a way to develop closer cooperation bilaterally or regionally and to gain a competitive edge.

Income Generation and Commercial Trade

In the last decade, some countries have placed more emphasis on economic and income-generating opportunities attached to the crossborder delivery of education. New franchise arrangements, foreign or satellite campuses, online delivery, and the increased recruitment of fee-paying students are examples of a more commercial approach to internationalization. The fact that education is now one of the 12 service sectors in the General Agreement on Trade in Services (GATS) is positive proof that importing and exporting education programs and services is a potentially lucrative trade area. Trade in higher education is a multi-billion dollar business internationally which is expected to increase significantly. Therefore, countries are showing increased interest in the potential for exporting education for economic benefit. The development of new international and regional trade agreements is now providing regulations which will decrease barriers to trade, thereby increasing the commercial side of international crossborder trade in education (Knight, 2002).

Nation Building/Institution Building

An educated citizenry and workforce, and the capacity to generate new knowledge are key components of a country's nation-building agenda. Many countries lack the physical/human infrastructure and the financial resources to offer higher education opportunities to their citizens. Traditionally, international academic projects, as part of development and technical assistance work, have been considered an important contribution to the nation-building efforts of a developing country. International development work, based on mutual benefits for all partners, continues to be a key aspect of the internationalization of postsecondary education. However, there is a discernible shift from an aid/development approach to one focused on trade for commercial purposes. While some countries are interested in exporting education to generate income revenue, other countries are interested in importing education programs and institutions for nation- and capacity-building purposes.

These four emerging, yet primary, rationales are more closely linked to the political and economic categories of rationales, whether it is for technological, economic, or scientific advancement or competitiveness.

Social/Cultural Development and Mutual Understanding

The social and cultural rationales, especially those that relate to the promotion of intercultural understanding and national cultural identity are still significant; but perhaps, in some countries their importance does not carry the same weight as economic and political rationales. Whether in light of the pressing issues and challenges stemming from culturally based clashes within and between countries, it is not yet clear that more importance will be attached to social/cultural rationales and mutual understanding. It may be optimistic, but it would be reassuring to think that social and cultural rationales for internationalization will be given equal importance to economic and political bases.

INSTITUTIONAL-LEVEL RATIONALES

Of course, there is a close link between national-level and institutional-level rationales, but it is not always as close as one would expect. Many factors are involved, one of which is how much the internationalization process is a bottom-up or top-down affair in any given country. It is probably accurate to say that, in countries where internationalization is not given much prominence at the national level, institutional-level rationales have greater importance and may differ substantially from one institution to another. Furthermore, myriad factors influence institutional-level rationales. They include mission, student population, faculty profile, geographic location, funding sources, availability of resources, degree of institutional autonomy, and orientation to local, national, and international interests. Again, the four traditional categories of rationales apply to institutions, but it appears that the emerging rationales of greater consequence are these:

International Profile and Reputation

Traditionally, prominence has been given to the importance of achieving international academic standards, however they may be defined. This motivation is still important but it appears to have been subsumed by the overall drive to achieve a strong worldwide reputation as an international, high-quality institution. This drive relates to the quest for name recognition in an attempt to attract the brightest of scholars, a substantial number of international students, and, of course, high-profile research and training projects.

One could say that education institutions have always been competitive in trying to achieve high academic standards and, more recently, an international profile. However, a not-so-subtle shift has developed toward achieving an international reputation in order to successfully compete in a more commercial environment. Institutions and companies are competing for a market share of international fee-paying students, or for-profit education and training programs, or for education services like language testing and accreditation services. The interest in branding is leading institutions to seek accreditation or quality assurance services by national and international accrediting bodies, some of which are very trustworthy and some of which are not so reputable. Accreditation is becoming an industry unto itself, and it is clear that institutions and providers are making serious efforts to create an international reputation and "name brand" for themselves or a network of partners to gain competitive advantage. Therefore, the desire to have international recognition—whether it is for academic, economic, social, or political purposes—is clearly growing, but one must ask at what price?

Quality Enhancement/International Standards

For most institutions, internationalization is not an end in itself but a means to an end. The contribution that the international dimension makes to improve the quality and relevance of higher education in relation to international standards is often articulated as a rationale and goal of internationalization. Given the more interconnected and interdependent world of today, it is important that higher education, through a strengthened international dimension in teaching and research, serves the needs of individuals, communities, countries, and society at large.

At a more practical level, internationalization is proving a useful tool in assisting institutions to benchmark and gain innovative solutions to ongoing management, academic, and research-related challenges. This is yet another aspect where internationalization can help to strengthen the quality of higher education institutions and the primary functions of teaching/learning, research, and service.

Student and Staff Development

At the institutional level, it appears that there is renewed emphasis on internationalization as a means of enhancing international and intercultural understanding and skills for students and staff. The first contributing factor is the escalating numbers of national, regional, international, and cultural conflicts, which are pushing academics to help students understand global issues and appreciate international/intercultural diversity. The growing emphasis on the knowledge society makes continuous upgrading of knowledge and skills important for students. The mobility of the labor market, and the increase in cultural diversity of communities and the work place, require that both students and academics acquire increased understanding of and demonstrated abilities to work and live in a culturally diverse or different environment.

On the other hand, the increased emphasis on accountability and outcomes-based education is resulting in a substantial effort toward identifying student and staff competencies developed through internationalization initiatives. Lastly, the development of information and communication technologies, especially the internet, has highlighted the need for deeper knowledge and understanding of the world and has provided new opportunities for gaining that understanding.

Income Generation

On the other side of the ledger from human (student and staff) development is the motivation of economic development. There is no question that some institutions are increasingly looking for internationalization activities as a way to generate alternative sources of income. Public institutions are caught in the squeeze of decreased public funding and increased operational costs, all taking place in an environment of increased accountability and growing competition.

The motivation to undertake internationalization in order to generate income is a complex issue. The purpose or use of the income generation is often questioned—not in terms of where or how the money is being spent—but rather in terms of whether it is profit oriented or for cost recovery. This is not an issue with clear answers, as most public institutions would argue that they are, by definition, not for profit and that therefore any surplus from internationalization activities would be used to subsidize other initiatives on campus. Others would suggest that any income generated from internationalization activities should be reinvested to enhance under-funded aspects of internationalization.

Another factor related to income generation is the emergence of new commercial corporate providers (Garrett, 2005) who are primarily in business to generate income on a for-profit basis. Thus, while more importance is being attached to the economic rationale for internationalization at the institution/provider level, the issue is becoming more complicated as it introduces larger questions related to commercialization/commodification of education with crossborder delivery of education programs and services playing a major role.

Strategic Alliances

Once again strategic alliances can be seen as both a rationale for and as a means of achieving internationalization. There is no question that the number of bilateral or multilateral educational agreements has increased exponentially in the past decade. During the early stages of the internationalization process, institutions are often reacting to the multitude of opportunities to establish international institutional linkages. These linkages can be for different purposes—academic mobility, bench-marking, joint curriculum or program development, seminars and conferences, and joint research initiatives. It is often the case that institutions cannot support a large number of agreements, and thus many are inactive and mainly paper-based arrangements. As institutions mature in their approach to internationalization, they tend to put more effort into developing strategic alliances in which purposes and outcomes are clearly articulated.

An important trend is the development of networks. Networks tend to have clearer and more strategic objectives but, in many cases, are more difficult to manage than bilateral agreements because of the complexities of working with so many different education systems and cultures. All in all, the rationale for developing key strategic international education alliances at both the national and institutional level is not so much an end in itself but rather is a means of achieving academic, scientific, economic, technological, or cultural objectives.

Research and Knowledge Production

The complexity and costs involved in higher education institutions' role in the production and distribution of knowledge should not be minimized. Given the increasing interdependence among nations, it is clear that there are global issues and challenges that cannot be addressed at the national level only. International and interdisciplinary collaboration is central to solving many global problems such as those related to environmental and health challenges, international crime, and others. National governments are therefore making the international dimension of research and knowledge production a primary rationale for the internationalization of higher education, and many institutions are articulating this goal as a key motivation for internationalization given its role in the turmoil caused by this transitional period.

All in all, the rationales driving internationalization vary from institution to institution, from government department to government department, from stakeholder to stakeholder, and from country to country. Differing and competing rationales contribute to both the complexity of the international dimension of education and its impact. A final point to emphasize is that, in spite of the complexity of rationales, it is of fundamental importance for an actor—whether an institution, commercial provider, public or private stakeholder, non-government organization, governmental department or intergovernmental agency—to clearly articulate its motivations for internationalization, as policies, programs, strategies, and outcomes are all linked and guided by explicit and implicit rationales.

APPROACHES TO INTERNATIONALIZATION

Why Approaches?

Given the changing—even chaotic—world, in which higher education is functioning, it is important to acknowledge that individual countries, education systems and even institutions/providers are facing specific challenges and opportunities with respect to the international dimension of higher education. This means, of course, that there are many different approaches to addressing the process of internationalization.

An "approach" is different from a "definition." Even though different countries (or even institutions within a country) may hold a common interpretation or definition of "internationalization," their implementation plan may vary due to different priorities, culture, history, politics, and resources. An approach is not fixed. Approaches change during different periods of development. In many cases, countries or institutions believe that they are using different approaches at the same time, or they believe that they are in a transition period from one approach to another. There is no right approach. The notion of approach is introduced here to help describe and assess the manner in which internationalization is being conceptualized and implemented.

The following section presents generic approaches at the national level. They illustrate aspects of internationalization that a country or even region could emphasize in attempting to develop and implement a position, policy, or strategy to address the international dimension of postsecondary education.

National- or Sector-Level Approaches

Five different categories of approaches at the sector level are described. They are not mutually exclusive categories, nor are they presented in any particular or progressive order. They describe dominant features of the way that a country or the education sector has decided to proceed with internationalization.

Programs. The internationalization of higher education is seen in terms of providing funded programs that facilitate opportunities for institutions and individuals to engage in international activities such as mobility, research, linkages, development projects, foreign language training, etc.

Rationales. The internationalization of higher education is presented in terms of why it is important for a national higher education sector to become more international. Rationales vary enormously and can include competitiveness, human resources development, strategic alliances, income generation, commercial trade, nation building, and social/cultural development.

Ad hoc. The internationalization of higher education is treated as an ad hoc or reactive response to the many new opportunities being presented for international delivery, mobility, and cooperation in higher education. Different national government departments or agencies are individually involved in specific activities but there is no coordinating mechanism.

Policy. The internationalization of higher education is described in terms of policies that address or emphasize the importance of the international or intercultural dimension in higher education. Policies can be set by a variety of sectors including education, foreign affairs, immigration, science and technology, culture, or trade. In many case, the policies are not developed into programs and thus remain a paper commitment to the international dimension of higher education.

Strategic. Internationalization of higher education is considered to be a key element of a national strategy to achieve a country's goals and priorities, both domestically and internationally and includes a well-developed plan across a variety of government departments and agencies involving concrete policies and funded programs.

APPROACHES TO INTERNATIONALIZATION AT THE INSTITUTIONAL LEVEL

The differentiation of higher education provision means that institutions have different guiding missions, values, priorities, and rationales. These differences impact the approach taken to internationalization, confirming that there is not "one way" or "a right way" to internationalize and that one should not conceptualize internationalization by a "one size fits all" approach. Six possible approaches, which are not necessarily exclusive of one another, include the following:

Activity. Internationalization is described in terms of activities such as study abroad, curriculum, academic programs, international students, institutional linkages and networks, development projects, and branch campuses.

Outcomes. Internationalization is presented in the form of desired results such as student competencies, increased profile, and more international agreements, partners, or projects.

Rationales. Internationalization is described with respect to the primary motivations or rationales driving it. They can include academic standards, income generation, cultural diversity, and student and/or staff development.

Process. Internationalization is considered to be a process in which an international dimension is integrated in a sustainable way into the three primary functions of an institution: teaching/learning, research, and service to society.

Ethos. Internationalization is interpreted as the creation of a culture or climate on campus that promotes and supports international/intercultural understanding and focuses on campus-based or "at home" activities.

Abroad/crossborder. Internationalization is seen as the crossborder delivery of education to other countries through a variety of delivery modes (face to face, distance, e-learning, etc.) and through different administrative arrangements (franchises, twinning, branch campuses, etc.).

It is interesting to note that the "process" and "ethos" approaches focus on the primary functions of a higher education institution, including curricular, extracurricular, and organizational aspects. The "rationales" and "outcomes" approaches attach more weight to the motivations and expected results of internationalization than to the activities or strategies themselves. The "activity" approach, which is still probably the most common approach, highlights the actual program initiatives that form part of the internationalization efforts. Finally, the "abroad" or "crossborder" approach accentuates the linkages with other countries and focuses on the mobility of education across borders.

It is important to emphasize that these approaches are not mutually exclusive nor are they meant to eliminate other approaches. The purpose of developing these two frameworks is to help institutions and policymakers reflect on the dominant features of their current approach to internationalization or what approach they would like to adopt in the future. It is a useful and revealing exercise to analyze whether the dominant approach being used is consistent and complementary to the rationales and values driving the efforts to internationalize.

INTERNATIONALIZATION STRATEGIES, PROGRAMS, AND POLICIES

Another principal feature of an analytical framework for internationalization focuses on the actual strategies, programs, and policies that are used at the institutional/provider, sector, and national level. There is a hierarchical dimension to the use of these three terms. "Strategies" reflect the most concrete level and include the academic and organizational initiatives at the institutional level. "Programs" reflect a more comprehensive approach to internationalization and "Policies" set out the overall framework. It is also important to note that national and institutional values, perspectives, and rationales underpin and frame strategies, policies, and programs.

Strategies at the Institutional/Provider Level

The term "strategies" refers to both program and organizational initiatives at the institutional/provider level. The notion of a more planned, integrated, and strategic approach is therefore implied in the use of the word "strategies." Tables 2.2 and 2.3 provide information and examples of academic and organizational strategies at the institutional level and have been updated to reflect both the growth in the

CHAPTER TWO

Table 2.2. Academic strategies

Acadamic Strategies	
Academic programs	Student exchange programs, foreign language study, internationalized curricula, area or thematic studies, work/study abroad, international students, teaching/learning process, joint/double degree programs, cross-cultural training, faculty/staff mobility programs, visiting lectures and scholars, link between academic programs and other strategies
Research and scholarly collaboration	Area and theme centers, joint research projects, international conferences and seminars, published articles and papers, international research agreements, research exchange programs, international research partners in academic and other sectors
External relations: domestic and crossborder	*Domestic:* Community-based partnerships with NGO groups or public/private sector groups, community service and intercultural project work, customized education and training programs for international partners and clients *Crossborder:* International development assistance projects, crossborder delivery of education programs (commercial and noncommercial) Branch campuses, international linkages, partnerships, and networks Contract-based training and research programs and services, alumni abroad programs
Extra-curricular	Student clubs and associations, international and intercultural campus events, liaison with community-based cultural and ethnic groups, peer support groups and programs

Source: Knight (2004).

Table 2.3. Organization strategies

Governance	Expressed commitment by senior leaders, active involvement of faculty and staff, articulated rationale and goals for internationalization, recognition of the international dimension in institutional mission/mandate statements, and in planning, management, and evaluation policy documents
Operations	Integrated into institution-wide and department/college-level planning, budgeting, and quality review systems; appropriate organizational structures; systems (formal and informal) for communication, liaison, and coordination; balance between centralized and decentralized promotion and management of internationalization; adequate financial support and resource allocation systems
Services	Support from institution-wide service units, i.e., student housing, registrariat, fundraising, alumni, information technology; involvement of academic support units, i.e., library, teaching and learning, curriculum development, faculty and staff training, research services; student support services for incoming and outgoing students, i.e., orientation programs, counseling, cross-cultural training, visa advice
Human resources	Recruitment and selection procedures that recognize international expertise; reward and promotion policies to reinforce faculty and staff contributions; faculty and staff professional development activities; support for international assignments and sabbaticals

Source: Knight (2004).

commercial crossborder strategies of internationalization and also the increased interest in the internationalization of "at home" activities. This approach is probably more applicable to the traditional public and private higher education institutions than to new providers, as the latter are often more oriented to teaching activities than to research or community service or may be delivering by distance.

Strategies and a strategic approach are at the core of the success and sustainability of internationalization at the institutional level; but because the national/sector level is now covered in the definition and analytical framework, it is necessary to broaden the concept of organizational strategies to the national or sector level by introducing the terms "policies" and "programs."

Programs and Policies

The analytical framework deliberately includes policies and programs at all three levels as illustrated in Table 2.4 Programs can be seen in a more macro way than strategies and are used as one of the policy instruments or, more generally, as one of the ways in which policy is actually translated into action.

At the national-sector level, all policies that impact or are impacted by international dimension of education are included. They can involve policies related to foreign relations, development assistance, trade, immigration, employment, science and technology, culture and heritage, education, social development, industry and commerce, and others.

Table 2.4. Policy and programs at all three levels

Level	Policy	Programs
National	Education and other national-level policies relating to the international dimension of higher education, i.e., cultural, scientific, immigration, trade, employment policies	National or subregional programs, which promote or facilitate the international dimension of higher education. Can be provided by different government departments or nongovernment organizations. May be oriented to different international aspects, i.e., academic mobility programs, international research initiatives, student recruitment programs, etc.
Sector	Policies related to the purpose, functions, funding, and regulation of higher education	Programs offered by and for the education sector specifically. Can be provided by any level of government or by public or private organizations.
Institutional	Policies that address specific aspects of internationalization and/or policies that integrate the international dimension into the primary mission and functions of institution and sustain it. See Table 2.3 for examples.	Programs such as those identified in the section labeled "Academic Programs" in Table 2.2.

Source: Knight (2006b).

CHAPTER TWO

At the education sector or system level, all policies that relate to the purpose, licensing, accreditation, funding, curriculum, teaching, research, and regulation of postsecondary education are included. These education-related policies have direct implications for all kinds of providers—public and private, for-profit or nonprofit, and commercial.

In terms of the discussion on policies, it is prudent to be aware that many of the policies related to the international dimension of education will impact both the public education institutions and the commercially oriented providers. This is why it is imperative that policies at both the national/sector and institutional levels are included in an analytical framework.

At the institutional level, policies can be interpreted in different ways. A narrow interpretation would include those statements and directives that refer to priorities and plans related to the international dimension of the institution's mission, purpose, values, and functions. Examples could include the institutional mission statement or policies on study abroad, student recruitment, international linkages and partnerships, crossborder delivery, international sabbaticals, etc.

A broader interpretation of policies at the institution level would include all those statements, directives or planning documents, which address implications *for* or *from* internationalization. If the institution has taken an integrative and sustainable approach to internationalization, then a very broad range of policy and procedure statements would be implicated, ranging from quality assurance, planning, funding, staffing, faculty development, admission, research, curriculum, student support, contract, and project work.

The purpose of this chapter has been to examine the key components of a conceptual model of internationalization that will guide and respond to the changes and challenges facing higher education. The updated definition of internationalization examined here will constitute the working definition for the remaining chapters. The bifurcation of internationalization into two streams—at home and abroad—was discussed, but the emphasis was on their interdependence rather than on their role as separate components of the internationalization process.

One of the more complicated but critical aspects of understanding internationalization is the diversity of rationales that drive institutions to internationalize and that guide countries to give more importance to and invest more deeply in the international dimension of higher education. These motivations are often not explicit and are gradually changing to reflect the international competitive environment of the knowledge society and the role of higher education in the knowledge industry. Finally, the academic and organizational strategies at the institutional level, and the policies and programs at the national level received attention because they are essential factors in operationalizing a commitment and plan to internationalize.

Note: This paper is based on J. Knight (2006b), "Internationalization: Concepts, complexities and challenges," in J. Forest & P. Altbach (Eds.), *International handbook of higher education* (pp. 207–228). Dordrecht, Netherlands: Springer Academic Publishers; and J. Knight, (2004), "Internationalization remodelled: Definitions, rationales and approaches," *Journal for Studies in International Education,* 8(1), 5–31.

RELATED REFERENCES

Altbach, P. G., & Knight, J. (2006). The internationalization of higher education: Motivations and realities. In *NEA Almanac of Higher Education* (pp. 27–36). Washington, DC: National Education Association.
Arum, S., & Van de Water, J. (1992). The need for a definition of international education in U.S. universities. In C. Klasek (Ed.), *Bridges to the future: Strategies for internationalizing higher education* (pp. 198–206). Carbondale, IL: Association of International Education Administrators.
Cambridge, J., & Thompson, J. (2004). Internationalization and globalization as contexts for international education. *Compare, 34*(2), 161–175.
Deardoff, D. (2006). Identification and assessment of intercultural competence as a student outcome of internationalization. *Journal of Studies in International Education, 10*(3), 241–266.
de Wit, H. (2002). *Internationalization of higher education in the United States of America and Europe: A historical, comparative and conceptual analysis*. Westport, CT: Greenwood Press.
de Wit, H., Jaramillo, I. C., Gacel-Avila, J., & Knight, J. (Eds.). (2005). *Higher education in Latin America: The international dimension*. Washington, DC: World Bank.
Enders, J., & Fulton, O. (2002). *Higher education in a globalizing world: International trends and mutual observations*. Dordrecht, Netherlands: Kluwer.
Garrett, R. (2005). *Mapping the education industry. Part 2: Public companies–relationships with higher education*. London: Observatory on Borderless Higher Education.
Haug, G., & Race, J. (1998). Interregional cooperation in higher education in Europe. *Journal of Studies in International Education, 2*(2), 5–34.
Knight, J. (1994). *Internationalization: Elements and checkpoints*. Canadian Bureau for International Education, Research Paper No. 7. Ottawa: CBIE.
Knight, J. (1999). Issues and trends in internationalization: A comparative perspective. In S. Bond & J. P. Lemasson (Eds.), *A new world of knowledge: Canadian universities and globalization*. Ottawa, Canada: International Development Research Centre.
Knight, J. (2004). Internationalization remodeled: Definitions, rationales, and approaches. *Journal for Studies in International Education, 8*(1), 5–31.
Knight, J. (2005) An internationalization model: Responding to new realities and challenges. In H. de Wit, I. C. Jaramillo, J. Gacel-Avila, & J. Knight (Eds.), *Higher education in Latin America: The international dimension* (pp. 1–38). Washington, DC: World Bank.
Knight, J. (2006a). *Internationalization of higher education: New directions, new challenges*. 2005 International Association of Universities Global Survey Report. Paris: International Association of Universities.
Knight, J. (2006b). Internationalization: Concepts, complexities and challenges. In J. Forest & P. Altbach (Eds.), *International handbook of higher education* (pp. 207–228). Dordrecht, Netherlands: Springer Academic Publishers.
Knight, J., & de Wit, H. (Eds.). (1999). *Quality and internationalization in higher education*. Paris: Institutional Management of Higher Education/Organization for Economic and Community Development.
Kushin, R. (Ed.). (2006). *The internationalization of higher education in South Africa*. Durban, South Africa: International Education Association of South Africa.
Nilsson, B. (2003). Internationalization at home: Theory and praxis. *European Association for International Education Forum, 12*.
Odin, J., & Mancias, P. (Eds.). (2004). *Globalization and higher education*. Honolulu, HI: University of Hawaii Press.
OECD. Organization for Economic and Community Development. (2002). *The growth of crossborder education: Educational policy analysis*. Paris: Organization for Economic and Community Development.
Some, D., & Khaemba, B. (2004). *Internationalization of higher education: The African experience and perspective*. Eldoret, Kenya: Moi University Press.
Teichler, U. (2004). The changing debate on internationalization of higher education. *Higher Education, 48*(1), 5–34.
Van der Wende, M. (1997). Missing links: The relationship between national policies for internationalization and those for higher education in general. In T. Kalvermark & M. Van der Wende (Eds.), *National policies for the internationalization of higher education in Europe* (pp. 10–31). Stockholm, Sweden: Hogskoleverket Studies, National Agency for Higher Education.

CHAPTER THREE

MONITORING THE QUALITY AND PROGRESS OF INTERNATIONALIZATION

INTRODUCTION

The internationalization of higher education will be remembered as one of the major challenges and accomplishments of the last two decades in the 20th century. The key question related to this statement is: For what will it be remembered? Will it be seen as a positive influence or one which had negative effects? To help answer these questions, more attention needs to be given to monitoring and evaluating the progress, quality, results, and impact of internationalization efforts.

Recent studies and surveys have shown an increase in the importance and attention given to supporting internationalization. This interest has translated into the active development of policies, programs, and infrastructure at both institutional and government levels. While this expansion and investment in internationalization are welcomed and needed, it is necessary to sharpen the focus on the evaluation of internationalization strategies and to make sure that we are "doing the right things" and "doing things in the right way."

The purpose of this chapter is threefold: to emphasize the importance of monitoring and evaluating internationalization initiatives; to introduce some preliminary measures to track the progress and quality of different elements and strategies of internationalization; and to review existing quality assessment and assurance instruments which can be applied to internationalization.

The Internationalization Cycle (Knight, 1994) identifies six major phases: (a) awareness, (b) commitment, (c) planning, (d) operationalization, (e) review, and (f) reinforcement. The phases are not discrete as there is considerable overlap between each, but there is a logic to the sequence of the stages in the cycle. As internationalization comes of age with movement through the different phases of the cycle, it is appropriate and timely to put more focus on review and evaluation. One approach to evaluating internationalization strategies includes the use of tracking measures, the subject of this chapter.

The proposed tracking measures should not be interpreted as performance indicators of internationalization. If internationalization is seen as a process, these tracking measures are meant to help in evaluating the progress and quality of the process. They are not intended to assess the results or impact of internationalization; however, evaluation of results is of critical importance and also needs to be addressed systematically.

CHAPTER THREE

RELATIONSHIP BETWEEN QUALITY AND INTERNATIONALIZATION

When one examines the relationship between quality and internationalization, there are two fundamental issues to consider (Knight & de Wit, 1999). The first one is a macro-level issue which relates to the question of the added value or qualitative difference that internationalization contributes to higher education. This is an outcomes or results-oriented approach. The second issue is more relevant to the institutional level and focuses on the quality of the individual and overall internationalization strategies. In other words, it asks: What is the quality of the internationalization initiatives that are undertaken from more of a process perspective?

The first approach focuses on integrating the international dimension into the regular, ongoing quality assessment and assurance systems of institutional reviews, including program/discipline audits. The second approach involves the development of a special quality review system or instrument to assess internationalization policies, programs, and initiatives. This chapter focuses on tracking measures of internationalization, which relate more to the second approach.

Meaning of Quality and Progress

The term "quality" is much used and misused in the field of higher education. It is a complex concept because it is often in the eye of the beholder; and given that there are many and diverse beholders/stakeholders in the education sector, it means that there are a broad range of meanings. Some interpret quality in terms of efficiency, effectiveness, and equity. Others describe quality in terms of perfection ("zero errors") and excellence. And still other stakeholders see quality as value for money. All can be correct if their basic assumptions are made clear.

Quality is a multidimensional concept and is grounded in values, cultures, and traditions of individuals, institutions, and countries. Therefore, it is essential to be clear about what meaning we are giving to the term. Harvey and Green (1993) attempted to develop a taxonomy of terms for the concept of quality. Their primary categories are:
- Quality as "excellence." This is a traditional understanding of quality which involves trying to do the best job possible. This interpretation is used very often in higher education.
- Quality as "zero errors." This interpretation centers on striving to be perfect. A "zero errors" approach is more appropriate for the manufacturing industry than for the education sector where it is hard to define, let alone achieve, perfection.
- Quality as "transformation." This view rests on the belief that development and evolution are the basis of quality. The focus is often on the development and empowering of students.
- Quality as "threshold." Quality is defined as a set of standards or norms or criteria which need to be met. The advantage of this approach is that the threshold or standard is objective and consistent. However, it has a steady state sense to it once the quality threshold has been achieved. The concept of standards is often

used in the certification or accreditation processes that are well known in the education sector.
- Quality as "enhancement." Continuous improvement is the backbone of this approach to defining quality. This approach is the mirror image of the "threshold" approach. While the advantages include a dynamic and constant improvement approach, it is often challenging to obtain an objective measure.
- Quality as "fitness for purpose." This interpretation is guided by the belief that it is difficult, if not impossible, to define quality in general and that quality therefore needs to seen as appropriateness for a specific purpose. If this is the case, the purpose needs to be clearly described or defined in terms of objectives or mission and quality can be demonstrated by achieving the objectives. This definition is frequently used in the higher education sector.

For the purposes of this discussion, "quality" is used in the context of trying to do the best job possible (excellence) and of continuous improvement to help meet stated objectives. Quality as fitness for purpose is also a defining feature as it is directly linked with the concept of progress.

Unlike quality, progress is a stand-alone and rather straightforward concept. The essence of the term is movement toward a desired objective or circumstance. The key element in this definition is the objective or circumstance. All too often, the objective is implied or not stated very clearly, so that it is difficult to assess it with either a qualitative or quantitative measure. It is assumed that the "desired objectives" are appropriate for the institution's overall mission. Progress, as already mentioned, is closely linked to the "fitness for purpose" definition of quality which stresses appropriateness for a specific objective.

EVALUATION OF QUALITY

Quality evaluation can be described as any process leading to judgments and/or recommendations regarding the quality of a unit, activity, or strategy. Different terms are used to differentiate among various approaches to quality evaluation. According to Woodhouse (1996), there are basically four different generic approaches: (a) general accreditation, (b) specialized or profession accreditation, (c) audit or review, and (d) quality assessment.

Accreditation is an evaluation of whether an institution qualifies for a certain status. Accreditation asks, "Are you good enough" to be approved? when approval implies admission to some category. Assessment is usually an evaluation that results in a grade, whether it be numeric or descriptive. Assessment asks "how good are your outputs?" Audit (or review) is a check on an institution's explicit or implicit claims about itself. A review or audit asks "Are your processes effective in achieving your objectives?" Fundamentally, the difference between an assessment and accreditation is that the former asks "How good are you?" and the latter asks, "Are you good enough?" An audit or review, therefore, asks, "How good are you at achieving your stated objectives?" The tracking measures are conceived as a review tool as they focus on the quality and progress toward achieving explicit objectives.

CHAPTER THREE

The term "quality assurance" refers to the policies, attitudes, actions, and procedures necessary to ensure that quality is being maintained and enhanced. It can involve different approaches which are collectively and generically referred to as quality assurance (Woodhouse, 1999).

QUALITY MATTERS: IMPORTANCE IN HIGHER EDUCATION

There are a number of reasons why quality assessment and assurance is more of a priority in many countries (El-Khawas, DePietro-Jurand, & Holm-Nielsen, 1998; QAA, 1998, Schofield, 1999). During the phase of rapid expansion and rationalization of higher education systems, some determination of quality is necessary to guide these developments. The increasing influence of the market approach to higher education is another catalyst influencing both the growth and downsizing of higher education systems. The number and diversity of new types of alternative providers, which are often outside the traditional education sector, raise new issues and challenges The increased emphasis on accountability for public sector funding in general and for education in particular is another major reason. This situation is intensified by the changing role of government in education resulting in decreased funding from government sources. All these factors contribute to an increasing preoccupation with quality and with quality assessment. In this context, quality assessment is usually seen in terms of greater accountability by the institutions to their various stakeholders.

The higher education sector around the world is also being impacted by new challenges, trends, and issues. They include privatization, decreased government funding, new teaching/learning/research technologies, globalization, the knowledge-based economy, increased competition, and new forms of collaboration. To respond proactively to these influences, quality assessment and assurance have been identified as means to help improve an institution's or program's relevance, efficiency, and effectiveness. Another reason is the growing emphasis on the outcomes-based approach to education, which leads to an increased interest in performance indicators. Tied to this trend is the consumer movement in which the student as client/customer is seen as shopping around for the best value for the money invested. Indicators of quality (perceived or real) are also important in this scenario as proved by the importance and controversy of the new international ranking systems of higher education institutions.

These trends and issues relate to higher education in general, but they are also pertinent to internationalization. Along with the increased importance of, commitment to, and investment in internationalization, there are increased expectations about the quality of the endeavors and the added value to higher education.

As a result of the increasing numbers of students who are traveling to other countries to undertake full degrees or even a semester of study, there is more interest in having indicators to assure prospective students of the quality and equality of degrees. The same situation applies to the growing number of full degree or certificate programs which are being exported to foreign countries. There is real concern on the part of the receiving countries that they are getting the same academic quality as the similar programs being offered at home institutions. Countries such as Hong Kong, Malaysia, and China are establishing quality control systems for imported programs, while simultaneously, exporting countries such as the United Kingdom and Australia are implementing quality assessment procedures for many of their exported programs. (See Chapter 7.)

There seems to be a myth accompanying the great leap forward in the internationalization of colleges and universities—the perception that the more international a university is, the better it is and the higher quality its programs are. Of course, one wants to believe and ensure that the international dimension of teaching/learning, research, and service is enhancing the quality of education, but do we have a way to prove it? At this point in time, colleges and universities are becoming increasingly competitive for both the domestic and international market of students. The international dimension (or the IQ—International Quotient!—however it may be measured) is being used as a strong marketing and branding feature.

For the most part, institutions are not gathering information systematically or consistently, nor are they undertaking evaluations of their internationalization efforts. As internationalization comes more of age, more questions will be asked about the quality of its strategies and the results or benefits accrued. These are fair and important questions. It is necessary to plan for and address these concerns. Different kinds of approaches and measures are required. The proposed tracking measures are but one tool to help collect and analyze the information necessary for evaluating internationalization.

Finally, the direct experience of developing, testing, and revising the Internationalization Quality Review Process (Knight & de Wit, 1999) has led to the realization that institutions need a way to monitor internationalization and collect information on an ongoing basis. Institutions often spend too much time describing in very vague terms the status of the internationalization. More precise, relevant measures of explicit objectives and targets will help provide the information necessary to analyze strengths and areas of improvements. With the information collected from the tracking measures, institutions can proceed to the more important step of analyzing how to maintain areas of strength, improve areas of weakness, and ensure that internationalization goals and objectives are being met. This is, in turn, a precursor to analyzing the results and outcomes of internationalization endeavors.

INTRODUCTION TO INTERNATIONALIZATION TRACKING MEASURES

The term "tracking measure," as opposed to "performance measure" or "indicator," has been consciously used to emphasize progress, rather than output. Tracking measures use quantitative data captured by numbers, ratios, or yes/no responses as well as qualitative information expressed as opinions and judgments. According to Einstein, "Not everything that can be counted counts, and not everything that counts can be counted." This supports the importance of using both quantitative and qualitative measures. Furthermore, the two types of approaches are usually stronger when used together.

CHAPTER THREE

Tracking measures can provide a single snapshot of what is happening at a given moment in time. Or, if used longitudinally, they can be described as "monitors of the pulse," signaling shifts in trends, either positive or negative. Tracking measures over time are likely to be more significant and useful than their comparative value at any one time, because positive trends will focus on how to preserve what is being done right and negative trends will highlight opportunities for improvement.

To identify appropriate tracking measures is a challenge. They need to be relevant, clear, reliable, consistent, accessible, and easy to use. If inappropriate tracking measures are developed, the process of collecting the information can be a time-consuming and bureaucratic waste of resources. Therefore, institutions need to be vigilant about their choice of tracking measures. Such measures need to be pertinent to the desired objective and limited to the most relevant, or more effort will be put into collecting the information than on analyzing it. Finally, the tracking measures need to stand the test of time, as they should be used over a period to get a true picture of progress toward reaching the objective and whether there is any improvement.

PRINCIPLES GUIDING THE DEVELOPMENT OF INTERNATIONALIZATION TRACKING MEASURES

An internationalization tracking measure is a measure which tracks the progress and quality of an internationalization element or strategy toward achieving a desired objective or target. Eight principles have guided the development of internationalization tracking measures:

1. The internationalization tracking measures are focused on two aspects: *progress and quality.* Progress is measured by a quantitative and/or qualitative measure and assesses movement toward achieving objectives and targets. Quality is measured by the opinion or judgment of those doing the assessment. It is a qualitative judgment of the level of excellence achieved and improvement needed.
2. The proposed tracking measures are based on the assumption that the progress and quality of internationalization efforts can be measured *according to the objectives and targets set by the institution.* One of the key challenges involved is making the objectives and targets more explicit. It is impossible to know whether the goal has been reached or has been well done if it has not been clearly defined or stated.
3. The tracking measures relate to both *organizational strategies* (i.e., policies, procedures, and structures) and *program strategies* (i.e., student and faculty mobility, curriculum, research, institutional agreements, and international students). (See Chapter 2.) This principle assumes that, if an international/intercultural/global dimension is to be integrated and sustained, then both activities and policies/structures need to be addressed and evaluated.
4. The tracking measures are *more oriented to evaluating the process of internationalization then the outcomes or impacts.* For instance, they do not attempt to measure the degree to which internationalization efforts have increased the knowledge or skills of the graduates or their employability. But they *do* attempt

to measure how well the institution has met its objective of internationalizing the academic experience (through curriculum, teaching/learning processes, study abroad initiatives) so that students will gain a deeper understanding of international issues and increased intercultural skills.
5. Internationalization tracking measures *point out where improvement is desirable and necessary;* they do not provide explicit directions on how to improve.
6. There is *no ideal or optimal measurement profile* of an internationalized higher education institution. The tracking measures are not intended to be used to achieve a quality standard of what an internationalized institution would look like.
7. The adage that the "whole is greater than the sum of its parts" applies to the use of the tracking measures. Tracking each element or strategy has merit, but how the different *elements work together in an integrated and strategic manner* is equally important; and therefore the relationships between and among tracking measures need to be analyzed.
8. Tracking measures fit into the *review phase of the internationalization cycle.* Therefore, to gain full benefit from them, they need to be used on a regular basis and over a period of time so that they can inform the ongoing planning, implementation, and reinforcement of the internationalization plan.

THE INTERNATIONALIZATION TRACKING MEASURE CHART

The purpose of the tracking measure chart is to collect information which can be used to analyze what improvements are necessary, desirable and feasible. The chart in Table 3.1 ensures that objectives, targets, and the level of achievement are clearly stated. When used appropriately, the chart can signal where there are problems to be addressed and why improvement is required. The conceptual framework for the charts is introduced in the table, then elaborated on in the following section.

Explanation of the Chart

The following section explains the purpose and use for each column. This information will help the user better understand the intent of the chart and help in the use of the charts.

Time period. It is extremely important to determine a realistic time period for setting objectives/targets and their eventual evaluation. Tracking measures can be updated on a frequent basis which allows for the ongoing monitoring of the progress and quality. The determination and evaluation of the significance of the measures at the end of the period are essential for setting priorities and planning the next cycle.

Column 1. Element/Strategy. A comprehensive internationalization plan consists of different elements or strategies. Each institution will give different levels of importance to individual strategies. "Elements" and "strategies" are terms which can be used interchangeably. They refer to the organizational strategies (e.g., policies, structures, resources) and to program areas (e.g., curriculum, research, projects).

CHAPTER THREE

Table 3.1. Chart for formatting internationalization tracking measures

Time Period: Date to Date					
Strategy/ Element	Tracking Measure	Objective or Target Quantitative or Qualitative	Progress Quantitative Measure	Progress Qualitative Measure	Quality Qualitative Measure
			Actual Number or Yes/No	Degree of Progress	Level of Quality
			0	1 2 3	A B C D
Column 1	Column 2	Column 3	Column 4	Column 5	Column 6
"Elements" refers to the major components or strategies of an institution's overall plan for internationalization. They can be organizational strategies (policies, structures, resources) or program strategies (i.e., international agreements, curriculum, student mobility).	A tracking measure is the tool used to assess a particular aspect of the element or strategy.	A clearly stated objective or target is a prerequisite to assessing progress and quality. The objective or target can be expressed in narrative or numerical terms.	This column provides the current level of achievement either in numerical terms or, in a few cases, with a yes/no response.	A judgment on the level of progress is stated in this column. It is critical to identify areas where improvement is required.	The level of excellence or amount of improvement needed to fully achieve the stated objective or target is included in this column. It signals where strengths need to be maintained or where improvements are required.
Legend	Progress:	0 = none	1 = low	2 = medium	3 = high
	Quality	A = Needs significant improvement	B = Needs some improvement	C = Adequate	D = Excellent

Column 2. Tracking measure. The tracking measure is designed to monitor and measure a particular aspect of the internationalization element. It is imperative that the tracking measures assess the presence and functioning of policies, and procedures as well as programs. The examples provided below are considered to be important individually and as a set. Some may not be particularly relevant to an institution's articulated priorities and in this case should be eliminated. In other cases, institutions may want to add measures that are particularly relevant to their plan.

Column 3. Objective/Target: Quantitative or qualitative response. Quality and progress are more effectively measured if there is an explicit objective or target stated. In too many instances, goals and objectives are implicit and vague. It is therefore important to state clearly whether the specific aspect described by the measure is (a) a priority for the institution and (b) has been articulated in terms of a measurable objective or target.

The user will find that several measures are purposely not defined in numerical terms. In these instances, it is more likely that the user will answer "yes" or "no" or by indicating whether this item is a priority for the institution. On the whole, this column is more important for measures requiring a numerical response. It is directly linked to Column 4.

Column 4. Progress, quantitative measure, actual number. The purpose of this column is to present and compare the actual numbers (ratios, percentages, etc.) as compared to the target numbers identified in the previous column. The differences between the target (Column 3) and the actual numbers (Column 4) will show the degree of progress being made toward achieving the objective.

Column 5. Progress, qualitative measure, degree of progress. It is important to know the perceived degree of progress toward achieving the stated objective. Quantitative numbers do not tell the whole story. The intent of this column is to have the user reflect on what degree of progress is really being made and why. The information is used to determine ways and means of either maintaining the high degree of progress or to improve where there is a low level.

Column 6. Quality, qualitative measure, level of quality. In essence, this column addresses the level of excellence achieved and the amount of improvement needed. The rating scale has four indicators: A = significant improvement needed, B = some improvement needed, C = adequate, and D = excellent. Assigning an actual designation helps the user to subjectively assess the quality. This is descriptive information only and will not be of any use to institutions unless the next step of analysis is taken. Action to either maintain excellence or implement the necessary improvements needs to be identified, agreed upon, supported, implemented, and then evaluated. This description demonstrates that the use of tracking measures is cyclical.

Suggested Tracking Measures

The set of tracking measures for key areas of internationalization presented below can be considered as examples. Institutions will want to customize the measures to make sure they are relevant and useful to their particular programs and priorities. An important aspect to remember is that they should be clear, easily measured, and capable of being used over time.

Planning and Review

The international dimension is acknowledged in the institutional mission statement.

The rationale, goals, and benefits of internationalization are clearly articulated in institutional policy or planning documents.

A comprehensive internationalization strategic/long-term plan supported by annual operational plans is in place.

A direct link exists between the internationalization strategic plan and the institution's overall long-term plan.

Country-specific plans to coordinate diverse international activities in priority countries are in place.

CHAPTER THREE

Table 3.2. Sample chart

CHART OF INSTITUTIONAL ACADEMIC AGREEMENTS AND COOPERATION

Time Period: September 2007 – September 2008

Strategy/ Elements	Tracking Measure	Objective or Target	Progress	Progress				Quality			
		Quantitative or Qualitative	Quantitative Measure	Qualitative Measure				Qualitative Measure			
			Actual Number	Degree of Progress				Level of Quality			
				0	1	2	3	A	B	C	D
Institutional Academic Agreements and Co-operation	Percentage of departments with international agreements	60%	40%		x			x			
	Total number of international academic agreements	45	38			x				x	
Includes bilateral or multilateral relationships	Number of international academic agreements active during the past two years	25	18		x			x			
Types of activities include: student and faculty exchange, joint research projects, curriculum design and delivery, etc.	Number of agreements which are multidimensional	30 (out of 45)	15	x				x			
	A strategic approach and set of criteria used for selection of countries and partners.	to be developed by June 2009				x				x	
	Internal evaluation system assesses agreements on a regular basis.	to be revised by Sept 2010					x				x
	Desired geographic balance is achieved.	high priority		x				x			
	Desired developing/developed country balance is achieved.	low priority			x				x		
	Desired discipline balance is achieved.	medium priority				x				x	
Legend	**Progress:** 0 = none		1 = low			2 = medium				3 = high	
	Quality A = Needs significant Improvement		B = Needs some improvement			C = Adequate				D = Excellent	

48

Review and evaluation mechanisms for the internationalization program and organization strategies are operational.

Specific improvement plans are developed and implemented after evaluations are complete.

Faculty/Staff Involvement

Number of faculty/staff participating in international institutional exchange through agreements.

Number of faculty/staff participating in overseas research, development, or training projects.

Number of visiting international faculty/staff collaborating with domestic personnel.

Number of departments with faculty/staff directly involved and supported in international activities.

Number of faculty/staff receiving external grants/support for international academic activities.

Number of faculty/staff receiving internal grants/support for international academic activities.

Professional development workshops available on a regular basis to support involvement in overseas projects such as teaching, training, consulting, benchmarking, etc.

Faculty/Staff Appointment, Promotion, Tenure, Recognition

Hiring policies and practices include criteria for international expertise where relevant.

Promotion and tenure policies and practices include criteria for international achievements.

Explicit recognition is given to faculty/staff for leadership, innovation, or excellence in internationalization pursuits.

Institutional Academic Agreements and Cooperation

Percentage of departments with active international agreements.

Total number of international academic agreements.

Number of international academic agreements active during the past two years.

Number of agreements which are multi-dimensional.

Existence of a strategic approach and set of criteria for the selection of partners and countries.

An evaluation system that assesses agreements on a regular basis.

Achieving desired geographic balance.

Achieving desired developing/developed country balance.

Achieving desired discipline balance.

Advisory and Support Services for Students' Study Abroad

Available study abroad opportunities are widely promoted to all students.

Counseling services are provided for outgoing and incoming students.

Pre-departure preparation is provided for all outgoing students.

Re-entry debriefing and support are available for all returning students.

Appropriate safety and legal processes are in place for study-abroad students.

CHAPTER THREE

Workshops for faculty on integrating study abroad experiences into the curriculum and research are provided.

Cross-cultural communication workshops for students and faculty/staff members are provided.

Student Exchange Programs

Number of active student exchange agreements.

Total number of outgoing undergraduates per year.

Total number of outgoing graduate students per year.

Percentage of total student enrollment represented by outgoing undergraduate/graduate students.

Number of incoming exchange undergraduates per year.

Number of incoming exchange graduate students per year.

Number of different departments sending or receiving students on exchange.

Internships or placements, field trips, work-abroad projects

Number of different schools/departments offering opportunities.

Number of different courses providing international field trips.

Total number of students participating in internships, field trips, work projects.

Strong link with curriculum, teaching/learning, and research.

Advisory and Support Services for International Students

Trained academic and social/cultural advisor(s).

Social/cultural/peer programs for international and domestic students.

Counseling on visa, health, employment, and security issues.

Academic monitoring and support services.

Links provided to local community services and activities.

Number of International Students on Campus

Total number of full-time, international, fee-paying students on campus.

Percentage of total student enrollment that this number represents

Percentage of departments with international students enrolled.

Achievement of desired geographic and cultural balance.

Curriculum and Teaching/Learning Process: Integrating an International/Intercultural Perspective

A review process is in place to identify and monitor the integration of international, comparative, global, or intercultural perspective or issues.

Workshops and funding are offered to provide faculty assistance in internationalizing curriculum.

International scholars, visiting experts, and local international/multicultural groups are regularly involved.

International students and returned study-abroad students are integrated as resources in the classroom.

Communication technology is used so students can do joint assignments with students in other countries.

Strong links are established between development projects, international field research, and curriculum.

Curriculum: Foreign Language Study
   Number of foreign languages taught at undergraduate level.
   Percent of undergraduate students taking foreign language studies as a major or minor.

International Courses and Programs
   Number of undergraduate and graduate level programs specifically designed with international content or placement.
   Desired balance across disciplines achieved.
   Number of joint or double degrees with international institutions.

Research and Scholarly Activities
   Advisory services and funding support for faculty/staff to develop international research projects or links.
   Number of active international collaborative research agreements.
   Number of departments with formal research projects with international partners,
   Percentage of all externally funded research initiatives which involve international partners.

International Development Projects
   Number of currently operating international development projects.
   Balance of distribution of projects across departments/centers.
   Academic contribution of project to curriculum and research activities.
   Number and distribution of faculty/staff and students involved in and benefiting from project.
   Whether projects have strong links to other internationalization activities.

Crossborder Academic Programs
   Guidelines/criteria for choosing international partners and determining academic and feasibility of proposed initiatives.
   Coordinating mechanism in place to monitor selection, implementation, and evaluation of crossborder academic programs.
   Training/briefing and recognition given to faculty/staff who teach in program.
   Strong links with other international activities in same country or region.
   Evaluation procedures in place for all crossborder activities.

Organizational Structures
   A designated office with responsibility for providing support, resources, and monitoring of the overall internationalization plan/strategy.
   A mechanism (committee, unit, position) with the responsibility of coordinating the different units and offices and direct operational responsibility for international initiatives.
   Central university services (library, student services, housing, etc.) that provide active support, where appropriate, for the internationalization plan and efforts.

Financing of International Efforts
   A mechanism is operational for allocating resources to support internationalization at both central and local levels.
   A cost/revenue allocation system exists for fees/revenue from international activities.

CHAPTER THREE

A sustainable funding base has been established for core internationalization activities.

International initiatives are included in the institution's external fund-raising campaigns.

GUIDELINES ON USING THE TRACKING MEASURES

The way in which the different elements are integrated and reinforce each other is critical to developing a successful and sustainable internationalization plan. Attempts have been made in the tracking measure lists to address the relationship and link between and among strategies. However, the very format of separate lists for each strategy is not conducive to promoting a holistic and integrated approach. Users are encouraged to stress the relationship of one element to another during the self-assessment use of the tracking measures.

The tracking measures are not specifically designed for comparison between or among institutions in a benchmarking type of exercise. Some of the tracking measures can be interpreted in several different ways, a factor that negates the value of a cross-institution comparison. However, they can easily be adapted for this purpose by the use of common definitions by an interested group of institutions or by the selection of tracking measures pertinent to their overall goals for internationalization. Given this approach, then tracking measures could be used effectively in a benchmarking context.

Qualitative measures by definition are subjective. They are the opinions and judgments of those doing the assessment. Because of this characteristic, it may be prudent to avoid having only one person undertake the evaluation.

The tracking measures can be used in the self-assessment phase of many quality assessment exercises. For instance, they could provide a systematic way for institutions to collect some of the necessary information for the Internationalization Quality Review process (see Chapter 4) or other evaluation schemes. They have been designed to be used as a "stand-alone" self-assessment procedure or as part of other quality assessment procedures.

Tracking measures are intended to be used as one part of an evaluation exercise for those institutions with an overall internationalization plan in place. However, institutions that are in the initial phase of developing a strategic plan for internationalization may find the concept of tracking measures useful.

A REVIEW OF QUALITY EVALUATION INSTRUMENTS

The purpose of this section is to identify and briefly describe several quality assessment instruments which are being applied to the international dimension of higher education (Knight, Adams, & Peace Lenn, 1999). These include: Codes of Practice, GATE principles, IQRP, ISO 9000 guidelines, and benchmarks. An examination of these instruments illustrates the evolution in the tools being developed to assess and assure the quality of international education. They also reflect the complexity and diversity of quality review processes.

Codes of Practice for International Students

Codes of practice are quite traditional approaches used to address the quality assurance of specific international activities, but they almost never address the progress dimension at all. For the most part, these codes of practice are statements of principles and can be interpreted as moral imperatives in defined areas of internationalization. Codes of practice are very common at the national level.

For example, the United Kingdom Council for Overseas Student Affairs (UKCOSA), in conjunction with the British Council, educational institutions, and professional organizations were among the first organizations to develop a "Code of Practice for Educational Institutions and Overseas Students." The UKCOSA code is an example of the kind of approach used in the mid-1980s to ensure ethical and responsible recruitment practices and support services for international students studying in the United Kingdom.

As the size of the market for international students increased, codes of practice took on more importance and were often broadened in scope. The "Code of Ethical Practice in International Education" developed by the Canadian Bureau for International Education (CBIE, 1996) is a good example. Interestingly, it uses the term "International Education," not "International Students" and covers many different types of activities. The CBIE code is essentially a statement of principles which all members accept by virtue of their membership in CBIE. It does not articulate protocols for the monitoring or enforcement of the code.

The set of principles by the Australian Vice-Chancellors Committee (AVCC, 1998) is an example of how codes evolve to respond to changes in providing international education. The AVCC revised two of its existing codes of practice and has combined them into a new "Code of Ethical Practice in the Provision of Education to International Students by Australian Universities." The first part of the revised code contains "Guidelines for Universities Providing Courses to International Students." They cover 10 major points, for example, promotion and marketing, agents and partners, admission, pre-arrival information for international students studying in Australia, university infrastructure, and debriefing for offshore students returning home. The second set of guidelines included in the code addresses the issue of fees refunds for international students.

More recently, new codes of practice have been developed for delivering programs to students in other countries using a variety of delivery modes and partnership arrangements. (See Chapter 7.) While codes of practice have been developed and adopted by national organizations for many years, they remain a generic type of quality assurance instrument. In general, they do not include any kind of an external regulatory system. Instead such a code appeals to the ethics and conscience of the institutions and the staff who are involved in international student mobility programs, and it tries to develop a set of values and principles to guide the process.

The Global Alliance for Transnational Education (GATE) Principles

Transnational education, as defined by GATE (1997), "denotes any teaching or learning activity in which the learners are in a different country (the host country)

CHAPTER THREE

to that in which the institution providing the education is based (the home coutry)." This situation requires that national boundaries be crossed by information about the education, and by staff and/or educational materials.

GATE's "Principles for Transnational Education" (1997) guide the provision of transnational education. (In 2003 GATE was transferred from Jones International and is now part of the United States Distance Education Association). The principles serve as a code for good practice which institutions should adhere to when offering transnational education. They are summarized below.

1. Goals and objectives: Transnational courses must be guided by goals and objectives that are understood by the participants who enroll in them. They must fit appropriately within the provider's mission and expertise.
2. Standards: The provider must assure students receiving education/education(al) credentials through transnational courses that the provider has approved the courses, that they meet its criteria for educational quality, and that the same standards are applied, regardless of the place or manner in which the courses are provided.
3. Legal and ethical matters: Transnational courses must comply with all appropriate laws and approvals of the host country.
4. Student enrollment and admission: Participants in transnational courses must be treated equitably and ethically. In particular, all pertinent information must be disclosed to the participants. Each participant must hold full student status or its equivalent with the provider organization.
5. Human resources: The provider must have a sufficient number of fully qualified people engaged in providing the transnational courses, and their activities must be supervised and regularly evaluated as a normal activity of the provider.
6. Physical and financial resources: The provider must assure an adequate learning environment and resources for the transnational courses, and must ensure that adequate resources will continue to be available until all obligations to enrolled participants are fulfilled.
7. Teaching and learning: Transnational courses must be pedagogically sound in teaching methods and in learners' nature and needs.
8. Student support: The provider must ensure that students have adequate support services to maximize the potential benefit they receive from the transnational courses.
9. Evaluation: Transnational courses must be regularly and appropriately evaluated as a normal part of the provider organization's activities. The results of the evaluations must be used to improve these courses.
10. Third parties: Where third parties, such as agents or collaborating institutions, are involved, explicit written agreements must spell out roles, expectations, and obligations

Internationalization Quality Review Process (IQRP)

The Internationalization Quality Review Process (Knight & de Wit, 1999) is a process whereby individual institutions of higher education assess and enhance the quality of their international dimension according to their own stated aims and objectives. The review process includes procedures, guidelines, and tools to be adapted and used in both a self-assessment exercise and an external peer review. The purpose of IQRP is to help institutions improve their internationalization work; it is not a certification or accreditation process.

The IQRP was developed by the Programme on Institutional Management of Higher Education (IMHE) of the Organisation for Economic Co-operation and Development (OECD) in consultation with the Academic Co-operation Association (ACA). The IQRP's starting point is the institution's own stated aims and objectives. The review process assesses the extent to which institutions actually achieve the aims and objectives which they set for themselves. The assessment of the relationship between objectives and actual achievement focuses on the core of the quality issue. See Chapter 4 for details on using the IQPR guidelines.

The framework is organized into these major parts:
1. Summary of the higher education system
2. Summary of the institutional profile
3. Analysis of the (inter) national context
4. Policies and strategies
5. Organization and support services
6. Academic programs
7. Research and scholarly collaboration
8. Students
9. Faculty and staff
10. External relations and services
11. Conclusions

The IQRP guidelines and framework are designed to apply to a great variety of circumstances. They can be used by small and large institutions, comprehensive or specialized institutions, private or public institutions, and in developed or developing countries. The guidelines are flexible enough that the IQRP can be used by institutions wishing to assess a well-developed institutional plan or those in the process of developing a strategy. Therefore, while the review process is intended to be international in application, acknowledgment and recognition of differences among institutions and countries is essential.

The ISO Set of Standards

ISO 9000 is a generic term for the International Standards Association family of standards and guidelines relating to the quality assurance of management systems. In short, the standards specify requirements for what the organization should do to manage processes which influence quality.

The ISO standards originated in the manufacturing industry. Their relevance to education is growing as education is increasingly being seen as a service industry. The current emphasis on the quality of education services is leading governments to demand that colleges and universities publicly demonstrate that they not announce their quality status but provide evidence for it. As a result, institutions are searching for concrete and coherent quality assurance systems that provide evidence in ways acceptable to an external audit process. The ISO 9000 family of standards has thus entered the education sector as one of these standardized external audit procedures. ISO 9000 standards are seen as a reliable means of providing quality assurance over the broad range of institutional processes and, in some cases, the design of the educational product itself. ISO is not a certifying authority. It publishes agreed standards but does not certify the outcome.

In an education setting, some of the management processes amenable to ISO 9002 application include student admissions, staff selection and development, strategic planning, teaching and learning, research and project administration, international activities, and financial planning and accounting. At the most fundamental level, ISO is concerned with documenting the management systems and the compliance with those systems.

Quality assurance processes provide a means of demonstrating the institution's commitment to its clients both domestic and international. As a way to illustrate how ISO standards are equally important and appropriate for international initiatives, several key areas of internationalization activities which lend themselves to an ISO 9000 review are listed below. Each category includes examples of the management processes that could be documented and monitored for quality compliance (Adams, 1998).

Institutional Strategy and Policy
    Development of appropriate missions, strategies, and values
    Relationship of the internationalization strategy to institutional strategy, mission, and values
    Explicit articulation of the rationale, goals, and objectives for internationalization
    Policy statements to enable and monitor internationalization activities
    Relationship of international initiatives and programs undertaken to the international strategy

Students
    Provision for international experience as part of academic course credit for 10% of students
    Promotion and access to study-abroad opportunities
    Academic, cultural, and logistical support for incoming/outgoing students
    Student satisfaction
    Cross-cultural briefing and support
    Articulation arrangements
    Relationship to internationalization of the curriculum strategy
    Program evaluation

Offshore Programs
    Development of offshore degree programs (defined as a range of delivery modes and direct teaching that provide opportunities for students to study and obtain a foreign degree completely or partially in their own country)
    Contract development and maintenance
    Selection of partners and representatives
    Student admission standards compared to those of the degree-granting country

Processes for the transfer of offshore students to the degree-granting country
Relationship of courses taught transnationally with domestic courses
In-country cultural and ethical standards
In-country regulatory and tax advice
Marketing, recruiting, and admissions procedures
Student support

International Students
Recruitment of international fee-paying students
Marketing and recruiting strategy for international students
Publications strategy
International student admissions
International student support
Cross-cultural teaching and learning strategies
Cross-cultural training for teaching and administrative staff
English language standards of entry and support
Acceptance of overseas qualifications for entry and advanced standing
Relationship between domestic and international standards of entry
Selection and support of recruiting agents
International student performance and graduation rate

Curriculum and Teaching/Learning Process
Explicit and implicit internationalization of the curriculum
Cross-cultural teaching and support
Staff development
Relationship to student and staff mobility
Resources available for project development
International internship and cooperative education openings for students
External funding performance
Use of best international professional practice case studies
Relationship of language teaching to student and staff mobility.

There are other key areas of internationalization where management procedures can be documented, monitored, and improved. These could include the development of strong collaborative arrangements with overseas institutions in the areas of student/staff mobility, best practices benchmarking, collaborative research, joint teaching activities, and international training and consulting both commercially and through aid-funded projects.

In summary, ISO 9002 attempts to provide a coherent means of assuring the quality of international education by requiring a strategic framework and processes for detailed implementation and auditing of these strategies. Where appropriate, ISO 9001 can go one step further and address the actual design of the product or, in other words, assess and ensure the quality of the design of education or training programs.

Performance Indicators

As already discussed, demands for accountability from external bodies, plus the ongoing quest for improvement, have led to a growing preoccupation with performance indicators for the higher education sector.

CHAPTER THREE

Several definitions of "performance indicators" are found in the literature. One well-known definition describes performance indicators as "ratios, percentages, or other quantitative values that allow an institution to compare its position in key strategic areas to peers, to past performance or to previously set goals" (Taylor, Meyerson, & Massey, 1993). This is similar to, but at the same time slightly different from, the definition suggested by AUCC (1995). A performance indicator is a policy-relevant statistic, number, or qualitative description that provides a measure of whether the university, some aspect of it, or the university system is performing as it should.

Performance indicators have a comparative dimension or a reference point that permits a value judgment to be made about the institution or system. The comparison or reference point may be a goal or an objective, an absolute standard, a past value (comparison over time), or a comparison across institutions, regions, or countries. The second definition includes absolute standards and qualitative measures while the first one does not. This difference is a point of debate as there are serious questions whether quantitative numerical measurements can truly assess the complexity of the issues being measured and, furthermore, who is setting or determining the standards.

There is a tendency to refer to all indicators as performance indicators. There are some measures which are expressions of performance in the sense that they have a fixed point of reference that operates as a norm or standard. The key questions are whether the standard is selected or imposed, and whether it is institution-specific or system-wide. These questions are the source of much debate and some dissatisfaction about the use and misuse of performance indicators. Generally, performance indicators are a category of management indicators. They are often indicators of output.

The debate surrounding performance indicators has been active during the last decade. A considerable number of major studies and reviews have been undertaken. The discussion has tended to focus on a few critical questions: How effectively can quantitative performance indicators truly capture the quality of the educational experience and the value of research outcomes? Is it possible to define valid sector-wide indicators given the diversity in institutional profiles? How will the indicators be used? Will they inform funding decisions? How much work will be involved in their collection? There is growing awareness and agreement, however, that while performance indicators do not provide a substitute for qualitative judgment, when used and interpreted appropriately, they can provide some measure of organizational health.

The fact that indicators are prevalent does not mean that there is a consensus about them. Nor is there a consensus about how indicators should be used or what questions they should inform. Despite various attempts to generalize about quality, in the end indicators operate best at the program level within individual institutions. It has been suggested that the higher the level of their aggregation, the less useful quality indicators become.

To date, there has not been a lot of work on the development or use of performance indicators for internationalization. This may be a mixed blessing.

Benchmarking

Benchmarking is a quality management tool—and yet another term with myriad definitions. Key themes include measurement, comparison, identification of best practices, and improvement. A collective definition of benchmarking could refer to the analysis of process, activities, and performances compared within or between organizations. The objectives of this comparison exercise is to assess an institution's standards, obtaining information for self-improvement and implementing changes to affect improvement.

An Australian study (McKinnon, Walker, & Davis, 1999) focused on developing key benchmarks for inter-university and, in some cases, intra-university comparison. The study included both criterion-based and quantitative benchmarks. Internationalization was among the nine different themes included in the study. For the internationalization theme, seven different benchmarks were developed and piloted: the institution's internationalization strategy, its culture of internationalization, balance with the onshore international student program, financing the internationalization program, students' exposure to international experience, the management of offshore delivery, and overseas institutional activity. It is interesting, but not surprising, that there is considerable overlap among these seven benchmark areas.

The two approaches to benchmarking used in the McKinnon study are very different but complementary. The "criterion reference" approach simply defines the attributes of good practice in a specific area. For example, one aspect of good practice for internationalization is the area of students' exposure to international experience both directly and indirectly through staff. It is described as follows: 25% of academic staff will have had recent research, teaching, or practice supervision experience lasting more than four weeks in an overseas country within the last three years, and 25% of home campus students will have had substantial interaction (in excess of five hours of contact) with international visiting academics. The second approach, "quantitative benchmarks," is used to measure normative and competitive levels of achievement. An internationalization example is "the percent of the undergraduate cohort studying abroad."

This study is an important step forward and it will be interesting to see whether institutions decide to use these internationalization benchmarks and for what purposes. Competition for the international market of students and offshore programs is very stiff in Australia, and benchmarking can serve many purposes in this context.

FINAL WORDS

At this stage in the maturation of internationalization, the importance of monitoring the progress and quality of our internationalization efforts needs to be emphasized over and over again. First, it is critical to assure different stakeholder groups that the process of internationalization is being evaluated on a consistent basis and, second, that improvements are being made to ensure that the international dimension of teaching/learning, research, and service is contributing to the relevance and quality of higher education.

CHAPTER THREE

The concepts of quality and quality review of internationalization have been the focus of much discussion. The concept of internationalization tracking measures has been introduced as one approach institutions can consider to monitor and review their internationalization strategies. A number of different approaches and instruments are being used to assess the quality of internationalization efforts. (See Chapter 4.) It is a positive sign to have a variety of different instruments available to institutions. The "one size fits all" philosophy is not appropriate as it does not acknowledge the individuality and different cultures of higher education institutions.

Note: This chapter is based on J. Knight (2000), *Taking the Pulse: Monitoring the Quality and Progress of Internationalization,* Millennium Research Series, Monograph #2. Ottawa: Canadian Bureau for International Education.

RELATED REFERENCES

Adams, T. (1998). *ISO and the international dimension of higher education.* Unpublished paper.
American Council of Education. (2005). *Measuring internationalization at community colleges—at comprehensive universities–at liberal arts colleges–at research universities.* A series of four monographs. Washington, DC: American Council on Education.
AUCC. Association of Universities and Colleges of Canada. (1995). *A primer on performance indicators.* Research File Vol. 1, No. 2. Ottawa, Canada: AUCC.
AUCC. Association of Universities and Colleges of Canada. (1998). *Code of ethical practice in the provision of education to international students by Australian universities.* Canberra, Australia: Australian Vice-Chancellors Committee.
Brennan, J. (1997). Authority, legitimacy and change: The rise of quality assessment in higher education. *Higher Education Management, 9*(1).
CBIE. Canadian Bureau for International Education. (1996). *Code of ethical practice in international education.* Ottawa: CBIE.
De Winter, U. (Ed.). (1996). *Internationalization and quality assurance: Goals, strategies, and instruments.* Occasional Chapter No. 10. Amsterdam, Netherlands: European Association for International Education.
El-Khawas, E., DePietro-Jurand, R., & Holm-Nielsen, L. (1998). *Quality assurance in higher education: Recent progress, challenges ahead.* Washington, DC: World Bank.
GATE. Globalization Alliance for Transnational Education. (1997). *Certification manual.* Washington, DC: GATE.
Harvey, L., & Green, D. (1993). Defining quality. *Assessment and Evaluation in Higher Education, 18*(1), 9–34.
HEQC. Higher Education Quality Council. (1996). *Code of practice for overseas collaborative provision in higher education.* London: HEQC.
Knight, J. (1994). *Internationalization: Elements and checkpoints.* Ottawa: Canadian Bureau for International Education.
Knight, J. (1999). *A time of turmoil and transformation for internationalization.* CBIE Research Monograph, No. 14. Ottawa: Canadian Bureau for International Education.
Knight, J. (2000a). *Progress and promise: The 2000 year AUCC report on internationalization at Canadian universities.* Ottawa: Association of Universities and Colleges of Canada.
Knight, J. (2000b). *Taking the pulse: Monitoring the quality and progress of internationalization.* Millennium Research Series, Monograph 2. Ottawa: Canadian Bureau for International Education.
Knight, J., & de Wit, H. (Eds.). (1999). *Quality and internationalization in higher education.* Paris: OECD/IMHE.
Knight, J., Adams, T., & Peace Lenn, M. (1999). Quality assurance instruments and their relationship to IQRP. In J. Knight & H. de Wit (Eds.), *Quality and internationalization in higher education* (pp. 207–224). Paris: OECD/IMHE.

Kristofferesen, R., Sursock, A., & Westerheijden, D. (1998). *Manual of quality assurance: Procedures and practices.* Turin, Italy: European Training Foundation.

McKinnon, K. R., Walker, S. H., & Davis, D. (1999). *Benchmarking in universities: Manual.* Canberra: IDP Australia.

Schofield, A. (1999). *Benchmarking in higher education: An international review.* London: Commonwealth Higher Education Management Service.

Smith, A. (1994). *International education: A question of quality.* Occasional Chapter No. 7. Amsterdam, Netherlands: European Association for International Education.

Smith, D. (2000). *And how will I know if there is quality?* Toronto, Canada: Ontario Council of Universities.

QAA. Quality Assurance Agency for Higher Education. (1998, October). Quality assurance: A new approach. *Higher Quality* [newsletter], No. 4.

Taylor, E., Meyerson, J., & Massey, W. (1993). *Strategic indicators for higher education: Improving performance.* Princeton, NJ: Peterson's Guides.

Woodhouse, D. (1996). Quality assurance: International trends, preoccupations and features, assessment and evaluation. *Assessment and Evaluation in Higher Education, 21*(4), 247–257.

Woodhouse, D. (1999). Quality and quality assurance. In J. Knight & H. de Wit (Eds.), *Quality and internationalization in higher education* (pp. 29–40). Paris: OECD/IMHE.

Wende, M. van der. (1999). Quality assurance of internationalization and internationalization of quality assurance. In J. Knight & H. de Wit (Eds.), *Quality and internationalization in higher education* (pp. 225–235). Paris: OECD/IMHE.

CHAPTER FOUR

AN INTERNATIONALIZATION QUALITY REVIEW PROCESS AT THE INSTITUTIONAL LEVEL

In many countries, developing an institution-wide internationalization strategy which is linked to the overall university mission and strategic plan is a relatively recent phenomenon and, in some cases, is still in the early stages of development. Thus, a major project of evaluating international work and strategy in 1997 was a project before its time . The Institutional Management of Higher Education Program (IMHE) of the Organization for Economic and Community Development (OECD) recognized the importance, not only of institutions' developing the internationalization strategy but, more specifically, of monitoring and reviewing the implementation and operation of the action plan. As a result, a major project was undertaken in 1997 to develop a tool designed to help higher education institutions that are in the process of evaluating their internationalization strategy or are in the early stages of developing the international plan. The evaluation tool is a set of guidelines to undertake an Internationalization Quality Review Process (IQRP). This chapter presents the guidelines and discusses some of the lessons learned by different types and sizes of institutions around the world that have used the guidelines—either for quality assessment and assurance purposes or to assist in the design of an internationalization plan.

INTRODUCTION TO IQRP: PURPOSE AND PRINCIPLES

The Internationalization Quality Review Process (IQRP) is a process whereby individual institutions of higher education assess and enhance the quality of their international dimension according to their own stated aims and objectives. For institutions that wish to design, implement, or evaluate an internationalization strategy, having a framework that assists them in this process is important.

The review process includes procedures, guidelines, and tools to be adapted and used in both a self-assessment exercise and an external peer review. The purpose of IQRP is to help institutions improve their internationalization work; it is not a certification or accreditation process.

The IQRP is developed by the Programme on Institutional Management of Higher Education (IMHE) of the Organisation for Economic Co-operation and Development (OECD) in consultation with the Academic Co-operation Association (ACA) in Brussels.

The purpose of the IQRP is to help institutions of higher education assess and improve the quality of their international dimension by focusing on:
– the achievement of the institution's stated goals and objectives for internationalization;

CHAPTER FOUR

- the integration of an international dimension into the primary functions and priorities of the institution;
- the inclusion of internationalization as a key element in the institution's overall quality assurance system.

The starting point for the review is the institution's own stated aims and objectives. The review process assesses the extent to which institutions actually achieve the aims and objectives which they set for themselves. The assessment of the relationship between objectives and actual achievement is the core of the quality issue. The internationalization of higher education is the process of integrating an international dimension into the teaching, research, and public service functions of the institution. The purpose of the self-assessment process is to critically evaluate a variety of aspects related to the quality of the international dimension of the institution. The more emphasis given to self-assessment, the more self-assessment will function as a means of training and assisting the institution to take responsibility for its own quality improvement. Self-assessment should not be seen as an exercise to produce information for the external peer review team, but rather as an opportunity to conduct an analysis of the extent and quality of internationalization initiatives.

The purpose of external peer review is to mirror the self-assessment process and to provide feedback and analysis that are complementary to the institution's self-assessment from a different, external, and international perspective. The emphasis is not on actual fact-finding, inspection, or evaluation. While the review process is intended to be international in application, acknowledgement and recognition of differences among institutions and countries is essential.

The self-assessment and external peer review reports are for the use of the evaluated institution only. The reports are owned by the institution and can be published only by the evaluated institution or with its explicit approval. The review process is not intended to prescribe practices or advocate uniformity or standardization of internationalization approaches or procedures. There is no explicit or implicit comparison with other institutions involved. It is an exercise for self-improvement. This does not exclude the possibility that an institution may combine the IQRP with other quality-assurance procedures such as benchmarking, ISO 9000, GATE (Global Alliance for Transnational Education certification), or Total Quality Management.

The review process is seen as part of an ongoing cycle process of advocating, planning, implementing, rewarding, reviewing, and improving the institution's internationalization strategy.

THE OPERATIONAL FRAMEWORK OF IQRP

While the IQRP is guided by the institution's own goals and objectives for internationalization, major areas are common to many institutions. The review process will address these areas. It is presupposed that the emphasis and orientation of the self-assessment exercise are on analyzing the quality of the institution's international dimension. It should not merely be a description of the various internationalization initiatives. At the same time, it is recognized that, particularly for institutions that intend to use the IQRP to initiate an internationalization strategy, a qualitative and

QUALITY REVIEW PROCESS, INSTITUTIONAL LEVEL

quantitative inventory of international activities will be an important basis for the assessment.

SELF-ASSESSMENT PHASE

Role and Structure of the Self-Assessment Team

A self-assessment team (SAT) is formed at the institutional level and is given the mandate to (a) collect the necessary information, (b) undertake a critical analysis of the provision for and the quality of internationalization, as well as internationalization's contribution to higher education, and (c) prepare the self-assessment report.

The institution chooses the members of the team to reflect the internal organization and aims of the institution. Ideally, the SAT should consist of representatives of the administration, the academic staff, and the students. In order for the team to be functional and accomplish its task in a relatively short period of time, the group should be relatively small and the members should receive administrative support to undertake the work. The full endorsement and active involvement of the institution's leaders are essential for the success of the self-assessment team.

The SAT has a chairperson and a secretary. It is recommended that the key person in the institution responsible for internationalization strategy and policy be the chair of the SAT. The secretary is responsible for organizing the SAT's work and for coordinating the preparation of its report.

The SAT will be the direct counterpart of the peer review team (PRT). The SAT will exchange comments with the PRT on the self-assessment report prior to its visit, will prepare the program of the visit, and will discuss the draft peer review report with the PRT. The secretary of the SAT plays an important role in the liaison with the secretary of the PRT.

The Design of the Self-Assessment Process

It is important to emphasize that the whole purpose of the self-assessment is to analyze the international dimension, not merely to describe it. Collecting data to build a profile of all the different activities, programs, policies, and procedures related to the international dimension of the institution is only a first step, albeit an important and rather time-consuming step. Some institutions may not have mechanisms in place to make a quantitative and qualitative description of these activities, programs, procedures, and policies but still wish to use the IQRP as an instrument to assist in preparing an internationalization strategy. Drawing up a profile of the institution's internationalization dimension is a major undertaking but well worth the effort. The analysis of an institution's performance and achievements according to its articulated aims and objectives for internationalization is critical in assessing and eventually assuring the quality of the international dimension and the contribution that internationalization makes to the institution's primary functions. The process must provide directions for improvement and change of the internationalization strategy of the institution.

CHAPTER FOUR

The Self-Assessment Outline is intended to serve as a practical guide for the process of analyzing the aims and objectives, the performance and achievements, the strengths and the weaknesses, and the opportunities and threats regarding the international dimension of the institution.

The outline is a starting point and a guide for the institution to undertake the preparation of their self-assessment. It is not intended to be a coercive structure. There may be questions and issues included in the outline which are not relevant or appropriate to the mandate of the specific institution. In other instances, there may be important items which have not been included in the outline which the SAT wants to address; these aspects should be added to the outline.

The self-assessment report should give an adequate profile of the institution, reflecting its particular directions, priorities, and effectiveness. It is aimed at giving directions for improvement and change. This self-assessment should not primarily be regarded as a descriptive exercise but rather as a critical analysis of the institution's performance and achievements in the field of internationalization. Besides providing the necessary information, an analysis should be made of strong and weak points (indicating how well the various internationalization efforts are being realized) and formulating potential avenues to improvement.

Terminology often differs from country to country and from institution to institution. Institutions should use the terminology which they find appropriate for their situation. It would be helpful to add a note of explanation so that the peer review team understands the use of terms in their institutional context.

Outline for the Self-Assessment Report

Context
a. Summary of the higher education system
   Provide a brief description of the higher education system in the country and indicate the position of your institution in the system.
b. Summary of the institutional profile
   Provide key general data on: age of the institution, student enrollment (undergraduate/graduate), number of faculty and staff, faculties and departments
   State the mission of the institution.
   Provide key data on the international dimension of the institution:
   - percentage of foreign students (undergraduate/graduate, as compared to total enrollment)
   - percentage of foreign staff (as compared to total number of staff)
   - numbers of incoming and outgoing students per year (home country/destination)
   - give a summary of the history of internationalization efforts in your institution.
c. Analysis of the (inter)national context for internationalization in terms of opportunities and threats. Make reference to national and regional policies and programs of relevance for the institution's international dimension.

Internationalization Strategies and Policies

What is the institution's stated policy and strategy for internationalization?

What is the relationship between the internationalization strategy and the institution's overall strategy, and what links exist with other relevant policy areas?

How has the decision-making process for internationalization policy been structured, and what systems exist to facilitate the introduction of new policies?

What meaning does your institution give to internationalization?

Why is internationalization important to your institution?

Indicate the directions, priorities, and objectives for internationalization.

How is internationalization valued with respect to the institution's overall mission and goals by the different actors in the institution: administration, faculty, students?

How effective is the support and involvement given to internationalization by senior leaders and governing boards of the institution?

What is recommended to improve the strategies and policies for internationalization?

How can the support and involvement of administrators, faculty, and students be improved relative to the internationalization policies and strategies of the institution?

Organizational and Support Structures

a. Organization and Structures

What office/unit/position has the overall and ultimate policy-level responsibility for the internationalization of the institution?

Which unit(s) have direct operational responsibility for international activities?

What is the reporting structure, liaison and communication system (both formal and informal) between the various offices/units/persons involved in internationalization?

How effective are the existing organizations and support structures in relation to the strategic plan for internationalization?

What improvements are recommended to make the organization and support structure more effective in relation to the existing strategies and policies?

b. Planning and Evaluation

How is internationalization integrated into institution-wide and department-level planning processes, and is this integration effective?

What system is in place for the evaluation of internationalization efforts and what impact does it have on these efforts?

Does the overall quality assurance system (internal/external) include reference to internationalization, and if so, what is its impact?

What proposals for improvement in the planning and evaluation processes for internationalization are recommended?

c. Financial Support and Resource Allocation

What internal and external sources of support exist for internationalization, and how effective are these funds for the realization of the objectives and goals for internationalization?

What is the mechanism for the allocation of resources (at both central and departmental level) for internationalization and how effective are these mechanisms?

CHAPTER FOUR

What is the institution's process for seeking, securing, and maintaining internal and external funding for internationalization and are these processes effective?

What proposals for improvement in the fund allocation and fund-raising for the realization of the internationalization of the institution are made?

d. Support Services and Facilities

What specific services and infrastructure exist to support and develop international activities and how effective are they?

What level of support is available from institution-wide service departments and what is their impact?

To what degree do the facilities (e.g., libraries) and the extracurricular activities on campus include an international or cross-cultural dimension, and what is their impact?

What recommendations are made to improve the support services and facilities to bring them in line with the internationalization strategies and policies of the institution?

Academic Programs and Students

a. Internationalization of the Curriculum: Area and Language Studies, Degree Programs, and the Teaching/Learning Process

What area studies and language studies are offered across degree programs, and what is their impact on internationalizing the curriculum?

What interdisciplinary degrees are offered in international/regional studies, and how do they fit in the strategy for the internationalization of the curriculum?

What international/regional research and graduate centers belong to/are sponsored by the institution and what role do they play in the internationalization strategies and policies of the institution?

Are there degree programs which include options for area and language studies (including courses in intercultural communication and culture studies), and what is their impact?

How has the international dimension been integrated into the courses/units in the various disciplines, and how effective has this policy been?

What joint- or double-degree programs are offered by the institution in partnership with foreign institutions, and what is their impact on the curriculum and the students?

Does teaching include the use of examples, case studies, research, literature, etc., drawn from different countries, regions, and cultures and to what effect?

To what extent is the "international classroom setting" applied, i.e., are students encouraged to study together and to interact with foreign students?

To what extent is instruction given in languages other than the national language of the country?

What recommendations are made with respect to the future place of area and language studies in the institutional strategies and policies for internationalization?

What measures are recommended to improve the international dimension in the curriculum?

What recommendations are made to improve the internationalization of the teaching and learning process?

b. Domestic Students

What are the quantitative goals (if any) for the number of students studying abroad annually, are they being met, and how effective are the mechanisms of reaching these goals?

Do graduate students participate in international research projects and international networks? If so, how and what is the impact?

What policies and support services are in place to encourage students to participate in international and intercultural activities, and to support such participation? How effective are these policies and services?

Are students being informed and advised about international work/study/research opportunities, and are the mechanisms effective?

How are students being prepared for and debriefed from international academic experiences? Are these procedures effective, and what is their impact? What recommendations are made to improve the opportunities for students for an international dimension to their study (both at home and abroad)?

c. Foreign Students

What are the quantitative goals (if any) for the number of foreign students (both degree-seeking and exchange) and how effective are the measures taken to reach these goals?

What strategies does the institution have for attracting, recruiting, and selecting foreign degree-seeking students? What are the objectives behind these strategies, and how effective are they?

What strategies (bilateral and multilateral) does the institution have for attractting and selecting exchange students, and how effective are they?

What is the level of academic success and integration (educational and social) of foreign (exchange and degree-seeking) students?

How is social guidance and academic counseling for foreign (exchange and degree-seeking) students organized?

Is there a difference in objectives, impact, and attention between the strategies for foreign degree-seeking students and exchange students?

What measures should be taken to improve the strategies for the recruitment, selection, and integration of foreign degree-seeking and/or exchange students?

Study Abroad and Student Exchange Programs

What is the range of programs available for study abroad and student exchange? How effective are these programs?

How effectively are study abroad periods integrated into the curriculum? Have the transfer and recognition of credits been arranged in an adequate manner?

To what extent have international work experiences or internships been incorporated into the curriculum, and what is the impact of these arrangements?

How are study abroad and student exchange programs evaluated? In what way have the results of these evaluations been taken into account in the further delivery of these programs?

What measures are recommended for improving the quality of the study abroad and student exchange programs in the overall context of the internationalization strategies and policies of the institution?

e. Partnerships and Networks

What is the range of collaborative agreements with foreign partner institutions for education and how active/functional are these?

What other networks does the institution participate in and how effective are these?

What procedures exist for the establishment, management, and periodic evaluation of partnerships and linkages, and how well do these procedures function?

What is the relation between the policies and strategies at the faculty level and the central level, and how effective is that relationship?

What measures are recommended to improve the partnerships and networks in which the institution participates? What is their relation to the strategies and policies of the institution?

Research and Scholarly Collaboration

Which collaborative agreements exist with foreign institutions/research centers/private companies for research, and how effective are these agreements?

To what degree is the institution involved in international research projects, and how successful/renowned?

How actively involved is the institution in the production of internationally published scientific articles, and what mechanisms are in place to stimulate such involvement?

What mechanisms are in place to stimulate the institution's performance in organizing international conferences and seminars? How effective are these mechanisms?

What support (internal and external) structures exist for international collaborative research, and how effective are these structures?

How are international research and their outputs linked to international teaching, and how is the connection monitored?

What opportunities and resources are available to stimulate the international dimension in research, and are they effective?

What recommendations are made to improve the international dimension of research, as part of the institution's strategies and policies?

6. Human Resources Management

What mechanisms are in place to involve academic and administrative staff in international activities (at home and abroad)? Please distinguish among research, teaching, publications, and development assistance. How effective are these mechanisms?

What mechanisms are in place to stimulate the presence of foreign academic and administrative staff members on campus (temporary/permanent) and how effective are they?

How is the teaching/research of visiting staff organized, and how effectively is it integrated into the curriculum?

Do appointment procedures seek staff from abroad? How effective are such efforts?

How is the selection and recruitment of new staff (academic and administrative) targeted at personnel who are internationally experienced/active? How effective are such policies?

Are there procedures for selecting staff for international education assignments and how effective are they?

What mechanisms are in place to guarantee that staff members possess the knowledge and skills required for teaching international programs and for carrying out other international assignments, and how effective are they?

What mechanisms are in place to guarantee that staff members have a command of foreign languages, and how effective are these mechanisms?

Are there mechanisms in place to guarantee that international teaching/research/development assistance experience counts toward promotion and tenure; and if so, how effective are they?

What recommendations are made to improve the international dimension of the institution's human resource management as part of its internationalization strategies and policies?

Contracts and Services

a. Forms of delivery

What is the provision of information technology (IT) based teaching delivery systems, or other methods of providing university courses abroad?

Is there a process (internal/external) to the institution for the evaluation of such programs; and if so, what is the impact of these evaluations?

What are the institution's strategies to attract, recruit, and select students and staff for such programs abroad, and how effective are these strategies?

What measures are recommended to improve the quality of these systems and their relationship to the institutions overall strategy?

b. Development Assistance

What is the institution's involvement (as a contractor or partner) in development projects, how are they perceived by the faculty, and what is their impact on the teaching and research functions of the institution?

What is the link between development assistance projects and other internationalization activities of the institution?

What policies/procedures exist for the development, management, and evaluation of development projects, and what is the effect of these procedures on the projects and on the institution's strategy?

What measures are recommended to improve the quality of the development projects and to improve their integration in the institution's overall strategy?

c. External Services and Project Work

How active is the institution in external services (e.g., contract education, training, consultancy), and to what extent do these services include an international or cross-cultural dimension?

What is the impact of these services on the internationalization strategy of the institution?

What measures are recommended to improve the quality of these services and their relationship to the internationalization strategy of the institution?

CHAPTER FOUR

Conclusions
What are the main conclusions from the self-assessment on internationalization?
What are the main concerns and challenges for the institution with regard to the further development of internationalization?
What are the main recommendations to the institution for the further improvement of its international dimension?
Are the goals for the internationalization of the institution clearly formulated?
Are these goals translated into the institution's curriculum, research, and public service functions, and if so, is the institution providing the necessary support and infrastructure for successful internationalization?
How does the institution monitor its internationalization efforts?
How must the institution change in order to improve its internationalization strategies?
What specific topics or questions would you like to bring to the attention of the review team?

THE SELF-ASSESSMENT REPORT

After the self-assessment exercise has been completed, the preparation of the self-assessment report is the next step in the IQRP. The report should be limited to a maximum 20–30 pages plus possible annexes. It should follow as much as possible the general pattern of the Self-Assessment Outline as described above. It should be recognized that not all the categories and questions in the outline may be appropriate or relevant for each institution. It is also important to stress that the self-assessment team may add issues not covered by the framework but considered relevant. Thus, the self-assessment outline should be considered as a guide only, intended to introduce many of the areas and issues to be considered and to encourage the teams to undertake an analytical approach.

It is assumed that the self-assessment report will be more than a description of the type and extent of internationalization efforts; it is meant to critically assess and address ways to assure and improve the quality of the institution's internationalization of its teaching, research, and public service functions.

The language of the self-assessment report will in part be guided by the make-up of the peer review team (PRT). During the initial stages of the IQRP, the secretary of the SAT will decide, in collaboration with the secretary of the PRT, the working language of the PRT site visit and also the language of the self-assessment report. If a language other than the national language is used for the SAT report and PRT reports, it is assumed that the supporting documents, such as data annexes, can be in the institution's national language.

The peer review team members are to receive the self-assessment report at least two months prior to the visit. The institution sends one copy of the SAT report for each PRT members plus two additional copies for the IQRP archive (with the institution's permission) to the secretary of the PRT.

THE PEER REVIEW PHASE

Membership of the Peer Review Team

The Peer Review Team (PRT) can vary in size but requires a minimum of three members and usually consists of three to five members; all must be external and independent of the institution undergoing the IQRP. The experts appointed to the PRT are to have a general understanding of quality assessment and assurance, and will have particular expertise in the internationalization of higher education.

It is recommended that the PRT chairperson be a senior academic with expertise in university governance and preferably in the development and management of international relations/programs of institutions of higher education. Knowledge of recent developments in the internationalization of higher education globally is also essential. The expertise and experience of the other members should preferably relate to the priority areas of the institution's aims and objectives for internationalization. They should be knowledgeable in academic culture and governance. It is considered an additional asset to have a team member with prior experience in quality assurance review exercises.

The composition of the PRT is primarily international, but it does include one member from the institution's home country or a member with considerable experience in and knowledge of higher education in the country (but not related to the institution itself). At least one member of the PRT should come from another continent than the institution's home country. The first person will provide the PRT with insight in the national context; the second person will provide the PRT with a perspective beyond the regional context.

One member of the PRT will serve as secretary and be responsible for organizing the work of the PRT and for coordinating the preparation of its report. The secretary of the PRT is also the liaison person with the secretary of the SAT for the response of the PRT to the self-assessment report, and the preparation of terms of reference of the site visit.

The institution will be responsible for all costs related to the peer review. It is important to clarify and agree upon all the financial aspects of the review before individuals are invited to become members of the PRT.

Responsibilities of the Peer Review Team

The task of the PRT is to examine the goals for the institution's internationalization plan and whether they are clearly formulated; how these goals are translated into the institution's curriculum, research, and public service functions; and if the institution is providing the necessary support and infrastructure for successful internationalization; how the institution monitors its internationalization efforts; and how the institution changes in order to improve its internationalization strategies.

The PRT members will receive the self-assessment report at least two months prior to the visit. After thoroughly reviewing it, the PRT may provide general comments to the self-assessment team prior to the site visit. Then the PRT will pay a

CHAPTER FOUR

two-to-three-day visit to the institution and produce a detailed report (20–30 pages) for the institution no later than two months after the site visit.

DESIGN OF THE PEER REVIEW PROCESS

Ideally the PRT meets once before the actual site visit to discuss the self-assessment report, finalize the terms of reference for the visit, and agree on the division of labor among the team members. It is preferable that this meeting occur at the institution where the IQRP is carried out and also include a meeting with the self-assessment team to discuss the comments on the self-assessment report and to prepare the program.

It is acknowledged that, in many cases, expense and time will not permit such a preparatory visit. In that case, the secretary of the PRT will establish active communication with the other PRT members to receive their comments on the self-assessment report and suggestions for the terms of reference and the program of the site visit. It is also recommended that the secretary will pay a preparatory visit to the institution to discuss the comments on the self-assessment report and finalize the terms of reference and the program with the SAT. The PRT will hold a half- or full-day planning meeting on site prior to the commencement of the official PRT program.

Based on the PRT's initial review of the self-assessment report, they will decide whether they need additional information before the site visit. Prior to the site visit, the PRT will prepare a list of specific issues to be addressed and list the individuals/ groups with whom they will meet. They will forward this list to the self-assessment team.

The institution will prepare a detailed schedule for the PRT visit, which may vary in length between two and four days. It is recommended that the schedule includes meetings with the self-assessment team, the leadership of the institution, the chief academic and administrative staff responsible for international activities, and related support services. The team should also meet key persons among selected administrative and academic staff, students and graduates, and, if possible, representatives of other bodies (both in and outside the institution) responsible for or involved in international activities. Where appropriate, it may be useful to visit the units that support student and staff involvement in internationalization in addition to visiting other related facilities (i.e. library, residences) of the institution. In some cases it may be appropriate for PRT members to visit off-shore locations.

At the end of the site visit, the PRT meets with the SAT to comment on the site visit and discuss the plans for the preparation of the PRT report and its presentation to the institution. The PRT then also meets with the senior leaders of the institution to give a brief oral and preliminary report on the visit.

The Peer Review Team Report

The major issues to be addressed in the PRT report are the following:
– Is the institution's self-assessment report on internationalization sufficiently analytical and constructively critical?

- Are the strengths and weaknesses of the institution's international activities clearly articulated, and are the plans for improvements clearly presented and realistic?
- Is the institution achieving the aims and objectives it has set for itself?
- How do the institution's vision and goals relate to the development and sustainability of its international activities?
- What action is required of the institution, including a continuing role for the self-assessment team, in order to monitor progress and provide continuing impetus?

The PRT prepares a draft report and sends it to the chairperson of the SAT within two months after the site visit. The draft version of the PRT report is meant for review and comment before the final version is submitted. This step provides the institution with the opportunity of correcting any factual errors and errors of interpretation. The institution provides feedback to the PRT within two weeks of the receipt of the draft version of the report. It is the PRT's decision whether to include the recommended changes in the report. After putting the report in final form, the PRT sends five copies to the institution. From that point, the institution has complete ownership of the report. The report is strictly confidential if the institution wishes to consider it as such. It is the institution's decision about how many additional copies it will make for internal and external use. Follow-up activities and any other use of the PRT report are the institution's responsibility.

However, it is suggested that both the self-assessment report and the PRT report be made available at least internally. Given that the self-assessment process has taken place with active participation by many individuals and groups in the institution, it may be important that they are included in an open discussion or planning session about the comments and suggestions made in both the SAT and PRT reports. In other words, the use and follow-up to the reports is an integral part of the process of assessing, assuring, and improving the internationalization efforts of the institution.

FOLLOW-UP PHASE

It is recommended, in particular in those cases in which the IQRP is used to start the process of developing an internationalization strategy, that the institution includes in the IQRP a follow-up phase, one and a half to two years after the PRT report has been delivered. This follow-up phase could take place with or without the involvement of an external peer review. As part of this follow-up phase, the Self-Assessment Team will write a document analyzing the progress in implementing the recommendations made by the SAT and PRT and the internationalization strategy. It will make recommendations for further actions. This report might be the basis of a one-to-two-day site visit by the PRT to give their views on the progress and the recommendations for further action.

Preferably, the decision to include a follow-up phase in the IQRP should be made at the beginning of the IQRP or, at the latest, at the end of the PRT visit. This timing is particularly important should the institution desire to include a peer review visit in the follow-up phase.

CHAPTER FOUR

Practical Issues in Using IQRP

During the IMHE/OECD project, the IQRP was tested in a number of different types and sizes of institutions in a variety of countries. Valuable insights and information were obtained on the various ways the IQRP can be used to assess and enhance the international dimension of higher education. This section discusses the experiences gained and lessons learned from the case studies and reflects on the application of IQRP to institutions who will use IQRP in the future.

The Commitment to Undertake an IQRP

Implementing a quality review of the internationalization strategy involves a significant commitment of time and resources and, therefore, makes sense only under certain conditions. The institution must be clear about the rationale for undertaking a quality review of the international dimension. The different constituency groups, including the senior leaders, administrators, faculty, and students need to be committed to all stages of the review: the decision to undergo the review, the self-assessment, the peer review, and the implementation of conclusions and recommendations. There must be a clear identification of procedures following up on the review and how to implement any recommendations. Finally, there must be awareness about the resource implications of the review itself and the recommendations.

Description Versus Analysis in the Self-Assessment

One of the greatest challenges—and perhaps one of the most striking aspects—of the self-assessment exercise was the tendency for the SAT report to be more descriptive than analytical. This is easily understood and can happen for a variety of reasons. In some cases, preparing the SAT report was the first time that the institution had attempted to systematically collect information on all of its the international initiatives and policies. Developing a comprehensive picture of the nature and extent of internationalization activities can be very revealing but overwhelming. In situations where this type of inventory did not exist, the SAT tended to focus more on collecting data than on analyzing the findings. If the membership of the SAT was too focused—for example, if only international office personnel were involved—the depth and breadth of the analysis could be compromised and possibly biased.

For the SAT report to be useful to the institution, a clear articulation of goals and objectives/targets for internationalizing the institution is critical. The importance of having an explicit rationale, along with clearly stated goals and objectives, cannot be overstated. The rationale, goals, and objectives will guide the entire exercise. Given that IQRP's underlying principle is to assess and assure the achievement of the aim and objectives, it is critical that they be clearly stated. The analysis of the strengths, weaknesses, opportunities, and threats (SWOT) of internationalization strategies is at the heart of the IQRP. Therefore, a SWOT analysis is critical to ensuring that the SAT report is more than a catalogue of internationalization initiatives. A second factor central to ensuring an analytical approach is the selection of the chair and members of the SAT and the type of support that is available to the team.

Membership of SAT

It is important to have, as the SAT head, a senior leader of the university who is directly involved in or responsible for the institution's internationalization. This requirement is important for a number of reasons. First is the strong message sent to the community about the importance of the international dimension and the IQRP. Second is the leader's familiarity with the institution's internationalization work in particular but also its more general policies and governance. The third relates to the benefit of having a senior person's insight and influence for the implementation of the final recommendations for improvement.

To ensure that different constituencies of the institution are involved and to avoid the appearance that the review is a top-down process, it is important to have representatives of the teaching and administrative staff as well as students on the committee. Experience has shown that it is also worthwhile to have members who are involved in international activities as well as those who are not. A committee comprised only of internationalization champions and promoters can easily yield a skewed picture of the commitment and support for internationalization. Individuals who are not directly involved plus internationalization "nay sayers," who are always active on campus, bring different perspectives to the analysis and can make useful contributions. That being said, one has to be aware of the size of the SAT. Of course, it will differ according to the institution but a team of four to six is often most effective.

Consultation with the wider community in the institution is critical, and such consultation can be sought in a variety of ways to ensure that a broad cross-section of views is heard. The views and voices of both domestic and international students play a central role in the self-assessment process. In some cases, it may also be appropriate for the SAT to have a member external to the institution.

The IQRP guidelines are deliberately flexible so that they can be adapted and used in the most effective way according to the goals and characteristics of the institution. An important point, which merits repeating, is the necessity of the university community being involved in and committed to the process of internationalization. Both the self-assessment exercise and peer review are constructive ways to increase awareness of, involvement in, and commitment to internationalization. It is for this reason that special attention needs to be given to the composition of the SAT and the best approach for the self-assessment exercise.

Peer Review Team Members

As with the SAT, the composition of the PRT is also crucial. A number of factors should be taken into consideration when selecting the members and building the best team. First, it is assumed that all members are external to the institution and do not have any vested interests or biases. It is important to have at least one member who knows the local context and culture and can brief the other team members on

CHAPTER FOUR

any critical local issues. It is equally important to have at least one team member who is external to the country or region and is knowledgeable about different education systems and policies. Expertise and practical experience in internationalizing an academic institution is absolutely essential; theoretical understanding is not enough. Experience in a senior academic management position is also advisable so that both policy and operational issues are understood.

While it is an advantage to have quality assessment expertise represented on the team, it is not an absolute necessity. In fact, knowledge of best practices of internationalization in different types of institutions around the world is probably more useful to the peer review process. Experience has shown that diversity of backgrounds of the team makes for a perceptive and robust review.

The process of undergoing a self-assessment exercise is at the heart of quality assessment and assurance. The PRT is the second step and acts as a mirror to the findings and conclusions of the SAT process and report. While there may be some hesitation in making recommendations prior to the PRT site visit, it is strongly suggested that the SAT think through and articulate the conclusions and recommendations prior to the PRT visit, then review and revise them after the PRT visit and report. As already stated, ownership and commitment to improvement are important outcomes of the IQRP—especially true for the conclusions and recommendations.

Timing of the IQRP

There are three major points to be made with respect to the timing of the IQRP exercise. The first one relates to the stage of development of the institution relative to internationalization. The original expectation was that institutions already well along the path of internationalization would be most interested in undertaking an IQRP. However, one of the unexpected outcomes of the project has been the value of the IQRP guidelines as a tool for strategic planning for institutions that are in early stages of internationalization.

The second factor relates to the institution's priority placed on and its preoccupation with quality reviews. In the past several years, increasing importance has been given to quality reviews for both accountability and improvement reasons. While this is a positive sign, there is also a greater risk that "quality review fatigue" syndrome will be experienced. It is therefore important to be sensitive to the timing of IQRP with respect to other evaluation or audit exercises to avoid undue pressure on or expectations for the institution. However, experience has shown that IQRP is compatible with other quality review systems and that there are potential benefits in combining IQRP with other review exercises.

The length of time it takes to complete an IQRP is obviously influenced by many factors which are usually institutionally based and which therefore differ from to institution to institution. Experience has shown that between three and six months is an appropriate period in which to complete the exercise. Taking more time can result in "review fatigue," making it difficult to sustain a high level of commitment and participation. An extended SAT exercise may also be a sign of overemphasis on data collection rather than analysis. After completion and submission of the SAT report, it usually takes at least another three months before the PRT phase is finished and the final report is submitted. Therefore, one should aim to have the entire SAT and PRT stages finished within nine months. The institution can then focus on implementing the recommendation for improvements.

An Ad Hoc Versus Coordinated and Integrated Approach

An interesting and encouraging trend is the gradual shift toward a more strategic approach to internationalizing an institution. The process approach to internationalization has emphasized the concepts of integration and coordination and has deemphasized the "fragmented activities" approach.

The fact that the IQRP has been used as a planning tool as well as a review instrument illustrates that institutions are ready to think about internationalization strategies, not just as a series of isolated international activities. And furthermore, institutions are moving toward developing an overall institutional action plan that will integrate an international dimension into its teaching, research, and service activities. The new focus on strategic planning is helping to make internationalization a central part of the university mission and mandate, not a marginal, ad hoc, optional group of activities.

APPLICATION OF THE IQRP IN DIFFERENT CONTEXTS

Different Educational Contexts

One of the most complex issues in the design of the guidelines for the Internationalization Quality Review Process was to take into account the diversity of cultures and systems in higher education. As already stated, a guiding principle for the project was that the review process be international in application and that acknowledging and recognizing differences among institutions and countries is essential.

The project discovered that IQRP was useful and effective in different types of institutions in different regions of the world. The pilot case studies likewise demonstrated that IQRP is relevant to and adaptable to the following differences in educational contexts: (a) differences between private and public institutions, (b) differences between the universities and the non-university sector, (c) differences between large, comprehensive universities and specialized institutions, and (d) differences between undergraduate colleges, research universities, and professional schools.

Use in Different Cultural Contexts

A key challenge in developing the conceptual and operational frameworks for the IQRP was its application in different cultural contexts. Because IQRP is based on two fundamental principles—those of self-assessment and peer review—it was very important to be sensitive to different cultural orientations to these principles. The notion of "face" or "reputation" was of particular concern. Would the process of self-assessment result in a promotional or public relations report which would identify only strengths and accomplishments but gloss over areas needing improvement? Would the peer review report be credible and accepted if it focused on specific issues and activities which needed further development and enhancement? Would culturally based interpretations of the concepts of internationalization or globalization negatively influence the process of reviewing the international dimension? Would the need for an explicit rationale and clearly stated goals and objectives for an internationalization strategy be problematic in different cultures and regions of the world? These were the types of questions which were being asked during the final revision work of IQRP.

One of the most important principles guiding the design of the IQRP guidelines is that they respect and adapt to the individuality and fundamental cultural value and beliefs. Therefore, the frameworks and guidelines of IQRP have intentionally been developed to respect and accommodate different contexts—in particular, the cultural context.

Note: This chapter was adapted from J. Knight and H. de Wit (Eds.), (1999) *Quality and internationalization in higher education* (Paris: Institutional Management of Higher Education Program of the Organization for Economic Cooperation and Development), 259 pp.

CHAPTER FIVE

BORDERLESS, OFFSHORE, TRANSNATIONAL, AND CROSSBORDER EDUCATION:

Are They Different?

GROWTH AND COMPLEXITY OF INTERNATIONAL EDUCATION MOBILITY

In the past decade, the interest and growth in international academic mobility has exploded. It is not only the students, professors, and scholars who are moving around the world, but different kinds of providers—including private companies, traditional academic institutions, and professional associations—are taking academic programs to students in their home countries. Various types of program delivery methods are being used to offer a wide range of courses either through virtual or face-to-face contact. New types of partnerships including public/private, non-profit/for-profit, local/foreign, institutions/corporations are being formed to respond to the burgeoning demand for access to higher education and, in many cases, the appeal of a foreign academic qualification.

A report by IDP Australia (Bohm, Davis, Meares, & Pearce, 2002) predicts that the demand for international education will increase four-fold—from 1.8 million students in 2000 to 7.2 million students in 2025. These are staggering figures. They help to explain and forecast the growth in worldwide academic mobility. It is highly questionable whether this demand can be met solely through student mobility. The numbers and types of education providers and programs being delivered across borders will need to grow. Students may welcome foreign education institutions/providers in their home country, as more learners will be able to afford foreign tuition costs if they stay home and avoid the financial burden of travel and accommodation expenses. Furthermore, governments and employers may expect less brain drain if the students study at home.

The growth in the crossborder mobility of programs and providers raises important issues such as the licensing of providers, quality assurance of programs, equitable access, funding models, research, intellectual property, trade policies, recognition of qualifications, and joint ownership of curriculum. These issues are definitely central to the analysis of the new forms of international academic mobility. Nevertheless, it is difficult to address these issues, especially in terms of policies and regulations, if there is confusion about what "crossborder" or "transnational" or "offshore" or "borderless" education really means and involves. Clarity on definitions and types of providers and programs is more important in light of the diversity of actors involved. Second, the dearth of reliable statistical data at the national and regional levels (and often at the institutional level as well) is also becoming more problematic. Without solid information on the volume, type, destination, impact,

CHAPTER FIVE

and trends related to education being delivered across borders, it is difficult to build a foundation on which to develop national, regional, and international regulatory frameworks. Furthermore, there are few opportunities to undertake a comparative analysis within and between countries and regions.

This chapter explores the similarities and differences among the four terms—"borderless," "offshore," "transnational," and "crossborder" that are being used to describe or characterize the phenomenon of international higher education mobility. The purpose is to examine differences and similarities between ways various countries and organizations are using the terms and to identify key and common elements. Given the turmoil and turbulence of higher education internationally, this approach can facilitate a common understanding of what is being debated and, more importantly, what is being regulated. Of equal significance is the need for a clearer picture of the parameters and variables used in collecting and analyzing data at all levels—institutional, national, regional, and international.

In short, increased attention on students, education programs, and institutions/providers moving between countries is needed and welcomed. But to develop effective policy frameworks and guidelines requires a common understanding of the terms being used and the data being collected. The emphasis is on developing *a common understanding* of the terms for policy, regulations, research, and data collection purposes—not necessarily a *common language,* although the latter does facilitate the former.

It is important to be clear about the scope of this discussion. International higher education mobility includes the movement of ideas, information, people, programs, providers, technology, curricula, values, and knowledge. The focus of this chapter is on the movement of academic programs that lead to some type of qualification and on the mobility of institutions/providers. These providers include the more traditional institutions involved in teaching, research, and service as well as the new providers who focus more on the delivery of academic courses and educational support services.

As higher education evolves, so does the language or terminology. "International cooperation," "international relations," and "international education" were the most common terms used 40 years ago. These concepts were usually defined in terms of activities: development projects, foreign students, and international cultural agreements. About 20 years ago, the term "internationalization" emerged to take a more central place in higher education. It, too, was defined in terms of activities such as study abroad, area and language studies, and institutional agreements (Arum & Van de Water, 1992). However, the notion of internationalization also introduced the concept of "process" and broadened the meaning beyond activities. "Internationalization" became a more comprehensive term, encompassing institutional- and national-level goals, policies, strategies, and activities (Knight, 2004). It was used to refer to the international dimension of all aspects of higher education, not just specific activities.

As the term "internationalization" was being adopted, the notion of globalization started to gain more popularity. At first, the two terms were used interchangeably in the education sector. But soon efforts were made to distinguish between the globalization and the internationalization of education by situating globalization as a phenomenon that touched all aspects of society—including education—while internationalization was situated as both a response to and as an agent of globalization. Without trying to oversimplify the complexity of the debate about these concepts, it can be said that internationalization stressed the concept of relations between nation, people, and culture while globalization stressed the idea of a worldwide flow of people, technology, economy, ideas, knowledge, and culture but did not focus on (nor exclude) the relationships between countries. They are closely related and dynamic concepts but are purposely used differently in the context of education (Knight, 2005a).

TRANSNATIONAL AND OFFSHORE EDUCATION

Australia was one of the first countries to use "transnational education" in the early 1990s, as it wanted to differentiate between international students recruited to Australian campuses and those who were studying for Australian degrees offshore. Hence, "transnational education" became used to simply describe offshore international student enrollments regardless of whether the offshore students were studying through twinning, franchise, distance, or branch campus arrangements. It is interesting to note that terminology in Australia has evolved in such a way that "international education" usually refers to foreign students studying in Australia while "transnational education" refers to those studying offshore. In this conceptualization of "transnational," the focus is on the location of the student.

The Global Alliance for Transnational Education (GATE) was established as an independent organization in 1995. Over the years, GATE has changed in governance and ownership, but it still remains dedicated to disseminating good practices in transnational education and offering certification services. GATE (1997) was one of the first organizations to address the issue of quality assurance of education being delivered abroad and described transnational education as any teaching or learning activity in which the students are in a different country than the provider's home country. This situation requires that national boundaries be crossed by information about the educational content (including materials) and/or by staff. Once again, this description emphasizes the student's location but adds a new element: the location of the institution providing the education. The element of crossing borders is also made explicit.

UNESCO and the Council of Europe in their "Code of Practice on Transnational Education" (2001) describe transnational education in a similar way to GATE. This description presents transnational education as "types and modes" of delivering course content (up to whole programs) or services (such as distance education) in which the learners are located in a country different from the one awarding the degree or certificate. UNESCO/COE's description, however, goes further by including programs of nations different from the one in which it operates and also those independent "of any national education system." This comprehensive definition introduces important elements. It includes all types and modes of delivery, and specifies that the learner is in a different country than that in which the "awarding" institution is based. Thus, the idea of who awards the qualification becomes more important. Reference is also made to "stateless" types of programs and, by inference, institutions. These are important elements.

Both the GATE and UNESCO/Council of Europe definitions of transnational education are oriented and applicable to situations in which programs move across a border or in which the program or provider are virtual and delivering by distance formats. It is, however, unclear whether these definitions cover "new types" of providers, especially those that establish a physical presence in the country and obtain permission from the receiving country to offer "recognized" qualifications. In this scenario, the providers are clearly foreign "awarding" providers, but they are not located in a different country than the student. Is this type of situation included in a definition of "transnational education" that is based on having the student and awarding institution in different locations?

It is interesting to try to pinpoint the difference between "international education" and "transnational education." Clearly, the idea of a nation or country is common to both terms, leaving the prefixes "inter" and "trans" as the distinguishing feature. But do the two prefixes really explain the difference between the two concepts? In the Australian case, the literal meaning of the prefixes is almost irrelevant as a means of explaining the difference between international students studying in Australia or offshore. In the GATE and the UNESCO/COE cases, "transnational education" describes situations where students are not in the "source country" of the awarding institution. In other words, the programs from the awarding institution have been transported to students residing in other countries. The logic of why it is "transnational" rather than "international" is perhaps based on the need to have a term that differs from "international education" rather than from any substantially different meanings of "trans" and "inter."

BORDERLESS EDUCATION

The term "borderless education" first appeared in an Australian report by Cunningham, Ryan, Stedman, Tapsall, Bagdon, Flew, and Coaldrake (2000) and was followed by a similar type of study in the United Kingdom. Basically the term is described as the "blurring of conceptual, disciplinary and geographic borders traditionally inherent to higher education" (CVCP, 2000). The innovative and enlightening feature of this term is that it goes beyond geographic and jurisdictional boundaries to include temporal, disciplinary, and conceptual borders. Although this is the term's strength, it is also a possible weakness. Its contribution is at a conceptual level, but it remains fairly abstract and challenging to use in concrete and applied situations.

It is interesting to juxtapose the concepts of "borderless" education and "crossborder" education. The former term acknowledges the disappearance of borders while the latter term actually emphasizes their existence. Both approaches reflect contemporary reality. In this period of unprecedented growth in distance education and e-learning, geographic borders seem to be of little consequence. Yet, on the other hand, it is possible to detect a growing importance of borders when the focus turns to regulatory responsibility, especially issues of quality assurance, accreditation, funding, joint ownership, or intellectual copyright. "Borderless education" does not seem to be extensively used in operational or applied settings. Nevertheless, it is a useful concept for capturing the blurring and erosion of traditional academic boundaries and for that reason has played an important role in raising awareness about changes and challenges in the education sector.

CROSSBORDER EDUCATION

In many ways it seems ironic that the role of borders is actually stronger in a globalized world that encourages the free flow of people, ideas, goods, services, knowledge, capital, and technology. The introduction of new multilateral trade rules or immigration laws are examples where crossing borders into a different jurisdiction has significant implications. Hence, the notion of jurisdictional boundaries has increasing significance for many sectors including education. Primarily in response to the importance of borders, the more recent term "crossborder education" has emerged and is being more widely used as a comprehensive term. It includes many aspects of international academic mobility but primarily focuses on students and education programs and providers.

For instance, both UNESCO and OECD are giving serious attention to the issues related to crossborder higher education. Many of their recent working groups, forums, and publications have addressed the current challenges facing internationalization and have used the term "crossborder education" to focus on and capture the major changes related to academic mobility. Another example is the UNESCO (2004) position chapter on "Higher Education in a More Globalized World," which makes frequent reference to crossborder education as a key aspect of internationalization that deserves more attention in terms of quality assurance, research, and language of instruction. The Centre for Education, Research and Innovation (CERI) of the OECD has organized three regional meetings and produced two new publications that have addressed the quality assurance/consumer protection issues in crossborder education (OECD, 2004a) and the trade approach to internationalization (OECD, 2004b)

Both of these organizations have moved crossborder education higher on the policy agenda in response to member state interests. They have developed, with key education stakeholders, the UNESCO/OECD "Guidelines for Quality Provision in Crossborder Higher Education" (2005). This document's definition of crossborder education is:

> Higher education that takes place in situations where the teacher, student, programme, institution/provider or course materials cross national jurisdictional borders. Crossborder education may include higher education by public/private and not-for-profit/for-profit providers. It encompasses a wide range of modalities in a continuum from face-to-face (taking various forms from students traveling abroad and campuses abroad) to distance learning (using a range of technologies and including e-learning).

This is a very comprehensive description and clearly refers to people, programs, providers, and reference materials crossing borders using a variety of modalities. It makes national borders the central concept, as opposed to transnational education, which emphasizes the different locations of learner and awarding institution. The result may be the same, but the conceptualization is different.

CODES OF PRACTICE

Codes of conduct for education delivered between countries have been developed by several national university associations, quality agencies, and government departments. They are usually a set of principles to guide the practices of delivering programs to other countries and establishing partnerships with foreign providers. They are related to, but differ from, the codes for international student recruitment, as they focus on the movement of programs and providers, not on the students' movement.

The codes are intended for use by public and private higher education institutions. They have relevance, but no imperative, for other types of providers such as companies and professional associations. The codes differ in substance and perspective but they are similar in spirit and purpose. They have the goal of assuring quality in crossborder academic provision and maintaining the integrity of the academic credit and qualification. It is interesting to note the different terminology used in the titles of the codes: "overseas," "offshore," "transnational," crossborder" and "collaborative provision." This profusion serves as eloquent testimony to the diversity of terms currently being used. Examples of these codes include:

- Quality Assurance Code of Practice: Collaborative Provisions—UK Quality Assurance Agency
- Code of Ethical Practice in the Offshore Provision of Education and the Educational Services by Higher Australian Higher Education Institutions—Australian Vice-Chancellors Committee
- Principles of Good Practice for the Educational Programs for Non-US Nationals—New England Association of Schools and Colleges
- Code of Good Practice in the Provision of Transnational Education—UNESCO/CEPES and the Council of Europe
- Code of Conduct for CrossBorder/Transnational Delivery of Higher Education Programs—South African Ministry of Education
- Code of Practice for Overseas Education Institutions Operating in Mauritius—Tertiary Education Commission.

NONGOVERNMENTAL ORGANIZATIONS

A review of reports, seminars, and publications from nongovernmental organizations and professional associations from around the world shows increased attention and action directed to internationalization and, more specifically, to academic mobility. It is worth noting that, in many instances, internationalization is being interpreted only as academic mobility and, in some cases, only as commercial or trade-oriented activities. While this narrowing of focus often happens when new trends and issues are being addressed, it is important not to lose sight of the fact that internationalization is a phenomenon that is much broader than mobility. It relates to the international, intercultural, and global dimensions of teaching, research, service, and delivery. It covers campus-based activities as well as mobility initiatives between countries. This is precisely why it is necessary to examine new terms such as "transnational education" and "crossborder education" in relation to each other and context with existing terms such as "internationalization."

The heightened awareness about new opportunities and potential risks involved in education crossing borders has produced declarations such as the 2004 "Sharing Quality Higher Education across Borders: A Statement on Behalf of Higher Education Institutions Worldwide." This statement was developed by four groups: the International Association of Universities (IAU), the American Council on Education (ACE), the Council for Higher Education Accreditation (CHEA), and the Association of Universities and Colleges of Canada (AUCC). Even though this statement is essentially driven by three North American groups and one international association, its audience is higher education institutions, government agencies, and nongovernmental associations around the world. The title demonstrates once more the critical role played by the notion of "borders."

National and regional studies are being undertaken, and it is clear that individual countries prefer different terms. For instance, Australia and Europe generally use "transnational education," albeit in different ways. There appear to be more references to "transnational education" in Latin America while North America and the United Kingdom tend to use "crossborder education." Countries in Africa are using "crossborder education" and "transnational education" interchangeably with no clear definition for either term. The new code of practice from South Africa is a concrete example. This is a sign of the times, and it may well be that confusion over terminology is a necessary part of development and progress.

Whether the term is conceptualized by "location of learner and the awarding provider" or the "crossing of jurisdictional borders" may be a semantic subtlety, but there are genuine consequences from a regulation point of view. Clarity and consistency of terms are necessary within a country for national regulations to work and to create a common understanding of regional/international policies. That said, one is optimistic that the new Crossborder Guidelines developed jointly by UNESCO and OECD (2005) will bring some leadership to the current confusion about terminology and some convergence on shared understandings.

The way that the Observatory of Borderless Higher Education (OBHE) uses the terms is both interesting and revealing. OBHE, arguably the world's leading authority on borderless education, undertakes/commissions leading-edge applied research on a broad spectrum of related issues. A review of OBHE reports and briefing notes illustrates the panorama of new terminology, particularly in relation to students, programs, and providers moving between countries. Because authors of OBHE reports originate from different countries, sectors, and disciplines, the resulting wide diversity of terms is not surprising, but it does contribute to the confused terrain. The term "borderless education" is used in a broad and conceptual way. As an umbrella term, it is efficient and covers a very broad spectrum of terms and topics. The problem begins when different meanings are given to the same term in different contexts (such as transnational education) and when related terms are used interchangeably.

GENERAL AGREEMENT ON TRADE IN SERVICES (GATS)

The introduction of education as a tradable service is relatively new territory for the higher education community. The GATS is a worldwide agreement administered by the World Trade Organization aiming to further liberalize trade in services. GATS has introduced a new set of rules and principles to govern the import and export of any service—including education—and has developed four principal modes of trade of service:

Mode 1: "Crossborder supply" focuses on the service crossing the border. It does not require the consumer to physically move. Examples in higher education include distance education and e-learning.

Mode 2. "Consumption abroad" means that the consumer moves to the country of the supplier. In education, this means that students take all or part of their education in another country.

Mode 3. "Commercial presence" means that a provider establishes a commercial facility in another country to provide a service. Examples in higher education include branch campuses or franchising arrangements.

Mode 4. "Presence of natural persons" means that persons travel to another country on a temporary basis to provide service. In the education sector, they would include professors or researchers.

It is clear that crossborder supply is one of the four modes of trade. "Crossborder education" in the GATS context is focused primarily on distance education and therefore has a much narrower interpretation than "transnational" or "crossborder education" as used by the education sector. However, one similarity in interpretation bears mentioning, and that is the element of commercial practice prompted by the profit motive. There is a perception in the education community that crossborder education has a close link to commercial and for-profit education, which, of course, is the focus of the GATS four modes of trade (Knight, 2005a, 2005b). The same perception exists about transnational education, especially in the Australian context. From a European perspective, there is less emphasis on the commercial business of transnational education although it certainly is increasing in many Eastern and Western European countries.

This discussion has illustrated how various countries, governments, and associations attach different meaning to similar terms and often, similar meanings to different terms. Table 5.1 provides a summary of the approaches used to define the phenomenon of delivering education between countries and identifies key elements.

Table 5.1. Summary of definitions and key elements

Stakeholder and Source	Date	Key Elements	Definition
GATE- Global Alliance for Transnational Education	1996	Location of learner and providing institution	Transnational education denotes any teaching or learning activity in which the students are in a different country (the host country) to that in which the institution providing the education is based (the home country).
Report on the "Business of Borderless Education" CVCP	2000	Blurring of borders	Borderless education refers to the blurring of conceptual, disciplinary, and geographic borders traditionally inherent to higher education
UNESCO and Council of Europe Convention on the Recognition of Qualifications: "Code of Practice for Transnational Education"	2001	Location of learner and awarding institution	All types and modes of delivery of higher education study programs, or sets of courses of study, or educational services (including those of distance education) in which the learners are located in a country different from the one where the awarding institution is based.
UNESCO/OECD "Guidelines for Quality Provision in Crossborder Higher Education"	2004	Crossing of national jurisdictional border	Higher education that takes place in situations where the teacher, student, program, institution/provider, or course materials cross national jurisdictional borders.
OBHE Report on Transnational Education and Regulations	2005	Between countries	Transnational education is used to designate higher education provision offered by one country in another and to exclude provision in which only the student travels abroad.
IAU, CHEA, ACE, AUCC Statement	2004	Role of borders	"Sharing Quality Higher Education across Borders"
GATS Agreement	1994	Service moves across border, not the consumer	Crossborder supply focuses on the service crossing the border, which does not require the consumer to physically move

Source: Knight (2005b).

CHAPTER FIVE

Two common themes characterize the definitions in Table 5.1 The first is the concept of crossing borders, and the second is that the learner is located in a different country than the awarding institution. Is this a case of two different approaches meaning the same thing? On the surface, perhaps. But closer inspection raises the question of whether the crossing (jurisdictional) borders will have more sustainability and perhaps greater significance during this period when new regulations and policy are being developed to deal with licensing, quality assurance, intellectual property, foreign ownership, profit, and the implications of GATS rules.

The concept of learner and awarding institution being located in different countries is attractive because it is student/education oriented rather than regulation-oriented. However, it is more applicable to program mobility than provider mobility and may be eclipsed by the fact that "stateless" providers (meaning those having no affiliation with a national education system in a home or sending country) can readily establish a physical presence in a host country and provide education courses and services to resident students and clients. This fact may negate the basic tenet of transnational education (student and awarding institutions in different countries). Therefore, the term "crossborder education" may be more relevant to the challenges presently facing the delivery of international education to students through program and provider mobility. Hence, this chapter will use the term "crossborder education." The notion of "borders" refers to jurisdictional borders at national, subregional, or regional levels.

DATA COLLECTION

One of the most conspicuous challenges in trying to analyze crossborder education is the lack of data. While there are more data and informed analysis on the movement of students across borders, the paucity of information on program and mobility creates an undesirable environment of speculation, confusion, and often misinformation. This situation can have negative consequences in terms of confidence in the quality and dependability of crossborder education provision and impedes the analysis needed to underpin solid policy and regulatory frameworks.

Australia is the leader in terms of having up-to-date and fairly comprehensive data from universities on the volume, types, award level, and discipline of crossborder program delivery. The Australian Vice-Chancellors' Committee (AVCC), as well as Australia's Department of Education, Science, and Technology (DEST) collect, analyze, and publish these data annually. In New Zealand, the International Policy and Development Unit of the Ministry of Education undertook a major survey in 2005 of crossborder delivery in all tertiary institutions, but this practice is not yet conducted annually. The U.K. Higher Education Statistics Agency started to collect information in academic years 2002–2003 and 2003–04 on U.K. education programs offered abroad. This is the first time it has gathered this data, so many wrinkles still need to be ironed out of the process and report. Countries with well-developed licensing and quality assurance procedures (e.g., Hong Kong, Singapore, Malaysia, and South Africa) have data on incoming programs and providers; but again, they are exceptions, not the rule.

The question at hand is whether the data being collected can be compared across countries or regions. In other words, are similar definitions of terms and indicators being used? The answer is probably no. As already discussed, much variation exists in how key terms are defined and what variables are priority areas for collecting data. The following list provides some examples of questions that need to be thought through as institutions or countries move forward in their efforts to determine what to measure in crossborder education initiatives and how to measure it. These questions focus on program and provider mobility, not on student mobility.

- What aspects of crossborder education are included?
  Domestic programs that are being sent/exported to other countries
  Foreign programs that are being received/imported
- What kind of providers/institutions are included?
  "Recognized" and/or "non-recognized" providers
  Universities and colleges (public and private)
  Specialized, technical, vocational institutes (public and private)
  Commercial companies (national and international)
  Corporate universities
  Other types of providers such as professional associations or NGOs
  Networks and partnerships
  Others
- What is/are the unit/s of measurement?
  Number of enrolled students/graduates
  Number of programs
  Number of different providers
- What types of arrangements are included?
  Commercial or fee-based programs (usually for-profit oriented)
  Academic exchanges or linkages (usually nonprofit)
  Development cooperation (usually externally funded and nonprofit)
- What level of qualifications/awards are included?
  Foundation or pre-degree studies
  Specialized certificate or diploma
  Undergraduate/bachelor's degree
  Graduate level/master's and/or Ph.D.
  Other
- What mode of delivery is included?
  Virtual, distance, electronic
  Face to face, classroom-based
  Combination
- What forms of program delivery are included?
  Twinning
  Franchising
  Articulation
  Validation
  Double/joint degree
  Other

CHAPTER FIVE

- What kinds of provider mobility/presence are included?
  Branch or satellite campus
  Stand-alone institution
  Virtual university
  Study or testing center
  Local/foreign mergers/acquisitions
  Other
- What length of programs are included?
  Short term (less than one semester)
  Semester
  Year
  Multiple year
- What type of study arrangements are included?
  Full-time
  Part-time
  Self-study
- What countries are involved:
  As destination countries for exported education?
  As sending countries for received/imported education?
- Who recognizes, assures quality, accredits the program and/or qualification?
  Sending institution/provider
  Receiving institution/provider
  Sending country quality assurance agency
  Receiving country quality assurance agency
  Profession accreditation agency
  Third country or international quality assurance agency
  Other
- Who actually awards the degree?
  Institution/provider delivering the education
  Collaborating partner/provider in receiving country
  Third party
  Members of network delivering the education
  Other
- What disciplines and/or subjects are taught?

These are only some of the questions that could be asked in trying to collect data on programs and providers crossing borders. The list is illustrative only, certainly not exhaustive. It demonstrates the number of different variables to be taken into consideration. More importantly, it identifies the need for some common understanding of what specific terms or variables mean. For instance, what is meant by a "recognized/non-recognized," level of qualification, or type of program arrangements: twinning, articulation, double degree, validation, branch campus/stand-alone institution, or public/private, etc.? While it may be possible to have a common interpretation of these terms within one national higher education system, it is certainly a steep challenge to have common interpretations among different countries.

This problem is not unique to crossborder education. A similar situation existed (and is still ongoing) with the collection of statistics on the movement of students across borders. There are still enormous challenges in comparing the numbers and types of international students. Due to the relatively recent emergence of programs and providers moving between countries, perhaps there is the opportunity to develop common interpretations of terms so as to facilitate the collection and comparison of data. This is an important international project waiting to happen.

CHALLENGES AND QUESTIONS

The Definition Dilemma

In a field that is changing as much as international education, the challenge of finding common meanings for the same and similar terms will continue. Each country, association, or government agency will use terms that make sense from its perspective. What is needed is a concentration on the key and common reference points so that, when policy and regulations are being established at national, regional, or international levels, there is clarity on the meaning of the terms and, most importantly, on the implications.

The concept of "border" can be used as the key and consistent element in borderless, offshore, transnational, and crossborder education—in fact, for most terms describing international academic mobility. Yet, "border" is not the key concept for internationalization, which is a term much broader in scope and which refers to an international, intercultural, or global dimension to teaching, research, service, and, of course, now the delivery of higher education. Mobility is only one aspect of this generic term.

Given the current importance attached to jurisdictional borders in the mobility of students, professors, education programs, providers, and knowledge, the term "crossborder education" has been the preferred term in this chapter. The irony related to the importance of jurisdictional borders in a more globalized and borderless world is acknowledged. It may well be that with time—though perhaps this is wishful thinking—borders will not be the defining concept for education mobility. But at present, this is the case, and we must live with and be proactive about the consequences.

What is included or excluded in the notion of crossborder education? Again, there is no universal right or wrong answer to this question. Table 5.2 attempts to present a comprehensive interpretation of crossborder education and illustrate what are currently its principal elements. The mobility of students, professors, scholars, and experts has been part of higher education for centuries and is a pillar of academic mobility. The developments in program and provider mobility are certainly more recent and today are garnering much attention. This is why, when one refers to "crossborder education," the mobility of students is definitely included, but the current emphasis is on program and provider mobility.

CHAPTER FIVE

Table 5.2. Analysis of the term "crossborder education"

Components	*Types of Arrangements (Examples Only)*	*Approaches*	*Modes of Mobility*
People	Exchanges, semester or year abroad, full program, internships, field research, sabbaticals	Applicable to all components and types of arrangements	Applicable to programs, providers, and projects
Projects	Twinning, franchise, joint /double degree, articulation models	• Development cooperation externally funded, nonprofit	• Physical
Providers	Branch campus, mergers, independent institutions, teaching/testing centers	• Academic exchange self-funded, nonprofit	• Virtual
Projects	Research, curriculum, IT, capacity building, reference materials	• Commercial trade fee-based, for-profit	• Combination

Source: Adapted from Knight (2003).

The Need for Data Collection

This chapter is meant to deliver a strong message about the need to take the collection of data about crossborder education more seriously. It bears repeating that, without some reliable and valid information on the volume, type, and scope of crossborder education, it is an overwhelming challenge to develop sound policy and regulations to guide this growing sub-sector of higher education and to monitor new opportunities, risks, and benefits. The collection of data by an institution, association, or government needs to be guided by the intended purpose, use, and benefits of crossborder education, which are many and diverse.

Perhaps some lessons may be learned from the long experience of collecting statistics on students who study in foreign/other countries. The lack of common terms and definitions on the immigration status of students, lengths of stay, level of studies, type of qualification, etc., all contribute to the inability to compare data among countries with any level of confidence. The discrepancies between national-level data on international student numbers and flows and the data collected by OECD or UNESCO are well known but not always well understood. This problem is exacerbated when comparisons are being made between countries, which is, in fact, one of the major uses of the data. The gathering of data on the crossborder mobility of programs and providers is still nascent. It is therefore an opportune time to bring together an international team to study the issues, identify key variables, and develop definitions so that there can be some common reference points among countries in the way data are collected and analyzed. This step would be a definite and welcomed contribution to the field of international education, and the time to start such an initiative is now.

CONCLUDING COMMENTS

Even though, the mobility of students, professors, knowledge, and values has been part of higher education for centuries, it has only been in the last two decades that there has been significant growth in the mobility of programs and providers through physical and virtual modes of delivery. This recent development presents many new opportunities for increased access to higher education, for strategic alliances between countries and regions, for the production and exchange of new knowledge, for the movement of graduates and professionals, for human resource and institutional capacity building, for income generation, for the improvement of academic quality, and for increased mutual understanding. The list of potential benefits is long and varied.

But so is the list of potential risks. Risks can include an increase in low-quality or rogue providers, a decrease in public funding if foreign providers are providing increased access, non-sustainable foreign provision of higher education if profit margins are low, foreign qualifications not recognized by domestic employers or for further study, elitism in terms of those who can afford crossborder education, overuse of English as the language of instruction, and national higher education policy objectives not being met. Risks and benefits vary between sending and receiving countries, between developed and developing countries, and for students, institutions, companies, and employers. In light of the fast pace of crossborder growth and innovation, it is important that the higher education sector be informed and vigilant about the risks and benefits and, more importantly, about the need for appropriate policies and regulations to guide and monitor current and future developments.

The higher education sector is a much stronger actor in the knowledge society and has more room for influence. However, it also has greater chances of being affected by other sectors such as trade, science, technology, immigration, culture, and industry. Crossborder education is an increasingly important aspect of higher education and the time is opportune for the clarification of key terms, for the development of new policy frameworks/regulations to facilitate and monitor the increased growth, and for the strategic collection and analysis of data at institutional, national, and international levels.

Note: This chapter is adapted from J. Knight (2005b, October), *Borderless, offshore, transnational and crossborder education—definition, and data dilemmas.* Report of the Observatory on Borderless Higher Education (London: Observatory on Borderless Higher Education).

RELATED REFERENCES

Adam, S. (2001). *Transnational education. A study prepared for the Confederation of European Union Rectors' conference.* Geneva: Confederation of European Union Rectors' Conference.

Adam, S. (2003). *The recognition, treatment, experience, and implications of transnational education in Central and Eastern Europe.* Stockholm: Swedish National Agency for Higher Education.

Arum, S., & Van de Water, J. (1992). The need for a definition of international education in U.S. universities. In C. Klasek (Ed.), *Bridges to the futures: Strategies for internationalizing higher education* (pp. 198–206). Carbondale, IL: Association of International Education Administrators.

CHAPTER FIVE

AVCC. Australian Vice-Chancellors Committee. (2003). *Offshore programs of Australian universities.* Canberra, Australia: AVCC.
Bohm, A., Davis, D., Meares, D., & Pearce, D. (2002). *The global student mobility 2025 report: Forecasts of the global demand for international education.* Canberra, Australia: IDP.
Cunningham, S., Ryan, Y., Stedman, L., Tapsall, S., Bagdon, S., Flew, T., et al. (2000). *The business of borderless education.* Canberra: Australian Department of Education, Training and Youth Affairs.
CVCP. Committee of Vice-Chancellors and Principals. (2000). *The business of borderless education: UK perspectives.* London: CVCP.
DEST. Department of Education, Science and Training. (2003). *Higher education statistics collection.* Canberra: Commonwealth Government of Australia, DEST.
ESIB. National Unions of Students in Europe. (2002). *European student handbook on transnational education.* Brussels: ESIB.
GATE. Global Alliance for Transnational Education. (1997). *Certification manual.* N.p.: Author.
IAU (International Association of Universities), ACE (American Council on Education), CHEA (Council for Higher Education Accreditation), & AUCC (Association of Universities and Colleges of Canada). (2004). *Sharing quality higher education across borders: A statement on behalf of higher education institutions worldwide.* Paris: Authors.
Knight, J. (2003). *GATS, trade and higher education: Perspectives 2003–Where are we?* London: Observatory on Borderless Higher Education.
Knight, J. (2004). Internationalization remodeled: Rationales, strategies and approaches. *Journal for Studies in International Education, 8*(1), 5–31.
Knight, J. (2005). Crossborder education: An analytical framework for program and provider mobility. In J. Smart & W. Tierney (Eds.), *Higher education: Handbook of theory and practice* (Vol. 21, pp. 345–306). Dordrecht, Netherlands: Springer.
Knight, J. (2005b, October). *Borderless, offshore, transnational and crossborder education–definition, and data dilemmas.* Report of the Observatory on Borderless Higher Education. London: Observatory on Borderless Higher Education.
Krause, K. (2006). *Student voices in borderless higher education: The Australian experience.* London: Observatory on Borderless Higher Education.
Larsen, K., Momii, K., & Vincent-Lancrin, S. (2004). *Crossborder higher education: An analysis of current trends, policy strategies, and future scenarios.* London: Observatory on Borderless Higher Education.
McBurnie, G., & Ziguras, C. (2007). *Transnational education: Issues and trends in offshore higher education.* New York: Routledge.
New Zealand Ministry of Education. (2002). *New Zealand's offshore public tertiary education programmes: Initial stockade.* Auckland: International Policy and Development Department.
OECD. Organization for Economic and Community Development. (2002). The growth of crossborder education. In *Educational Policy Analysis.* Paris: OECD.
OECD. Organization for Economic and Community Development. (2004a). *Internationalization and trade of higher education: Challenges and opportunities.* Paris: OECD.
OECD. Organization for Economic and Community Development. (2004b). *Quality and recognition in higher education: The crossborder challenge.* Paris: OECD.
UNESCO. (2004). *Higher education in a more globalized world: Position chapter.* Paris: UNESCO.
UNESCO/COE. UNESCO & Council of Europe. (2001). *The UNESCO-CEPES/Council of Europe code of good practice for the provision of transnational education.* Paris: UNESCO.
UNESCO/OECD. (2005). *Guidelines for quality provision in crossborder higher education.* Paris: UNESCO/OECD.
Verbik, L., & Jokivirta, L. (2005). *National regulatory frameworks for transnational higher education: Models and trends. Parts 1–2.* Briefing Notes. London: Observatory on Borderless Higher Education.
Wilson, L., & Vlasceanu, L. (2001). *Transnational education and recognition of qualifications.* Bucharest: CEPES/UNESCO.

CHAPTER SIX

CROSSBORDER EDUCATION: PROGRAMS AND PROVIDERS ON THE MOVE

A fascinating but very complex world of crossborder education is emerging, adding its own burgeoning turbulence to the explosive field of international higher education. The last few years have been a hotbed of innovation and new developments. For instance, Phoenix University has become the largest private university in the United States (owned and operated by the Apollo Group) and is now present or delivering courses in Puerto Rico, Netherlands, Mexico, and Canada. Other Apollo companies are offering courses in Brazil, India, and China. The Netherlands Business School (Universitiet Nijnrode) has recently opened a branch campus in Nigeria, and Harvard is active in the Dubai Health Care City in the United Arab Emirates. Johns Hopkins University is operating programs in China and Italy. Furthermore, Jinan University will be the first Chinese university to open a branch campus outside China with Thailand as the projected location. Laureate Education (formerly Sylvan Learning Systems) has purchased all or part of private higher education institutions in Chile, Mexico, Panama and Costa Rica and owns universities in Spain, Switzerland, and France. Dubai has developed a "Knowledge Village"; and to date, universities from India, Australia, Canada, Ireland, Iran, Pakistan, and the United Kingdom are offering courses through franchising agreements and branch campuses. Columbia University and De Paul University from the United States has been active in Jordan since 2005 and Columbia University plans to open a branch campus there in 2009. Qatar Education City is another attractive place for foreign universities to establish undergraduate and graduate level programs; and thus far, Carnegie Mellon University, Georgetown University School of Foreign Service, and Cornell University are operational there. The University of Westminster (UK) is the key foreign academic partner in the new private Kingdom University of Bahrain and plays a similar advisory/provision role with new institutions in Nigeria, Uzbekistan, and Kazakhstan (OBHE, 2002–2007).

These are only a few examples of hundreds of new initiatives that have developed in the last 10 years. They involve higher education providers (including institutions and companies) delivering their courses and programs to students in their home countries. It is convincing evidence that international education is not just a matter of students who are moving across borders. Rather, we have now entered a new era of crossborder education driven by the knowledge society, ICTs, and the market economy that are increasing the demand for higher and continuing education. This demand is leading to increased crossborder education provision involving new types of education providers, new modes of delivery, new programs and qualifications, new partnerships and network models, and new national and regional regulations.

The purpose of this chapter is to delve into some of the trends, issues, challenges, and implications of these new developments in order to better understand crossborder education itself. The primary focus here is on the movement of education programs and providers across borders, not the mobility of students. The emphasis is on higher education; however, many of the issues and challenges apply to other levels. It is important to recognize that crossborder education comprises many different perspectives and issues depending on whether one is a receiving (host) country or a sending (source) country; this chapter aims to address both perspectives. The discussion of issues and challenges is primarily targeted to system-level policies and responsibility, not the individual institution.

Traditional higher education institutions are no longer the only international deliverers of academic courses and programs. International conglomerates, media and IT companies, and new partnerships of private and public bodies are increasingly engaged in the provision of education both domestically and internationally. The term "education providers" is now becoming a more common and inclusive term, encompassing both traditional higher education institutions and for-profit organizations and companies. This chapter uses the term "providers" to mean all types of entities that are offering education programs and services. There is some criticism directed toward the use of "providers" as it seems to accept the so-called marketization and corporatization agenda. Such awareness is a sign of the times; and indeed, every attempt is made in this chapter not to adopt the trade and commercial language of "suppliers," "consumption abroad," "commercial presence," etc. Finally, it is important to acknowledge the confusion regarding the meaning and use of the terms "transnational," "crossborder," "offshore," and "borderless" education as discussed in Chapter 4. The preferred term here is "crossborder education," as it is the presence of national borders which is central to many of the regulatory, quality, academic, and financial issues cast into high relief by the new mobility of programs and providers.

CROSSBORDER EDUCATION: A FRAMEWORK AND TYPOLOGIES

Crossborder education refers to the movement of people, programs, providers, knowledge, ideas, projects, values, curriculum, providers, and services across national boundaries. The scope is wide, but the focus of this chapter is primarily on programs and providers. Table 6.1 provides a framework for understanding the nature of crossborder education and illustrates two significant trends. The first trend is the vertical shift downward from student mobility to program and provider mobility. It is important to note that the number of students seeking education in foreign countries is still increasing; however, more emphasis is currently being placed on delivering foreign academic courses and programs to students in their home countries. The second shift is from left to right, signifying substantial change in orientation from development cooperation to competitive commerce, or in other words, from aid to trade. However, it would be an oversight not to recognize the substantial amount of crossborder activity that is happening under the category of academic exchange and linkage by higher education institutions.

A more detailed explanation of the framework provides further insight into some of the complexities and new challenges characterizing crossborder education. One of the first questions to ask is: "What are the defining factors/principles for a

Table 6.1: Framework for Crossborder Education

Category	Forms and Conditions of Mobility		
	Development Cooperation →	Educational Linkages →	Commercial Trade →
People Students Professors/scholars Researchers/ Experts/consultants	Semester/year abroad Full degrees Field/research work Internships Sabbaticals Consulting		
Programs Course Program Subdegree, degree Postgraduate	Twinning Franchised Articulated/ validated Joint/double award Online/distance		
Providers Institutions Organizations Companies	Branch campus Virtual university Merger/acquisition Independent institutions		
Projects Academic projects Services	Research Curriculum Capacity building Educational services		

Source: Adapted from Knight (2005a).

conceptual framework of crossborder education?" Many come to mind: What elements of education move? How does the movement occur? Why does education move? Where is this movement happening? Who is funding it? Who is awarding the qualification? Who is regulating it? Given the changing nature of the rationales driving crossborder education, the worldwide scope of delivery, and the new modes of provision, "why, how, and where" can be eliminated as the defining factors. Rather, the crucial category is "what" moves across borders. Four categories are suggested: people, programs, providers, and projects/service.

People

The first category covers the movement of people, whether they are students or professors/scholars/experts. Students are mobile in a number of ways. They can take

CHAPTER SIX

whole degrees in another country, participate in a study-abroad exchange program, undertake field work or an internship, register for a semester/year abroad program, etc. The funding for such crossborder education can be through exchange agreements, scholarships from government, public or private sources, and self-funding. Professors/scholars and experts can be involved in teaching and research activities, technical assistance and consulting assignments, sabbaticals, seminars, and other professional activities. These types of initiatives can be self- or institution-funded, be based on exchange agreements, involve contracts and fee for service, or be supported by public and private funding.

Programs

The program, not the student, moves in this category. The delivery of the program is often done through a partnership arrangement between international/foreign and domestic providers or can be an independent initiative by a foreign provider. The programs can be delivered by distance, face-to-face, or mixed mode. Franchising, twinning, and new forms of articulation and validation arrangements are the most common. In some cases, the program and qualification awarded is provided by the source country institution/provider, but the teaching and support is done in part or totally by a local institution/provider. In other cases, the foreign provider takes complete responsibility for delivering the academic program but may have a local business partner investing in the operation. Distance delivery of a program involves yet another set of circumstances.

Providers

The key factor in this category is that the institution/provider moves to have physical or virtual presence in the receiving/host country. The student does not move to the provider; rather, the provider moves to serve the student. The movement of a provider can involve a more substantial range of programs and academic/administrative support services—for example, by establishing a satellite campus or even a full institution. In other scenarios, the provider moves by purchasing/merging with a local institution. Virtual universities are yet another example of the provider moving across borders through distance delivery of selected programs. The providers can include private and public, for-profit or nonprofit, educational institutions, organizations, and companies. Both recognized bona fide institutions/providers and non-recognized rogue providers are included in this category

Projects/Services

A wide range of education-related projects and services needs to be considered when analyzing crossborder education. Such activities could include a diversity of initiatives such as joint curriculum development, research, benchmarking, technical assistance, e-learning platforms, professional development, and other capacity-building initiatives, especially in the area of information technology. The projects and services could be undertaken as part of development aid projects, academic linkages, and commercial contracts.

A second set of key factors relates to the fact that crossborder education occurs under different kinds of arrangements. Therefore, three different sets of conditions for crossborder delivery are proposed: (a) development cooperation/aid education projects; (b) academic exchanges and linkages; and (c) commercial trade initiatives.

TOWARD A TYPOLOGY FOR NEW CROSSBORDER PROVIDERS AND DELIVERY MODES

The number of new actors involved in the promotion, provision, and now regulation of crossborder education is increasing exponentially. Whether one is supportive or critical of the change, the reality is that the education sector in many countries is becoming a competitive and dynamic marketplace for both local and foreign providers.

Given the increase in demands for higher education, there are new providers, new delivery methods, and new types of programs. These new providers include media companies such as Pearson (UK) and Thomson (Canada); multinational companies such as DeVry (U.S.), Informatics (Singapore), and Aptech (India); corporate universities such as those run by Motorola and Toyota; and networks of universities, professional associations and organizations. Together they make for a fascinating array of entities involved in the new arena of crossborder education.

Generally, the new or alternate providers are mainly occupied with teaching/training or providing services and do not include a strong focus on research per se. They can complement, cooperate, compete, or simply coexist with the traditional public and private higher education institutions whose mandate is traditionally the trinity of teaching, research, and service. However, it is not just the new providers that are becoming increasingly interested in commercial crossborder initiatives. Conventional higher education institutions, both private and public, are also seeking opportunities for the commercial delivery of education programs in other countries; and to date it is estimated that they are delivering the majority of crossborder education programs (Larsen et al., 2004). The majority of these traditional providers are bona fide institutions that comply with domestic and foreign regulations (where they exist), but there is also an increase in rogue or low-quality providers that are not recognized by bona fide accreditation/licensing bodies. In addition, there is a worrisome increase in the number of degree mills operating around the world. These are often no more than web-based companies that sell certificates based on "life experiences" and do not deliver genuine education programs (Garrett, 2004).

The expansion in numbers and types of entities that provide education courses and programs across borders is causing some confusion. This confusion is exacerbated by the modes of crossborder program mobility and provider mobility. This general state of flux may well indicate progress and innovation, but it also begs for some kind of classification system or typology in order to make sense of the new playing field of crossborder education. Table 6.2 is an attempt to conceptually map the diversity of actors and to separate the type of provider from the form of crossborder delivery.

CHAPTER SIX

Table 6.2. Typology of traditional and new or alternative providers

Category of Provider	*Status*	Profit or Nonprofit	Comments
Traditional Higher Education Institutions: Oriented to Teaching, Research, Service to Society			
Recognized Higher Education Institutions	Includes public nonprofit, private nonprofit and private for-profit institutions. Usually part of home[a] national education system and recognized by national, bona fide licensing/accrediting body.	Can be nonprofit or for-profit oriented as an institution.	Many countries have a mixed system of publicly and privately funded HEIs, but there is a definite blurring of the boundary separating or distinguishing one type from another.
Nonrecognized HEIs	Usually private and not not formally part of a national education system. Includes HEIs that are not recognized by national bonafide licensing/accreditation body. If the non-recognized HEIs are of low quality, they are often referred to as "rogue" providers.	Usually profit oriented domestically and internationally.	Diploma mills sell degrees but do not provide programs of study and are related to crossborder education but are not true providers. Rogue providers are often "accredited" by self-accrediting groups or companies or by agencies that sell accreditation (accreditation mills).
New or Alternative Providers: Oriented to Teaching and/ or Commercial Services			
Commercial Company HEIs	Can be publicly traded or privately owned and include: 1. Companies that establish HEIs that may or may not be recognized by bona fide licensing/accrediting bodies and 2. Companies that focus more on the provision of services. Usually not part of home national education system.	Profit oriented.	Can include a variety of companies (i.e., media, IT, publishing) who provide education programs and support services. Can complement, cooperate, compete, or coexist with more traditional HEIs. Companies that provide academic programs and are publicly traded on a stock exchange are part of the Global Education Index developed by the Observatory on Borderless Education (Garrett, 2004)

(Continued)

Corporate HEIs	Usually part of a major international corporation and outside of national education system. Not usually recognized by national bona fide licensing/accreditation body. Not part of home national education system.	Not relevant.	The corporations that run their own education/training institutes provide programs for their employees only and are crossborder providers by virtue of being large multinational companies. They often collaborate with traditional HEIs especially for degree-awarding power.
Professional, government and non-government organizations and networks	Can be a combination of public/public or public/private or private/private organizations and HEIs.	Usually profit oriented.	The organizations/networks may or may not be part of home national education system; and they may or may not be recognized by national bona fide licensing/accreditation body. However, some of the individual partners may be.
Virtual HEIs	Includes HEIs that are 100% virtual. May or may not be part of home national education system and may or may not be recognized by national bona fide licensing/ accrediting body.	Usually profit oriented if delivering crossborder.	Difficult for receiving national education system to monitor or regulate international virtual HEIs due to distance delivery methods.

Source: Adapted from Knight (2005a).
[a] Home country = sending country.

It is worth highlighting the fact that whether a higher education institution is public or private is no longer the key factor differentiating the two types of traditional higher education institutions. The element of official "recognition" by the home (or sending) country is proposed as the element of differentiation. This shift illustrates the importance of a higher education institutions being in good standing and recognized by a bona fide agency that registers, assures quality, or accredits higher education institutions. This is a result of two developments. The first is the increasing emphasis on quality in all countries of the world for both domestic and international provision and the necessity of differentiating bona fide higher education institutions from low-quality and rogue providers.

The second relates to the blurring of boundaries between publicly and privately funded institutions and between the nonprofit and for-profit status of the higher education institution. This blurring has occurred because many public nonprofit higher education institutions receive funding from private sources and engage in some for-profit activities to diversify their sources of funding and increase income.

CHAPTER SIX

This pattern is especially evident in countries where government funding is not able to increase to meet growing demand and costs. At the same time, privately funded institutions are receiving public funds or subsidies and may be engaged in social nonprofit activities. Therefore, not only is there a mixed private/public higher education sector but there are also many institutions that engage in both for-profit and nonprofit activities especially in relation to crossborder activities. This is one reason why the public/private label is no longer an effective differentiating factor for crossborder education.

The category of "new and alternative providers" includes a diversity of private and public companies, organizations, networks, and institutions delivering education programs and courses in foreign countries. These new types of crossborder providers can be brick and mortar institutions or virtual universities. They are usually commercial in nature and for-profit in purpose. The description and classification of new crossborder providers is rather challenging. The tendency is to use the factors inherent to traditional higher education institutions and apply them to new providers. This orientation will probably change over time, especially if the "new or alternate providers" begin to receive subsidies from government or undergo the same accreditation processes that traditional universities undergo.

One of the central issues is who recognizes and gives any type of provider the power to award the qualifications in the home or sending country and/or in the host or receiving country. Some of the new providers are not part of a home institution of higher education or are not recognized by its national education system. They are, in effect, stateless, a situation that challenges the receiving country to determine its quality and legitimacy. This ambiguity may lead to receiving countries taking more responsibility to develop their own regulations to register and accredit foreign providers. (Verbik & Jokivirta, 2005).

Program Mobility

Crossborder mobility is defined in this volume as the movement of individual education/training courses and programs across national borders through face-to-face, distance, or a combination of these modes. Credits toward a qualification can be awarded by the sending foreign country provider or by an affiliated domestic partner or jointly.

It is clear that a key factor in program mobility is who awards the course credits or ultimate credential for the program. As the movement of programs proliferates, there will undoubtedly be further changes to national, regional, and even international regulatory frameworks. The question of "who grants the credits/awards?" will be augmented by "who recognizes the provider?" and whether the program has been accredited or quality assured by a bona fide body. Of critical importance is whether the qualification is recognized for employment or further study in the receiving country and in other countries as well. The perceived legitimacy, recognition, and ultimate mobility of the qualification are fundamental issues yet to be resolved.

Table 6.3. Typology of crossborder program mobility

Category	Description
Franchise	An arrangement whereby a provider in source country A authorizes a provider in another country B to deliver its course/program/service in country B or other countries. The qualification is awarded by provider in country A.
Twinning	A situation whereby a provider in source country A collaborates with a provider located in country B to develop an articulation system allowing students to take course credits in country B and/or source country A. Only one qualification is awarded by provider in source country A.
Double/Joint Degree	An arrangement whereby providers in different countries collaborate to offer a program for which a student receives a qualification from each provider or a joint award from the collaborating providers.
Articulation	Various types of articulation arrangements between providers in different countries permit students to gain credit for courses/programs offered/delivered by collaborating providers.
Validation	Validation arrangements between providers in different countries allow provider B in receiving country to award the qualification of Provider A in source country.
Virtual/ Distance	Arrangements where providers deliver courses/program to students in different countries through distance and online modes. May include some face-to-face support for students through domestic study or support centers.

Source: Knight (2005b).

Given that several modes for program mobility involve partnerships, a crucial question is: "Who owns the intellectual property rights to course design and materials?" What are the legal and moral roles and responsibilities of the participating partners in terms of academic, staffing, recruitment, evaluation, financial, and administrative matters? While the movement of programs across borders has been taking place for many years, it is clear that the new types of providers, partnerships, awards, and delivery modes are challenging national and international policies and regulatory frameworks and that there are more questions than answers at present.

Provider Mobility

The crossborder mobility of the provider is described in this volume as the physical or virtual movement of an education provider across a national border to establish a presence to provide education/training programs and/or services to students and other clients. The difference between program and provider mobility is one of scope and volume in terms of programs/services offered and the local presence (and investment) by the foreign provider. Credits and qualifications are awarded by the foreign provider (through foreign, local, or self-accreditation methods), by an affiliated domestic partner, or jointly.

Table 6.4. Typology of Crossborder Provider Mobility

Category	*Description*	*Examples*
Branch Campus	Provider in country A establishes a satellite campus in country B to deliver courses and programs to students in country B (may also include country A students taking a semester/courses abroad). The qualification awarded is from provider in country A.	Monash University from Australia has established branch campuses in Malaysia and South Africa. University of Indianapolis has a branch campus in Athens.
Independent Institution	Foreign provider A (a traditional university, a commercial company or alliance/network) establishes in country B a stand-alone HEI to offer courses/programs and awards.	The German University in Cairo, Phoenix Universities in Canada, and Puerto Rico (Apollo Group).
Acquisition/ Merger	Foreign provider A purchases a part of or 100% of local HEI in country B.	Laureate (formerly Sylvan Learning Systems) has merged with and/or purchased local HEIs in Chile, Mexico, and other LA countries.
Study Center/ Teaching Site	Foreign provider A establishes study centers in country B to support students taking their courses/programs. Study centers can be independent or in collaboration with local providers in country B.	Texas A&M has a "university center" in Mexico City. Troy University (USA) has MBA teaching site in Bangkok.
Affiliation/ Networks	Different types of "public and private," "traditional and new" providers from various countries collaborate through innovative types of partnerships to establish networks/institutions to deliver courses and programs in local and foreign countries through distance or face-to-face modes	Partnership between the Caparo Group and Carnegie Mellon University to establish campus in India. Netherlands Business School branch campus in Nigeria in partnership with African Leadership Forum (NGO).
Virtual University	Provider that delivers credit courses and degree programs to students in different countries through distance education modes and that generally does not have face-to-face support services for students	International Virtual University, Hibernia College, Arab Open University.

Source: Knight (2005b).

The virtual and physical movement of providers to other countries raises many of the same registration, quality assurance, and recognition issues of program mobility. But it also involves extra considerations, especially if a network or local/ foreign partnerships are involved. Setting up a physical presence requires paying attention to national regulations regarding status of the entity, total or joint ownership with local bodies, tax laws, for-profit or nonprofit status, repatriation of earned income, boards of directors, staffing, granting of qualifications, selection of academic programs and courses, etc. Provider mobility relates to Mode 3 of the GATS (see Chapters 9 and 10), and thus trade rules are at play here as well. For some countries, it means that strict regulations are being developed to closely monitor and, in some case, restrict new providers coming into the country. In other instances, incentives are being offered to attract high quality institutions/providers to set up a teaching site or full campus. This is especially true when "knowledge parks," "technology zones," or "education cities" are being developed to attract foreign companies and education/training providers. This proposed typology is still a work in progress, as it does not yet capture in detail the innovations that are occurring in relation to networks, partnerships, and other forms of collaborative provision. However, it does distinguish between program and provider mobility and their respective regulatory issues.

RATIONALES AND IMPACT

An examination of the rationales and impacts related to the increase in crossborder education requires a 360-degree view of the issues. Such an overview involves giving serious consideration to the diverse and often contradictory perspectives and expectations that different groups of stakeholders may have in both receiving and sending countries. This is not a straightforward or linear task of analysis. Rather, the viewpoints differ drastically from the perspective of a student, a provider, a governmental or nongovernmental body, and whether the perspective represented is that of the exporting or importing country. In short, the analysis of rationales and impacts can be rather complicated.

Rationales at the National/Country Level

Perhaps the best place to start is to look at the more macro-level rationales that are driving internationalization in general and determine which are appropriately applied to crossborder education. Traditionally, the rationales for internationalization have been presented in four groups: social/cultural, political, academic, and economic (Knight & de Wit, 1997). In the past several years, much has been written about changes in rationales both within and between this classification of rationales (Altbach, 2004; De Wit, 2002; Van Vught et al., 2003). These generic categories remain a useful way to analyze rationales; however, globalization has contributed to the blurring of the boundaries. It has therefore been necessary and useful to identify cross-cutting metarationales at both the country and the institutional/ provider level. The rationales for internationalization at the national/system level (Knight, 2004) are as follows:

Human resources development: Brain power. The knowledge economy, demographic shifts, mobility of the labor force and increased trade in services are factors driving nations to place more importance on developing and recruiting human capital or brain power through international education initiatives. In general, there is a positive stance toward what is being called brain circulation due to student and professional mobility. However, this phenomenon affects small and large, developed and developing countries in different ways. The term "brain chain" may be more relevant as it is often the larger and more developed countries that capture brain gain while smaller, less developed nations at the bottom of the brain chain experience more brain drain. Therefore, for some countries an increased brain drain is a genuine risk attached to student mobility, especially when international student recruitment policies are linked to aggressive immigration policies. Therefore, the smaller countries on the receiving end of crossborder programs and providers see them as effective means to lessen the chances of their tertiary education graduate staying abroad after they have finished their studies.

Strategic alliances. The international mobility of students, academics, and programs, as well as collaborative research and education initiatives, are seen as productive ways to develop closer geo-political ties and economic relationships among countries. Over the past 10 years, there has been a definite shift from alliances for cultural purposes to economic purposes. The development of strategic alliances is attractive to both sending and receiving countries and providers.

Income generation/commercial trade. For sending countries there is a strong motivation to use crossborder education as a means of generating income from fee-based education programs and services. More emphasis is now being placed on economic and income-generating opportunities. New franchise arrangements, foreign or satellite campuses, on-line delivery, and the increased recruitment of fee-paying students are examples of a more commercial approach to internationalization. The fact that education is now one of the 12 service sectors in the General Agreement on Trade in Services is positive proof that importing and exporting education programs and services is a potentially lucrative trade area.

Nation building/capacity building. While some countries are interested in exporting education to generate income, other countries are interested in importing education programs and institutions for nation-building purposes. The fact that the increased demand for education cannot always be met by domestic capacity makes importing foreign programs and providers an attractive option to help increase access to education and to augment/improve national capacity.

Socio/cultural development. There are mixed views and sometimes conflicting opinions related to socio/cultural rationales. On the one hand, there is the belief that national identity and indigenous customs can be maintained by having students stay in the home country while studying for a foreign qualification. A contrasting view questions how relevant and culturally appropriate course content and teaching/learning processes are when imported from other countries. A third opinion emphasizes the advantages to students who live and study in a country and culture different than their own. Such an experience opens their eyes and increases their international understanding and cross-cultural skills while at the same time they learn how their own country relates to the rest of the world. These kinds of experiences and insights are difficult to replicate in virtual or crossborder provision.

A report from the OECD's Centre for Education Research and Innovation focuses on "Internationalization and Trade in Higher Education: Opportunities and Challenges" (OECD, 2004). It provides case studies on the crossborder mobility of students, programs, and providers in North America, Europe, and the Asia-Pacific region. Four rationales for crossborder education are presented and analyzed: mutual understanding, skilled immigration, revenue generation, and capacity building. This is another helpful approach to examining rationales of crossborder education, especially those of the sending or exporting countries.

Student and Provider/Institution Perspectives

As already mentioned, it is important to examine the rationales and anticipated impacts from the viewpoint of students enrolled in crossborder courses/programs and that of the institutions/providers involved in delivering the education. Table 6.5 presents some differing perspectives on several key factors.

In a study sponsored by IDP, Davis, Olsen, and Bohm (2000) looked at issues and challenges regarding providers, partners, and policies of transnational education. They focused exclusively on traditional public/private universities who were engaged in providing courses and programs in other countries through branch campus, twinning, franchise, and other articulation-type activities. Although this study was completed in 2000 and the field has continued to evolve rapidly, the findings are still relevant and seem to be fairly representative in capturing the motives of conventional higher education institutions for being active in crossborder delivery of programs. According to the findings, the primary rationales for "offering educational programs offshore" are:

> 41% to generate additional sources of income
> 31% to increase the institution's profile and reputation
> 13% to internationalize the curriculum
> 9% to recruit international students to Australian campuses
> 6% to build the capacity of the offshore partner (p. 24).

The importance assigned to the rationales was also important. The lowest were providing opportunities for Australian students to study at offshore campuses and to provide staff development and opportunities through the teaching and management of offshore programs (p. 26).

Table 6.5. *Different Perspectives on Rationales and Impacts of Program and Provider Mobility*

Rationales and Impact	Enrolled Students in Home[a] Country	Institution/ Provider in Source[b] Country	Institution/Provider in Home Country
Increased access/supply in home country	Ability to gain foreign qualification without leaving home. Can continue to meet family and work commitments	Attracted to unmet need for higher education and training	Competition, collaboration or co-existence with foreign providers
Cost /income	Less expensive to take foreign program at home as no travel or accommodation costs. Tuition fees from quality foreign providers may be too high for majority of students	Strong imperative to generate a profit for crossborder operations. Fees could be high for receiving country	Varied rationales and impacts depending on whether institution/ provider is competing or cooperating with foreign providers
Selection of courses/ programs	Increased access to courses/ programs in high demand by labor market	Tendency to offer high-demand courses which require little infrastructure or investment	Need to offer broad selection of courses which may not have high enrollments and/or have major lab or equipment requirements
Language/ cultural and safety aspects	Can have access to courses in foreign and/or indigenous language. Remain in familiar cultural and linguistic environment. Post 9/11 students have stronger concerns about safety and security.	Language of instruction and relevance of curriculum to host[b] country important issues. If foreign language used, additional academic and linguistic support may be needed.	
Quality	Can be exposed to higher or lower quality course provision	Depending on delivery mode, quality may be at risk. Assurance of	Presence of foreign providers may be a catalyst for innovation and

(Continued)

		relevant and high-quality courses may require significant investment.	improvement of quality in courses, management and governance.
Recognition of Qualification	Foreign qualification has to be recognized for academic and employment purposes	May be difficult for academic award and for institution to be recognized in foreign country	Recognized home providers have an advantage and are attractive to foreign providers for award-granting powers
Reputation and Profile	Due to massive marketing campaigns international profile is often mistakenly equated with quality of provider/program	Profile and visibility are key factors for high enrollments and strategic alliances	Home (domestic) providers are challenged to distinguish between those providers with high/low profile and high/low quality

Source: Knight (2005a).
[a] Home country = sending country.
[b] Source or host country = receiving country.

These findings emphasize the importance of income generation and increased profile/reputation as the most powerful motivations for both national-level policy and institution-level providers in large exporting countries like Australia. At the same time, the potential of building capacity in foreign partners and domestic institutions alike was not seen as important—further evidence of the shift from academic collaboration and capacity building to commercialization and income generation.

The study also identified the challenges facing the movement of programs across borders. The participating institutions described the following issues as the major challenges facing them in the future: maintaining profile, operating within local legal contexts, and establishing comparable student outcomes. At the national level (identified as the "industry level" in the report) the key challenges were seen as: (a) quality assurance, (b) competition from other countries and non-university players, (c) finding in-country partners, (c) economic/investment issues, (d) enhancing the institution's reputation, (e) developing a national strategy and avoiding individualism (p. 28).

NEW DEVELOPMENTS IN PROGRAM AND PROVIDER MOBILITY AROUND THE WORLD

The growth and changes in crossborder program and provider mobility are remarkable. This section aims to provide a glimpse of these changes by identifying some of the new and interesting developments in crossborder education provision around the world. It is important to point out that this information reflects the mobility of programs and providers across borders, but it does not include any of the innovative activities oriented toward increasing student mobility or research/scholarship initiatives. The first part provides highlights of new crossborder activity

CHAPTER SIX

by region of the world. The examples have been taken from the Observatory on Borderless Higher Education's "Breaking News" service, bulletins issued monthly to track and report on the latest developments and trends in borderless education, and cited herein by month and year.

This section illustrates the scope of new developments in program and provider mobility, drawing them from just the last five years' reports by the Observatory on Borderless Education. The changes are occurring at such a fast pace that some of the new arrangements or providers may no longer be in existence. There are more examples from conventional higher education institutions than from commercial company providers or from corporate universities; however, the increase in these "new" types of providers should not be underestimated in terms of volume, innovation, and impact.

Middle East

The diversity of new developments in the Middle East makes it a very interesting region to study. For example, Poland has been approved to establish a new private medical institute in Israel where students will study for three years before moving to the Medical University in Gdansk for three more years of clinical study. They will then return to Israel for an internship (OBHE, November 2003).

Saudia Arabia is in the process of establishing new private universities with the involvement of foreign institutions and investors. For instance, the Prince Sultan Private University is being established in cooperation with the University of Arizona and UNESCO. In addition the Dar Al Faisal University is being founded in cooperation with the Stevens Institute of Technology (U.S.) and with financial investment from Boeing Company and the French defense firm Thales (OBHE, June 2003).

The most extensive developments are taking place in Education City in Qatar where Carnegie Mellon, Cornell University, Texas A&M, and Georgetown University School of Foreign Service, among other U.S. institutions, are providing a variety of programs through branch campus locations. This arrangement is similar to Knowledge Village in the United Arab Emirates where institutions from a greater diversity of countries including India, Iran, Canada, the United States, Belgium, Australia, the United Kingdom, and Ireland are delivering both bachelor's and master's degrees in subjects such as business, engineering, IT, interior design, and architecture. (Verbik & Merkley, 2006).

In Bahrain, a new Euro University is being planned in affiliation with the University of Hanover (Germany). Egypt is home to the American University, established more than 80 years ago; but in the last three years the German University in Cairo and the L'Université Française d'Egypte have been established. A new British University is under development. The partnership models between local and foreign partners are slightly different, thereby illustrating the creativity and diversity of new forms of collaboration. An interesting example is the franchise agreement by which the distance MBA program of Heriot-Watt University from the United Kingdom is being offered through the American University in Egypt (OBHE, March 2004).

Asia-Pacific

Vietnam is an emerging hotbed of activity with the development of the branch campus of RMIT University from Australia as 100% foreign-owned. The International College of IT and Management, established by Troy State University from the United States is another example of a foreign branch campus. And the number of active partnerships is growing. The University of Hué in Vietnam recently developed a franchised/joint degree bachelor's program in tourism with the University of Hawaii, and Hanoi University of Technology is currently offering master's and bachelor's degrees with higher education institutions from Belgium (1), France (8), Germany (1) Singapore (2), and the United States (1).

The Vietnamese government recently announced the development of the International University in Vietnam as another initiative to increase national capacity for higher education. It is expected that half the university teaching staff will be Vietnamese and the other half from foreign universities. The involvement of foreign institutions will build on and expand from the current links of Ho Chi Minh City National University (OBHE, January 2004). Thailand is another country of increasing importance for crossborder education and is an appealing destination for institutions and providers from Egypt, China, Australia, and the United States. For example, Al-Azhar Al-Sharif University in Cairo and Jinan University from China both plan to open a branch campus in 2005. Swinburne University of Technology (Australia) has been operating a branch campus since 1998, although it has changed its focus to industry training only. Troy State University from the United States has a teaching site in Bangkok for its MBA program and students can transfer to the United States depending on funds and visa requirements. Other institutions operating in Thailand include the Thai-German Graduate School of Engineering as well as 13 Australian and nine UK universities. (OBHE, March 2004).

In Singapore, the University of New South Wales (Australia) will establish the first 100% foreign-owned higher education institution. It received full approval to do so from the Singaporean government. It plans to offer undergraduate- and graduate-level programs and to develop a strong research capacity. Other well-respected foreign institutions offering education programs and training in Singapore through joint ventures, exchanges, and branch campuses include the Chicago University of Graduate School in Business, Shanghai Jiao Tong University, Stanford University, the German Technische Universitat Munchen, and Technische Universiteit Eindhoven from the Netherlands (OBHE, April 2004).

It is also interesting to note the exporting activities of Singapore institutions. For example, the National University of Singapore has developed a joint MBA with Fudan University aimed at both Chinese and Singapore students. Raffles LaSalle Limited from Singapore is a publicly traded company very active in providing programs in fashion and design in many Asian countries. It has a number of very innovative partnership arrangements and spans many countries. OBHE (December, 2003) describes it as "a remarkable instance of international partnership, combining a Singapore firm with branches in Australia, China, Malaysia, and Thailand, accreditation from an Australian state and a Canadian province, degrees from an

CHAPTER SIX

Australian and a UK university, and a number of in-county university and college partners."

The speed of change and innovation in India's higher education sector is unprecedented and includes both the import and export of programs and services. One of the more interesting initiatives is the partnership between the Caparo Group, a U.K. firm with interests in steel, engineering, and hotels, and Carnegie Mellon University (U.S.) to set up a new campus in India (OBHE, July 2003).

Africa

The Universitiet Nijenrode (Netherlands Business School), a private institution, has recently established a new branch campus in Nigeria in partnership with the African Leadership Forum (AFL) which is a nonprofit organization founded in 1988. This is one of the first such initiatives outside of South Africa (OBHE, April 2004). In South Africa in the last few years, there have been only a handful of foreign institutions with branch campuses including Monash and Bond from Australia, De Montfort (U.K.), and the Netherlands Business School. As a result of the recent review of all MBA programs offered in South Africa, three of the foreign institutions are leaving because of accreditation-related issues. Monash will remain (it does not offer an MBA program), and so will the U.K.-based Henley Management College, which is primarily a distance provider (OBHE, June 2004). South Africa is an example of a country where there has been a decrease in the number of foreign programs being offered, largely due to government regulations and accreditation processes. Kenya is home to two private nonprofit universities. The Aga Khan University from Pakistan opened a branch university campus in Kenya in 2002 which specializes in nursing education and Alliant International University from the United States provides education in social sciences and the humanities (OBHE, January 2004).

Mauritius is taking some bold new steps as it tries to establish itself as a "cyber island" by attracting foreign IT firms from the West and from India. A "knowledge center," described as a world-class integrated education and training complex, is a key aspect of its plans. To date, there are already more than 50 foreign universities and professional bodies offering programs locally. These programs tend to be at the diploma or certificate level and in specialized fields (OBHE, October 2003). The concept of attracting foreign education providers to support the education and training needs of the new "cyber island" may have positive consequences in terms of stemming brain drain or even in stimulating brain gain, but the impact on local education institutions is not yet known.

Europe

Russia is an example of a country undergoing major economic reform with major implications for the higher education sector. Many higher education institutions, for example, the Moscow International Slavonic Institute and the Moscow State University of Industry, are operating programs abroad in, for example, Bulgaria.

However, Russia is not only a sending country but also a receiving country of programs through joint/double degrees, twinning, and franchise arrangements. For instance, the Higher School of Economics has a double degree program with the London School of Economics. The Stockholm School of Economics is operating in St. Petersburg, and the University of Oslo's Center for Medical Studies is in Moscow. The UK Open University is active through 80 business training centers across the country. The University of Southern Queensland is partnering with Far Eastern National University in Vladivostok for program delivery (OBHE, October 2003). The Pune-based International Institute of Information Technology plans to offer its master's and Ph.D. courses through the newly established Russian-Indian Center for Advanced Computer Research in Moscow.

In Greece, the University of Indianapolis has been active for more than a decade, first through an articulation program whereby students start their studies in Athens and complete them in the United States. This model has now evolved into a campus in Greece called the University of Indianapolis Athens (OBHE, June 2004).

In terms of activities by private companies, Laureate Education owns part or all of the Universidad Europa de Madrid in Spain, Les Roches and Gilion Hotel School in Switzerland, and L'École Superiure du Commerce Exterier de Paris in France. Apollo International is offering its courses in the Netherlands, and Raffles La Salle from Singapore has recently signed an agreement with Middlesex University to offer its bachelor's and master's programs in fashion and design (OBHE, December 2003).

North America

To report on U.S. crossborder activities is a challenge because of the volume, diversity of providers, and types of partnerships. A review of the previous regional sections shows that U.S. higher education institutions and private companies are probably the most active and innovative in program and provider mobility around the world. Korea manifests several examples of U.S. program mobility through partnerships with local institutions and companies. For instance, Syracuse University, in conjunction with Sejong University in Seoul, offers a specially designed MBA program for Korean students. Duke and Purdue universities are also offering MBAs in Korea, and Stanford University is delivering online graduate and postgraduate courses, using alumni as local tutors (OBHE, August 2004). These types of crossborder activities from U.S. higher education institutions can be found in many Asian countries, for example, China, Vietnam, Thailand, Malaysia, Singapore, Philippines, and more recently India.

The Middle East is also a site for U.S. crossborder activity. The University of Missouri at St. Louis has been involved in the establishment of the first private university in Kuwait, the Gulf University of Science and Technology. The Missouri institution also has a similar relationship with the Modern College of Business and Science in Oman (OBHE, February 2004).

An important feature of U.S. crossborder activity concerns private and publicly traded companies. The Global Education Index (GEI), developed by the OBHE, is a system of classifying many of the largest and more active publicly traded companies who are providing education programs and services. A scan of more than 50 companies (Garrett, 2004) shows that the United States is home to the majority of these companies. Some of the better-known include Kaplan (owned by the *Washington Post*), the Apollo Group, DeVry, Career Education Corporation, and Laureate Education (formerly Sylvan Learning Systems). Kaplan owns 57 colleges in the United States but also owns the Dublin Business School, Ireland's largest private undergraduate institution. It is likely to be the first of many future purchases of foreign institutions (OBHE, December 2003). The Apollo Group owns Phoenix University, the largest American private university, and is aggressively seeking to broaden its foreign investments and holdings. Since 1995, Apollo has also owned Western International University (WIU) which runs a branch campus called Modi Apollo International Institute in New Delhi through a partnership with the KK Modi Group, an Indian industrial conglomerate. WIU has an agreement with the Canadian Institute of Business and Technology (CIBT) whereby CIBT offers WIU programs through its three business schools in Beijing (OBHE, October 2003).

Another smaller, but nonetheless interesting, initiative has been the establishment of Northface University by Northface Learning, Inc., which offers degree programs in IT and business and has the backing of IBM and Microsoft. This will be a company to watch in terms of future international expansion (OBHE, August 2004). The University of Northern Virginia is another small private university offering programs in business and IT; it has recently opened a branch campus in the Czech Republic and has delivery partnerships in China and India (OBHE, August 2004). These are only a few examples of the hundreds of new initiatives and partnerships by which U.S. higher education institutions and companies are delivering education courses and programs to other countries of the world.

The Al-Abram Canadian University in Egypt is Canada's first, and to date only, example of Canadian universities directly supporting the establishment of a new foreign university. The Al-Abram Organization is a large company that owns the Egyptian daily newspaper by that name. It is cooperating with McMaster University, École Polytechnique de Montreal, and the Université du Quebec in Montreal to establish a new private university that began enrolling students in September 2004. The Association of Canadian Universities and Colleges has played a role linking Al-Abram with Canadian partners and may have a role during the implementation phase (OBHE, March 2004).

Latin America

In Mexico, the University of the Incarnate Word (UIW), a private U.S. institution from Texas, opened a new campus in 2003. Other U.S. institutions with Mexican campuses include Endicott College, Alliant International University, and Texas A&M which has a "university center" in Mexico City (OBHE, September 2003). In 2000, Laureate Education purchased the Universidad del Valle de Mexico and is currently planning to open a new branch in Guadalajara. It also owns Universidad

Interamericana, a private university with campuses in Costa Rica and Panama (OBHE, November 2003) and parts of three private universities in Chile (OBHE, June 2003).

Bologna University from Italy is one of the few foreign institutions with a branch campus in Argentina. Florida State University has had a branch campus in Panama since 1999 (Verbik & Merkley, 2006). In terms of exporting, the Technical Institute of Monterrey (ITESM) in Mexico is well known for its online education programs, especially the MBA, delivered to many countries in Latin America.

These new initiatives illustrate the diversity of education activities by conventional higher education institutions and new commercial providers. They demonstrate the range of countries and types of partnerships being formed to promote, exchange, link, and especially sell higher education across borders.

One of the challenges related to crossborder education is a serious lack of solid data on the volume and type of crossborder program and provider mobility. Institutions and national education systems have invested a lot of effort in gathering reliable data on student mobility, but it is only in the last seven years that countries and international organizations are starting to track program and provider mobility. There are huge challenges in this data collection due to the lack of common set of terms and different systems of gathering data. However, Australia, New Zealand, and more recently the United Kingdom have been gathering statistics from the recognized higher education institutions on the extent of their crossborder education provision. A tentative analysis of crossborder activity in these three countries is included in this part of the chapter. It is described as tentative, for any analysis is only as good as the data, and there is no assurance that comparable aspects of crossborder delivery are being examined; nonetheless, it certainly provides interesting trend data. These three countries, who are primarily sending countries, are the leaders in trying to systematically gather quantitative data. Other countries, notably in Europe, are collecting descriptive data on crossborder provision primarily focused on intra-European mobility.

COMPARATIVE ANALYSIS OF CROSSBORDER ACTIVITY IN AUSTRALIA, THE UNITED KINGDOM, AND NEW ZEALAND

It is important to repeat and stress the caveat given above: A frustrating challenge in analyzing the implications of crossborder delivery of education programs is the lack of data. While more reliable information and informed analysis are available on the movement of students across borders, the paucity of information on program mobility creates an undesirable environment of speculation, confusion, and often misinformation. Among negative consequences are lack of confidence in the quality and dependability of crossborder education provision, further impeding the analysis needed to undergird solid policy and regulatory frameworks.

Australia is the leader in terms of having up-to-date and fairly comprehensive data from universities on the volume, types, award level, and discipline of crossborder program delivery. The Australian Vice-Chancellors Association and the

CHAPTER SIX

national Department of Education, Science, and Technology collect, analyze, and publish these data annually. In New Zealand, the International Policy and Development Unit of the Ministry of Education undertook a major survey in 2001 of crossborder delivery in all tertiary institutions, but this survey has not yet became an annual exercise. The U.K. Higher Education Statistics Agency collected information for the 2002–2003 academic year on U.K. education programs offered abroad—the first time it has gathered these data and published its findings. This is definitely a step forward.

An examination of the information from Australia, New Zealand, and the United Kingdom reveals differences in approaches to data collecting and interpretation. To the extent possible, a comparative analysis was done to check on noteworthy similarities and difference. To manage a degree of comparability, some of the raw quantitative data was converted into percentages, a step that required some rounding off of numbers. Consequently, the information presented in Table 6.6 is for illustrative purposes only. Furthermore, these three reports provide data only on exported programs—not on any crossborder education coming into their jurisdiction. However, it is probably fair to say that the number of crossborder programs and providers being imported into these three countries is insignificant compared to the number of outgoing programs and providers.

Not surprisingly, the crossborder activity of these three countries is fairly concentrated in the Asia-Pacific region. This pattern undoubtedly stems from geographical proximity, historical and linguistic ties, and most importantly the fact that many Asian countries do not have the capacity to meet the increasing local demand for tertiary level education.

Asia is certainly the region to watch for new developments. As this analysis shows, Malaysia, Singapore, China, and to a lesser extent Thailand, India, and Vietnam have been the most popular destination countries during the last five to 10 years. During this period, a maelstrom of new partnership types has developed through franchising, twinning, and articulation programs between foreign higher education institutions and local higher education institutions and private companies. These receiving countries have learned a great deal from their foreign partners and are currently being more proactive and strategic in exporting their own programs and providers to neighboring countries in Asia and the Middle East. They include a substantial number of private commercial companies such as Raffles LaSalle, Informatics, and Hartford in Singapore, Aptech and NIIT (National Indian Institute of Technology) from India, and SEG and Stamford College in Malaysia. Given that Asia will represent approximately 70% of the global demand in 2025 (Bohm et al., 2002), this part of the world will be the region to watch carefully for new trends and developments.

Table 6.6. Comparative data on programs offered across borders

	United Kingdom		Australia	New Zealand
Year Data Collected	2002–2003	2006	2003	2001
Percent of HEIs Delivering Crossborder Programs		87% of universities		47% of all (38) public HEIs (88% of universities)
Number of Students in Crossborder Programs	101,645	68,175	97,751	2,200 (increase from 380 in 1997)
Number of Crossborder Programs			1,569 programs	63 programs (increase from 6 in 1997)
Primary Locations	Hong Kong	Hong Kong Malaysia Singapora	China, Hong Kong, Singapore, Malaysia represent 70% of cross-border delivery	Malaysia 23% China 9% Australia 9% Hong Kong 6% Singapore 6%
Level of Degrees	Undergrad 56% Graduate 44%			Sub-degree 34% Undergrad 39% Post grad 27%
Primary Disciplines	Business 44% Joint degrees 21% Law 13% IT 8.5%		Business administration economics	Bus./commerce 15% Special medicine 15% Computer science 14% Management 13%
Spread of Activity among HEIs	10 institutions account for 81% of crossborder enrollments	12 institutions account for 74% of crossborder activity		3 institutions account for 55% of all crossborder program delivery
Mode of Delivery				42% through campus-based teaching 32% through distance only 26% used combination
Source of Data	HESA 2002–2003 London External 2002–2003, as reported by OBHE, July 2004	DEST Overseas Student Statistics 2006	AVCC Offshore Programs of Australian Universities 2003	Ministry of Education 2002

Source: Knight (2005b, upated 2008).

CHAPTER SIX

CONCLUDING REMARKS

The purpose of this chapter has been to explore the scope and practice of delivering education across national borders. There is ample evidence that demand for higher education in the next 20 years will outstrip the capacity of some countries to meet the domestic need. In fact, demand has already exceeded supply in many parts of the world. Students moving to other countries to pursue their studies will continue to be an important part of the international dimension of the higher education landscape. But student mobility will not be able to satisfy the enormous appetite for higher education from densely populated countries wanting to build human capacity to fully participate in the knowledge society—hence, the emergence and growing importance of crossborder education programs and providers.

A scan of trends, issues, and new developments in program and provider mobility shows a diversity of new types of education providers, new delivery modes, and innovative forms of public/private and local/foreign partnerships. New courses and programs are being designed and delivered in response to local conditions and global challenges, and new qualifications/awards are being conferred. The growth in the volume, scope, and dimensions of crossborder education has the potential to provide increased access and to promote the innovation and responsiveness of higher education, but this turmoil also brings new challenges and unexpected consequences. There are the realities that unrecognized and rogue crossborder providers are active; that much of the latest crossborder education provision is being driven by comercial interests and gain; and that mechanisms to recognize qualifications and ensure quality of the academic course/program are still not in place in many countries. These conditions present major challenges to the education sector. It is important to acknowledge the huge potential of crossborder education but not at the expense of academic quality and integrity.

Words like "diversity," "innovation," "complexity," "confusion," "opportunities," and "challenges" have been used repeatedly in this chapter to describe the development and evolution of crossborder education. Internationalization in the broadest sense means the process of integrating an international, intercultural, and global dimension into the purposes of higher education; into the primary functions of teaching, research, and service/outreach; and into the delivery of education at home and abroad. Academic cooperation, educational exchanges/linkages, and commercial provision are all part and parcel of internationalization and facilitate the mobility of students, programs, providers, and projects across borders. The education sector is not alone in looking for ways to guide, monitor, and regulate the movement of education programs and providers. It needs to work in close cooperation with other sectors and to play a pivotal role in ensuring that crossborder education reflects and helps to meet the individual country's educational goals, culture, priorities, and policies.

Note: This paper is adapted from J. Knight (2005a), "Crossborder education: An analytical framework for program and provider mobility," in J. Smart & W. Tierney (Eds.), *Higher education: Handbook of theory and practice* (Vol. 21, pp. 345–396). Dordrecht, Netherlands: Springer.

RELATED REFERENCES

Altbach, P. G. (2001). Higher education and the WTO: Globalization run amok. In *International education* (pp. 1–2). Boston: Newsletter of the Center for International Higher Education, Boston College.
Altbach, P. G. (2004). Globalization and the university: Myths and realities in the unequal world. In *Tertiary education and management*, No. 1.
AVCC. Australian Vice- Chancellors Committee. (2003). *Offshore programs of Australian universities*. Canberra: Australian Vice-Chancellors Committee.
Bhushan, S. (2006) *Foreign education providers in India: Mapping the extent and regulation*. London: Observatory on Borderless Higher Education.
Bohm, A., Davis, D., Meares, D., & Pearce, D. (2002). *The global student mobility 2025 report: Forecasts of the global demand for international education*. Canberra, Australia: IDP.
Connelly, S. (2006). *Models and types: Guidelines for good practice in transnational education*. London: Observatory on Borderless Higher Education.
Davis, D., Olsen, A., & Bohm, A. (Eds.). (2000). *Transnational education: Providers, partners and policy*. A research study. Brisbane, Australia: IDP.
DEST. Department of Education, Science, and Training of the Commonwealth Government of Australia. (2006). *Annual report: Higher education statistics collection*. Canberra, Australia: DEST.
De Wit, H. (2002). *Internationalization of higher education in the United States of America and Europe: A historical, comparative, and conceptual analysis*. Westport, CT: Greenwood Press.
ESIB. National Unions of Students in Europe. (2002). *European student handbook on transnational education*. Brussels, Belgium: National Unions of Students in Europe.
Feng, G. (2006). *Sino-foreign joint education ventures: A national, regional and institutional analysis*. London: Observatory on Borderless Higher Education.
Huang, F. (Ed.). (2006). *Transnational higher education in Asia and the Pacific region*. Hiroshima, Japan: Research Institute for Higher Education, Hiroshima University.
Garrett, R. (2004). *Transnational delivery by UK higher education. Part 2: Innovations and competitive advantage*. London: Observatory on Borderless Higher Education.
Garrett, R. (2005). *Fraudulent, sub-standard, ambiguous: The alternative borderless higher education*. Briefing Note. London: Observatory on Borderless Higher Education.
Garrett, R., & Verbik, L. (2004). *Transnational delivery by UK higher education. Part 1: Data and missing data*. London: Observatory on Borderless Higher Education.
Jokivirta, L. (2005). *Higher education crossing borders in francophone Africa: Parts 1 and 2*. Briefing Notes, November/December. London: Observatory on Borderless Higher Education.
Knight, J. (2004). Crossborder education: The complexities of globalization, internationalization, and trade. In M. Smout (Ed.), *Internationalization and quality assurance* (pp. 73–91). Pretoria: South Africa UniversityVice Chancellors Assocation.
Knight, J. (2005a). Cross-border education: An analytical framework for program and provider mobility. In J. Smart & W. Tierney (Eds.), *Higher education handbook of theory and practice* (Vol. 21, pp. 345–396). Dordrecht, Netherlands: Springer.
Knight, J. (2005b). *Cross-border education: Programs and providers on the move*. CBIE Millennium Research Monograph No. 10. Ottawa, Canada: Canadian Bureau for International Education.
Knight, J., & de Wit, H. (Eds.). (1997). *Internationalization of higher education in Asia Pacific countries*. Amsterdam, Netherlands: European Association for International Education.
Larsen, K., Momii, K., & Vincent-Lancrin, S. (2004). *Crossborder higher education: An analysis of current trends, policy strategies, and future scenarios*. London: Observatory on Borderless Higher Education.
McBurnie, G., & Ziguras, C. (2001). The regulation of transnational higher education in Southeast Asia: Case studies of Hong Kong, Malaysia, and Australia. *Higher Education, 42*(1), 84–105.
Middlehurst, R., & Woodfield, S. (2003). *The role of transnational, private and for-profit provision in meeting global demand for tertiary education: Mapping, regulation and impact*. Vancouver, Canada: Commonwealth of Learning and UNESCO.
New Zealand Ministry of Education. (2002). *New Zealand's offshore public tertiary education programmes: Initial stockade prepared by the International Policy and Development Department, Ministry of Education*. Wellington, New Zealand: Ministry of Education.

CHAPTER SIX

Observatory on Borderless Higher Education (OBHE). (2002–2007, cited by month and year). *Breaking news stories from 2002–2007*. London: Observatory on Borderless Higher Education. Available by subscription only.

Organization for Economic and Community Development (OECD). (2004). *Internationalization and trade in higher education: Challenges and opportunities*. Paris: Centre for Education Research and Innovation, OECD.

Van Vught, F., Van der Wende, M., & Westerheijden, D. (2003). Globalization and internationalisation: Policy agendas compared. In J. Enders & O. Fulton (Eds.), *Higher education dynamics*. Dordrecht, Netherlands: Kluwer Academic Publishers.

Verbik, L., & Jokivirta, L. (2005). *National regulatory frameworks for transnational higher education: Models and trends. Parts 1–2*. Briefing Notes. London: Observatory on Borderless Higher Education.

Verbik, L., & Merkley, C. (2006). *The international branch campus: Models and trends*. London: Observatory on Borderless Higher Education.

CHAPTER SEVEN

HIGHER EDUCATION CROSSING BORDERS:

Quality Assurance and Accreditation Issues

Internationalization is one of the forces which is having a profound effect on higher education in the beginning decade of the 21st century. Internationalization is a multifaceted process that is integrating an international dimension into the purpose, goals, functions, and delivery of higher education. One of the key elements of this internationalization is academic mobility/crossborder education. It is true that academic mobility across borders has been a central feature of higher education for centuries. The fact that "universe" is central to the concept of university demonstrates the presence of the international dimension since the founding of universities as institutions of higher education and research. While the international mobility of students and scholars are longstanding forms of academic mobility, it is only during the last two decades that more emphasis has been placed on the movement of education programs, higher education institutions, and new commercial providers across national borders.

The growth and changes in crossborder program and provider mobility are remarkable. There are new types of providers, new collaborative partnerships, new modes of delivery, and new types of awards and qualifications granted. This chapter examines the issues and questions concerning the quality assurance and accreditation of crossborder delivery that takes education to students in their own country. The focus is on academic programs and institutions/providers moving across borders–not the mobility of students.

ISSUES AND IMPLICATIONS

Registration of Crossborder Providers in Receiving Countries

A fundamental question is whether the institutions, companies, and organizations that are delivering award-based programs are registered, licensed, or recognized by the receiving country. The answer to this question varies. Many countries do not have regulatory systems in place to register out-of-country providers for various reasons, including lack of capacity or political will. If foreign providers are not registered or recognized, it is difficult to monitor their performance. It is a usual practice that, if an institution/provider is not registered as part of a national system, then regulatory frameworks for quality assurance or accreditation do not apply. This situation prevails in many countries; hence, foreign providers (bona fide and rogue) do not have to comply with the national regulations of the receiving countries.

Many questions and factors come into play where the registration or licensing of foreign providers are concerned. For instance, are different criteria or conditions applicable to providers who are part of and recognized by a national education system in their home country than to providers who are not? Does it make a difference if the provider is for-profit or non-profit, private or public, an institution or a company? What conditions apply if, in fact, the provider is a company that has no home-based presence and only establishes institutions in foreign countries? How does one monitor partnerships between local domestic institutions/companies and foreign ones? Is it possible to register a completely virtual provider? Clearly, there are challenges involved in trying to establish appropriate and effective national or regional regulatory systems for the registration of crossborder providers.

Often there are bilateral cultural/academic agreements in place to facilitate and monitor the foreign presence of education providers. However, the fact that education services are now part of bilateral and multilateral trade agreements introduces new regulations and questions. A key question facing national governments, as well as international organizations, is the extent to which the introduction of new national regulations to license, recognize, or accredit crossborder providers will be interpreted as barriers to trade and must therefore be modified to comply with new trade policies. All in all, the issue of regulating and licensing providers that deliver education across borders needs further attention by national education policymakers.

The Quality Assurance and Accreditation of Crossborder Education

During the past 10 years, increased importance has certainly been given to quality assurance and accreditation at the institutional and national levels. During that decade, more than 70 countries have developed new quality assurance mechanisms and national organizations. New regional quality networks have also been established. The primary task of these groups has been accrediting and regulating the quality of domestic higher education offered primarily by public and private higher education institutions. However, the increase in crossborder education by traditional institutions and new private commercial providers has introduced a new challenge (and gap) in the field of accreditation. Historically, national quality assurance agencies have generally not focused their efforts on assessing the quality of imported and exported programs, with some notable exceptions (described below). The key question now facing the sector is how to deal with the increase in crossborder education by traditional HEIs and, more importantly, the new private commercial providers who are not normally part of nationally based accreditation and quality assurance schemes.

As the discussion moves forward, it will be of strategic and substantive importance to recognize the roles and responsibilities of all the players involved in accreditation and quality assurance. These include individual institutions/providers, national quality assurance systems, nongovernment and independent accreditation bodies, professional bodies, and regional/international organizations—all of whom contribute to ensuring the quality of crossborder education. Much is at risk if rogue providers or fraudulent qualifications become closely linked to crossborder education. It will be important to work in a collaborative and complementary fashion to build a system that ensures the quality and integrity of crossborder education and maintains the confidence of society in higher education.

Diversity and Commercialization of Accrediting Bodies

Increased awareness of the need for quality assurance and/or accreditation has led to several new developments in accreditation, some of which are helping with the task of domestic and international recognition of qualifications, but some of which are only hindering and complicating matters. First, it is important to acknowledge the efforts of many countries to establish criteria and procedures for the recognition, quality assurance, accreditation, and approval of bona fide accreditors. At the same time, it is necessary to recognize the increase in self-appointed and rather self-serving accreditors, as well as accreditation mills that simply sell "bogus" accreditation labels.

Market forces are making the profile and reputation of an institution/provider and their courses more and more important. Major investments are being made in marketing and branding campaigns to achieve name recognition and increase enrollments. The possession of some type of accreditation is part of the campaign and assures prospective students that the programs/awards are of high standing. The desire for accreditation status is leading to a commercialization of quality assurance/ accreditation as programs and providers strive to gain as many "accreditation" stars as possible to increase competitiveness and perceived international legitimacy. The challenge is how to distinguish between bona fide and rogue accreditors, especially when neither the crossborder provider nor accreditor is nationally based or recognized as part of a national higher education system.

At the same time, there are networks of institutions and new organizations that are self-appointed and that engage in the accreditation of their members. These are positive developments when viewed as efforts to improve the quality of the academic offer. However, there is some concern that they are not totally objective in their assessments and may be more interested in generating income than in improving quality. While this caveat can apply to both crossborder and domestic provision, it is particularly worrisome for crossborder provision, as attention to national policy objectives and cultural orientation is often neglected.

Another worrisome development is the growth in accreditation mills. These organizations are not recognized or legitimate bodies, and they more or less "sell" accreditation status without any independent assessment. They are similar to degree mills that sell certificates and degrees with little or no course work. Different education stakeholders—especially the students, employers, and the public—need to be aware of these accreditation and degree mills, which are often no more than a web address and are therefore usually out of the jurisdiction of national regulatory systems.

Due to the increase in self-appointed accreditors and accreditation mills, the establishment of a registry of bona fide accreditors may be the necessary next step. It is no longer enough to have recognized higher education providers listed in a national database. It is now important to have a registry of approved accreditors. The European higher education community is now undertaking this step for its region.

It is probable that other sectors, in addition to education, will be interested in developing international quality standards and accreditation procedures for education. Those of the International Standards Organization (ISO) or other industry-based mechanisms (e.g., the Baldridge Awards) are examples of systems that might be applied or modeled for crossborder education. The education sector has mixed views on the appropriateness of quality standards being established for education by those outside the sector; some see merit to the idea while others see problems. At the same time, there are divergent opinions on the desirability and value of any international standards or criteria for accreditation, as such standards might jeopardize the sovereignty of national-level systems or merely contribute to standardization, not necessarily improve quality. This issue is complex, and many different actors and stakeholders are involved. However, given the realities of today's growth in the number and types of crossborder education providers and the prospect of increased trade and new trade rules, there is a sense of urgency about how to ensure the quality of imported and exported education providers and programs through accreditation processes, criteria or national regulations.

It is also important to acknowledge that a great deal of crossborder mobility of students, teachers, and programs occurs through non-commercial initiatives. Education activities that are part of development aid projects and international academic linkages and networks are good examples.

Recognition of Qualifications

The credibility of higher education programs and qualifications is extremely important for students, their employers, the public at large, and of course for the academic community itself. It is critical that the qualifications awarded by cross-border providers be legitimate and recognized for employment or further studies both at home and abroad. This is a major challenge facing the national and international higher education sector in light of new crossborder providers and programs.

UNESCO has long acknowledged the requirement of an international system to facilitate and ensure recognition of academic and professional qualifications. Regional UNESCO conventions on the Recognition of Qualification were established more than 25 years ago and have been ratified by over 100 member states in Africa, Asia, the Pacific, the Arab States, Europe, and Latin America. They are unique, legally binding instruments dealing with crossborder mutual recognition of qualifications. There is limited general awareness of these instruments except for the European regional convention, which in 1997 was updated jointly by UNESCO and the Council of Europe in the form of the Lisbon Convention. In 2001, the same two organizations established a Code of Good Practice for Transnational Education that is now a recognized part of the Lisbon Convention. At present, discussions are on-going about how these UNESCO conventions can be used as instruments to complement trade agreements and assure students, employers, and the public that there are systems in place to recognize academic and professional qualifications. Given the growth in academic mobility, the increased mobility of the labor force, and the fact that GATS is encouraging greater professional mobility, there is a clear and urgent need that national education policymakers address the issue of recognizing qualifications.

NEW NATIONAL, REGIONAL AND INTERNATIONAL INITIATIVES

Codes of Practice

Codes of conduct for crossborder/transnational education have been developed by several national university associations, quality agencies, and government departments. They are usually a set of principles that guide the delivery of programs across borders and the establishment of partnerships with foreign providers. They are intended for public and private higher education institutions but have relevance for nontraditional providers as well. The codes differ in substance and perspective. But they are similar in spirit and purpose—which is to assure quality in crossborder academic provision regardless of mode of delivery and partnership model, and to maintain the integrity of the academic qualification. Examples of these codes include:

- Quality Assurance Code of Practice: Collaborative Provisions, United Kingdom, http://www.qaa.ac.uk/academicinfrastructure/codeOfPractice/default.asp
- Code of Ethical Practice in the Offshore Provision of Education and the Educational Services by Higher Australian Higher Education Institutions, Australian Vice-Chancellors Committee, http://www.universitiesaustralia.edu.au/documents/publications/Principles_final_Dec02.pdf.
- Principles of Good Practice for the Educational Programs for Non-U.S. Nationals, http://www.neasc.org/cihe/overseas_programs.PDF.
- Code of Good Practice in the Provision of Transnational Education, UNESCO/CEPES and the Council of Europe, http://www.cepes.ro/hed/recogn/groups/transnat/code.htm.
- Code of Practice for Overseas Education Institutions Operating in Mauritius. Tertiary Education Commission. http://tec.intnet.mu.

These codes are not enforceable; they are guidelines only. But like the recently developed UNESCO/OECD Guidelines for Quality Provision in Crossborder Higher Education (discussed below), they are important awareness-building tools for the different actors in crossborder education and as such are very useful to education policymakers.

UNESCO/OECD Guidelines for Quality Crossborder Provision

It is timely that UNESCO and OECD (2005a) have jointly developed a set of "Guidelines on Quality Provision in Crossborder Education." These guidelines address six stakeholder groups in higher education: governments, higher education institutions/providers, student bodies, quality assurance and accreditation entities, academic recognition bodies, and professional associations. The purpose of the

CHAPTER SEVEN

guidelines is to encourage international cooperation and enhance the understanding of the importance of quality provision in crossborder higher education. The guidelines are designed to protect students and other stakeholders from low-quality higher education programs, accreditation and degree mills, and other disreputable providers. The guidelines are not legally binding but countries are encouraged to use them in the manner that is most appropriate for their national context. (See http://www.unesco.org/education/hed/guidelines).

One of the steps toward assuring the quality and accreditation of crossborder education is the development of national regulatory frameworks. To complement the guidelines, UNESCO and the Asia Pacific Quality Network (APQN) have prepared a "Toolkit on Regulating Quality Assurance in Cross-Border Education." This toolkit is designed to help both receiving and sending countries with the issues, models, benefits, and practical steps in establishing a regulatory framework for crossborder education (UNESCO/APQN, 2006). The following two sections briefly describe several contemporary national regulatory frameworks for outgoing and incoming crossborder providers. These examples have been taken from the Toolkit where more detailed information is available.

Examples of national regulations for sending countries. The responsibility for the quality assurance and/or accreditation process is shared differently according to the actors involved. The first line of responsibility lies with the providers themselves, the second with the sending country, and ultimately, of course, with the receiving (importing or host) country. This section looks at examples of several countries that have established procedures for evaluating domestic institutions that are active in such crossborder education initiatives as twinning, franchising, articulation, double/joint degrees, branch campuses, and others. It is interesting to note that these procedures and regulation are usually part of the national accreditation/quality assurance process for registered higher education institutions. This means that many of the nontraditional and private for-profit crossborder providers would not be covered by this regulation as they are often outside of a national higher education system of accreditation.

Australia. The situation in Australia is very interesting as Australian universities have the authority to accredit their own programs. National protocols/regulations do exist and set out a broad range of criteria and procedures for higher education approval processes across the whole sector. However, crossborder education is not part of these national protocols and, as a result, some Australian states have established their own. The entity with overall responsibility for quality assurance of universities is the Australian Universities Quality Agency. It is a nongovernmental body that includes as part of its mandate a regular cycle of quality audits of universities. These audits include a review of crossborder operations and include overseas site visits as necessary. (See www.auqa.edu.au.) To date, there is a policy to determine whether an overseas visit is required, but there are no specific criteria or guidelines specifically designed for evaluating different forms of crossborder provision.

Australia is well known for the exponential growth of its international education programs in the last decade, including recruiting students to both domestic-based institutions and to offshore programs and campuses. In 2005, the government developed a "Transnational Education Quality Framework" with four key elements: (a) better communication and promotion of Australia's quality assurance arrangements for transnational education and training, (b) increased access to and transparency of data and information about transnational activities, (c) efficient and effective quality assurance functions, and (d) the requirement that domestic and transnational education programs be equivalent in the standard of delivery and outcomes of program. In essence, it is an important communication and promotion program, but not a regulatory framework. (See http://aei.dest.gov.au.)

United Kingdom. The Quality Assurance Agency (QAA) (www.qaa.ac.uk) for Higher Education has oversight for the quality of crossborder initiatives undertaken by U.K. colleges and universities. However, the QAA does not register, approve, or accredit overseas programs. Instead it publishes a code of practice on foreign "collaborative provision and flexible and distributed learning," provides information on benchmark standards, conducts institutional audits regularly, but covers crossborder education only when foreign collaborative provision is an important part of the institution being reviewed. Thus, for the most part, evaluation of crossborder education is integrated into regular institutional audit programs but a separate code of practice exists which provides important reference points for the evaluation.

The code of practice for collaborative provisions addresses a number of key elements including: (a) responsibility for, and equivalence of, academic standards, (b) choosing a partner organization or agent, (c) assuring academic standards and the quality of programs and awards, (d) assessment requirements, and (e) external examinations for the students.

United States of America. The American model of quality assurance and accreditation differs from that of other countries. Instead of having one major national body responsible for accreditation activities, it has a large number of national, regional, and professional accrediting bodies that are private, nonprofit entities. These accrediting bodies have to be recognized by either the Council for Higher Education Accreditation and/or the United States Department of Education.

Many of these accrediting organizations develop their own policies and procedures for accrediting crossborder education programs that are part of U.S. higher education institutions. Some of them are also involved in accrediting new commercial providers that set up independent institutions overseas. There is no centrally determined policy for regulating the accreditation or quality assurance of U.S.-based higher education institutions and U.S. commercial companies, such as those listed in the Global Education Index (Garrett, 2004), that are delivering higher education programs abroad. The Council for Higher Education Accreditation (CHEA) serves as an important advocate and source of information on international accreditation issues and practices. It houses a database of recognized accreditors and information on degree mills. (See www.chea.org.)

CHAPTER SEVEN

It is also interesting to note that many of the regional accrediting bodies in the United States are hired by traditional or alternative providers in other countries to conduct an accreditation process on their institution. These foreign institutions benefit from the rigorous accreditation process and use the American status of accreditation as an important element in promotion campaigns to attract students, professors, and research funds. The CHEA has developed a set of guiding principles for these U.S.-based accreditors who are working on an international basis. This type of accreditation is different than the evaluation process of U.S.-based institutions who have overseas operations.

Examples of national regulations for receiving countries. As previously mentioned, Asia Pacific is the region with the greatest volume, scope, and variety in providing crossborder higher education. Thus, it is not a surprise that some major advances have been made in developing national regulations to monitor and assure the quality of crossborder education, including such joint initiatives as twinning, franchise, articulation, double/joint degrees, or independent projects such as branch campuses, virtual universities, or stand-alone institutions.

Peoples Republic of China. China is a hotbed of activity in terms of foreign entities establishing joint education ventures with Chinese partners. The demand for postsecondary education in China is enormous, given the population demographics and the desire of China to be a serious player in international economics and politics. China is one of the most interesting and desirable countries for commercial academic enterprises; and while it has opened its doors to these activities, it has done so with a national regulatory framework in place. In 2003 China established the "Regulations on Chinese and Foreign Cooperation in Running Schools." This law was supplemented the following year with additional regulations on implementation methods. (See http://www.cscse.edu.cn/Portal4/default533.htm.) These regulations require that all foreign institutions or companies collaborate with a local provider. Therefore, only joint ventures are permitted, and these partnerships must be authorized and accredited by the Chinese authorities.

If a foreign qualification is awarded, it must be recognized in the home country of the awarding institution. (This raises a question about the recognition and accreditation challenges of international providers that do not have a home-based awarding institution.) If a Chinese qualification is awarded, then the Chinese institution/partner is responsible for evaluating the standards of the foreign institution. However, foreign qualifications are not automatically recognized without a further step—seeking recognition of the foreign qualification by a national Chinese authority, the Chinese Service Centre for Scholarly Exchange. (See http://www.cscse.edu.cn/Portal4/default533.htm.)

The Chinese regulations are an interesting model to study with regards to accrediting foreign providers, given that joint ventures are mandatory. Experiences of foreign providers reveal that, while the regulations are clear on paper, implementation is still a challenge given the size and complexity of the higher education system in

China and the diversity of local/foreign, public/private, for-profit, and nonprofit partnerships that are being developed.

Malaysia. The Malaysian regulations for crossborder education provision are especially interesting as they address quality, cultural, and economic requirements. All foreign providers are subject to Malaysia's national quality assurance framework; but unlike China, foreign providers are not required to cooperate with a local institution or entity.

There are three levels of assessment in the Malaysian system. The first level is compulsory and provides approval to conduct programs of study. The second level sets a minimum standard which providers must meet if a qualification is to be offered. The third level involves an accreditation process, which is necessary if the qualification is to be recognized for employment purposes with the Malaysian public sector (government jobs). These rules apply to both domestic and foreign providers. The Malaysian Qualifications Authority (a new entity recently formed by the merger of the National Accreditation Board and the Quality Assurance Division of the Ministry of Higher Education) is now responsible for public and private, domestic and foreign quality assurance and accreditation work. (See http://apps.emoe.gov.my/qad/main.html.)

Malaysia has a long history of welcoming foreign institutions and companies that offer tertiary education programs. It is a good example of a country that has developed a public policy and regulations, including an accreditation process, to ensure that crossborder education (a) helps to meet national policy objectives, (b) is of a high quality, and (c) is economically sustainable.

Hong Kong. Hong Kong moved early to establish legislation for regulating higher and professional crossborder education. In 1997, it introduced a law to increase access to higher education for its population by allowing more crossborder education but at the same time ensuring consumer protection. (See http://www.doj.gov.hk/eng/laws.) Foreign providers may establish an education program in their own name or collaborate with a local institution. Registration is mandatory for all crossborder education providers delivering face-to-face or mixed mode programs. Each and every program must be formally registered; but interestingly, registering distance education programs is voluntary. In other words, programs offered face to face and by mixed mode must be registered; but if the same program is delivered by distance education, registration is voluntary. However, foreign providers who cooperate with a self-accrediting Hong Kong institution are exempted from mandatory registration. In addition to registering, crossborder education programs and providers may voluntarily apply for local accreditation by the Hong Kong Council for Academic Accreditation; to this point, it is not obligatory.

The Hong Kong regulations use comparability with the standards of home programs as the benchmark for quality for foreign institutions, companies, or networks. If foreign providers choose to adapt the content of their programs to be more relevant to local Hong Kong needs and norms, they are free to do so as long as they maintain comparability with home standards. A key assumption of this benchmark is that the provider has a home institution for comparability purposes. As pointed out in the typology of crossborder providers, not all of them have a home base that sets standards of quality nor are they necessarily accredited by a national quality assurance system.

New Zealand. While New Zealand has predominantly been considered an active exporter of education programs, more recently it has been seen as an importer of higher education as well. Currently, crossborder providers see possibilities of establishing joint ventures or stand-alone initiatives in New Zealand for both domestic and foreign students. In other words, foreign providers are establishing a base in New Zealand to attract foreign students. Hence, the New Zealand Vice Chancellors Committee, which oversees the quality assurance for universities, and the New Zealand Qualifications Authority (NZQA), which has responsibility for quality assurance of other tertiary-level institutions have new challenges to face in terms of quality assurance and the accreditation of foreign providers in their jurisdiction.

Foreign providers coming to New Zealand can choose whether to establish a joint venture with a local institution or a new entity. The latter option is available primarily for executive/professional training. Otherwise, all crossborder providers that will be delivering degree-level programs, or are registering domestic students who are eligible for tuition subsidies, or who are enrolling international students must be registered with the New Zealand Qualifications Authority and go through the same quality assurance procedures as domestic higher education institutions. (See http://www.nzqa.govt.nz.)

These are four different approaches to developing regulations to ensure that crossborder education providers are registered and, in most cases, undergo the same processes as domestic institutions in terms of quality assurance and accreditation. It is interesting to note which processes are mandatory and which are voluntary. In these examples, registration is obligatory as is some type of quality assurance but accreditation is optional depending on the level, mode of program delivery, and the type of local/foreign partnership that was been established.

MINIMIZING RISKS AND MAXIMIZING BENEFITS

For Sending Countries

It is important to emphasize that sending countries have a direct responsibility and vested interest in assuring the quality of the academic offer. The primary reasons are to ensure that students and foreign partner institutions are protected from low quality and rogue providers, that they have a relevant and high quality education experience, and that the qualifications they earn are recognized for further study and employment purposes.

But there are other reasons that sending countries need to have quality assurance or accreditation systems in place for crossborder education. Sending countries cannot afford to put their domestic and international reputations at risk by delivering low-quality academic programs in another country or having academic programs shut down before all students have completed their studies. A tarnished international profile in a increasingly competitive environment could have negative effects on the institution's ability to attract students, researchers, faculty, and research projects. Another macro rationale that drives a country's investment and interest in crossborder education is the opportunity for strategic political, economic, and technological alliances. This rationale has increasing importance in the knowledge economy. Therefore, if a country's reputation is jeopardized due to low quality provision overseas, the results could have far-reaching implications both domestically and internationally.

For Receiving Countries

The prospect of having foreign education providers deliver academic programs, establish new institutions, and collaborate with local institutions in joint ventures can bring many advantages to receiving countries. Potential benefits include increased access to higher and continuing education, more diversity in program offer, less brain drain of bright students to foreign institutions, and exposure to foreign teaching and education management systems. The list of potential benefits is long and varied. But so is the list of potential risks. Risks can include an increase in low quality or rogue providers, non-sustainable foreign provision of higher education if profit margins are low, foreign qualifications that are not recognized by domestic employers or for further study, elitism in terms of those who can afford crossborder education, and the overuse of English as language of instruction. Thus, it is critical that receiving countries are clear about the objectives and expected benefits of crossborder provision and that registration, quality assurance, and accreditation processes are in place to ensure high quality provision that contributes to national policy objectives.

The purpose of this chapter has been to explore the quality assurance and accreditation issues and practices in delivering education across national borders. There is ample evidence that the demand for higher education in the next 20 years will outstrip the capacity of some countries to meet the domestic need. Students moving to other countries to pursue their studies will remain important in the international higher education landscape. But student mobility will not be able to satisfy the enormous appetite for higher education from densely populated countries wanting to build human capacity so they can fully participate in the knowledge society—hence, the emergence and growing importance of crossborder education programs and providers.

A review of new developments in program and provider mobility shows a diversity of new types of education providers, new delivery modes, and innovative forms of public/private and local/foreign partnerships. New courses and programs are being designed and delivered in response to local conditions and global challenges, and new qualifications/awards are being conferred. The growth in the volume, scope, and dimensions of crossborder education has the potential to provide increased access, and to promote the innovation and responsiveness of higher education, but it also brings new challenges and unexpected consequences. There are the realities

CHAPTER SEVEN

that unrecognized and rogue crossborder providers are active; that much of the latest crossborder education provision is being driven by commercial interests and gain; and that mechanisms to recognize qualifications and ensure the quality of specific academic courses/programs are still not in place in many countries. These factors present major challenges to the education sector. It is important to acknowledge the huge potential of crossborder education but not at the expense of academic quality and integrity.

Note: This chapter is adapted from J. Knight (2006), "Crossborder higher education: Issues and implications for quality assurance and accreditation," a paper prepared for the Global University Network for Innovation (GUNI) and published in *Higher Education in the World 2007: Accreditation for Quality Assurance. What Is at Stake?* (pp. 134–146). Basingstoke, Eng.: Palgrave Macmillan.

RELATED REFERENCES

AVCC. Australian Vice-Chancellors Committee. (2003). *Offshore programs of Australian universities.* Canberra: AUCC.
Bohm A., Davis, D., Meares, D., & Pearce, D. (2002). *The global student mobility 2025 report: Forecasts of the global demand for international education.* Canberra, Australia: IDP.
Coleman, D. (2003). Quality assurance in transnational education. *Journal of Studies in International Education, 7*(4), 354–378.
Garrett, R. (2004). *Transnational delivery by UK higher education. Part 2: Innovations and competitive advantage.* London: Observatory on Borderless Higher Education.
Garrett, R. (2005). *Fraudulent, sub-standard, ambiguous: The alternative borderless higher education.* Briefing Note. London: Observatory on Borderless Higher Education.
Knight, J. (2005a). *Borderless, offshore, transnational and crossborder education: Definition and data dilemmas.* Report of the Observatory on Borderless Higher Education. London: OBHE.
Knight, J. (2005b). *Crossborder education: Programs and providers on the move.* CBIE Millennium Research, Monograph No. 10. Ottawa, Canada: Canadian Bureau for International Education.
Knight, J. (2006). Crossborder higher education: Issues and implications for quality assurance and accreditation. In *Higher education in the world 2007: Accreditation for quality assurance. What is at stake?* (pp. 134–146). Basingstoke, England: Palgrave Macmillan.
Knight, J. (2006). Programmes, providers, and accreditors on the move: Implications for the recognition of qualifications. In A. Rauhvargers & S. Bergan (Eds.), *Recognition in the Bologna Process: Policy development and the road to good practice* (pp. 139–168). Strasbourg, France: Council of Europe Publishing.
Larsen, K., Momii, K., & Vincent-Lancrin, S. (2004). *Cross-border higher education: An analysis of current trends, policy strategies and future scenarios.* London: Observatory on Borderless Higher Education.
Middlehurst, R. (2002). The developing world of borderless higher education: Markets, providers, quality assurance, and qualification. In *UNESCO first global forum on international quality assurance, accreditation and the recognition of qualifications in higher education* (pp. 25–38). Paris: UNESCO.
Middlehurst, R., & Woodfield, S. (2003). *The role of transnational, private and for-profit provision in meeting global demand for tertiary education: Mapping, regulation and impact.* Vancouver, British Columbia: Commonwealth of Learning and UNESCO.
Organization for Economic and Community Development (OECD). (2004a). *Quality and recognition in higher education: The cross-border challenge.* Paris: Author.
Organization for Economic and Community Development (OECD). (2004b). *Internationalization and trade of higher education: Challenges and opportunities.* Paris: Author.
Uvalic-Tromik, S. (2002) *Globalization and the market in higher education: Quality, accreditation and qualifications.* Paris: UNESCO/Economica.

UNESCO/APQN. Asia Pacific Quality Network. (2006). *Toolkit: Regulating the quality of cross-border education*. Bangkok, Thailand: UNESCO.

UNESCO & Council of Europe. (2001). *The UNESCO-CEPES/Council of Europe code of good practice for the provision of transnational education*. Paris: UNESCO.

UNESCO/OECD. (2005a). *Guidelines for quality provision in cross-border higher education*. Paris: UNESCO/OECD.

UNESCO/OECD. (2005b). *Draft proposal for proposed next steps for an international information tool on recognized higher education institutions*. Paris: UNESCO/OECD.

Verbik, L., & Jokivirta, L. (2005). *National regulatory frameworks for transnational higher education: Models and trends, Parts 1–2*. Briefing Notes. London: Observatory on Borderless Higher Education.

CHAPTER EIGHT

FINANCIAL ASPECTS AND IMPLICATIONS OF COMMERCIAL CROSSBORDER EDUCATION

DEVELOPMENTS IN COMMERCIAL CROSSBORDER EDUCATION

Crossborder education is a term that refers to the movement of education (students, researchers, professors, learning materials, programs, providers, knowledge, etc.) across national/regional jurisdictional or geographic borders. (See Chapter 6). It is forecasted that the demand for international/crossborder education will increase from 1.8 million international students in 2000 to 7.2 million international students in 2025 (Bohm, Davis, Meares, & Pearce, 2002). Furthermore, it is anticipated that 70% of this demand will be from the Asia-Pacific region. By all accounts, these are staggering figures and present enormous challenges and opportunities. It is not known what proportion of the demand will be met by student mobility, but it is clear that there will be exponential growth in the movement of programs and institutions/providers across national borders.

Two significant trends are visible in the increased mobility of higher education across borders. The first is the increase in program and provider mobility through a variety of new delivery modes including franchising, twinning, distance education, and branch campuses among others. It is important to note that the numbers of students seeking education in foreign countries is still increasing; however, delivering foreign academic courses and programs to students in their home countries is currently being emphasized. The second trend is the gradual but discernible shift in orientation from development cooperation to competitive commerce, or in other words—from aid to trade.

New Types of Higher Education Providers

The increase in the worldwide demand for higher education has resulted in a diversity of new providers delivering education across borders (OECD, 2004). The new providers include publicly traded companies, corporate universities, and networks of universities, professional associations, and organizations. However, it is not just new providers that have an increased interest in commercial crossborder initiatives. Conventional higher education institutions, both private and public, are also seeking opportunities for the commercial delivery of education programs to other countries. The majority of these universities are bona fide institutions that comply with domestic and foreign regulations (where they exist). But there is also an increase in rogue or low-quality providers who are not recognized by bona fide accreditation/licensing bodies in either the sending or receiving countries.

Crossborder education providers fall generally into two categories: (a) traditional higher education institutions (HEIs) who emphasize the triple missions of teaching, research, and service/commitment to society, and (b) the new or alternative providers who primarily focus on teaching and the delivery of education services (Knight, 2005).

Traditional higher education institutions include public nonprofit, private nonprofit, and private for-profit institutions. Many countries have a mixed system of publicly and privately funded HEIs. There is a definite blurring of the boundary between public and private institutions, as many public universities now find it necessary to seek private financing and to charge a tuition or service fee. On the other hand, in many countries private universities are eligible for public funds and engage in social nonprofit activities.

The new providers are diverse in nature but are typically described as a company or organization that provides education programs and/or services for profit purposes. They are more oriented to delivering education and training programs than undertaking research and scholarly activities. The new providers include publicly traded companies such as Apollo (USA), Informatics (Singapore), and Aptech (India), corporate universities such as those run by Motorola and Toyota, and networks of universities, professional associations, and organizations. These new types of crossborder providers can be brick-and-mortar institutions or virtual universities and can complement, compete, collaborate, or simply coexist with domestic higher providers and other crossborder providers.

The virtual and physical movement of providers to other countries raises issues related to registration, quality assurance, and recognition issues but there are additional factors to consider if a network or local/foreign partnership is involved. Setting up a physical presence requires attention being paid to national regulations regarding the entity's status, total or joint ownership with local bodies, tax laws, for-profit or nonprofit status, repatriation of earned income, boards of directors, staffing, granting of qualifications, selection of academic programs and courses, etc. For some countries, it means that strict regulations are being developed to closely monitor and, in some cases, restrict new providers coming into the country. In other instances, incentives are being offered to attract high-quality institutions/providers to set up a teaching site or full campus. This is especially true where "knowledge parks," "technology zones," or "education cities" are being developed to attract foreign companies and education/training providers.

The Observatory for Borderless Higher Education has developed a Global Higher Education Index (GHEI) of 49 companies that offer education programs and services which are publicly traded on a stock exchange (Garrett & MacLean, 2004). The index categorizes the 49 companies into five groups: (a) bricks and mortar institutions, (b) e-learning, (c) IT training, (d) publishers, and (e) software and consultancy firms and provides information on their revenue and net income. Table 8.1 lists the 41 companies in the first three categories; they can be seen as direct or indirect competitors with traditional nonprofit institutions.

These companies are involved in offering education programs and services on an international basis and fall into the category of new and alternative commercial crossborder providers. An analysis of these 41 companies reveals that 23 operate bricks and mortar institutions, 13 offer e-learning, and 5 provide IT training at

Table 8.1. Global Education Index (GEI) companies, 2003

Country	Company	Category	Net Profit*	% Profit**
Africa				
South Africa	Advtech	Bricks & mortar	5.6	10.47
	Primeserv	Bricks & mortar	0.4	0.80
Asia				
Australia	Garratt's Limited	Bricks & mortar	−0.7	−11.67
India	Aptech	IT training	2.3	2.70
	NIIT	IT training	0.9	0.56
	Tata Infotech	E-learning	6.1	6.60
Malaysia	FSBM Holdings	Bricks & mortar	−1.5	−10.14
	Hartford Holdings	Bricks & mortar	0.5	13.89
	Inti Universal Holdings	Bricks & mortar	8.5	20.05
	SEG International	Bricks & mortar	3.7	15.16
	Stamford College Holdings	Bricks & mortar	0.6	6.19
Philippines	Centro Escolar University	Bricks & mortar	4.5	24.46
	Far Eastern University	Bricks & mortar	3.0	26.09
Singapore	Horizon Education & Technologies	IT training	−32.9	−411.25
	Informatics Holdings	IT training	6.8	6.59
	Raffles LaSalle International	Bricks & mortar	3.1	28.44
Europe				
U.K.	BPP Holdings	Bricks & mortar	5.3	3.04
	Epic Group	E-learning	1.2	10.43
Ireland	SkillSoft Corporation	E-learning	−284	−279.80
North America				
Canada	Capital Alliance Group	Bricks & mortar	−1.5	−29.41
	Serebra Learning Corporation	E-learning	−0.5	−25.00
USA	Apollo Group	Bricks & mortar	247	18.43
	Career Education Corporation	Bricks & mortar	119.2	10.03
	Centra Software	E-learning	−7.9	−18.37
	Click2Learn	E-learning	−6	−20.62
	Concorde Career Colleges	Bricks & mortar	6.2	8.30
	Corinthian Colleges	Bricks & mortar	65.9	12.74
	DeVry	Bricks & mortar	61.1	9.00
	Digital Think	E-learning	−61.3	−145.61
	Docent	E-learning	−10.7	−35.31
	Ecollege	E-learning	0.9	2.44
	Education Management Corporation	Bricks & mortar	56.3	8.80
	EVCI Career Colleges	Bricks & mortar	2.6	12.87
	Health Stream	E-learning	−3.4	−18.68
	ITT Educational Services	Bricks & mortar	58.9	11.26
	New Horizons Worldwide	IT training	1.4	1.01
	PLATO Learning	E-learning	−1.7	−2.07
	Strayer Education	Bricks & mortar	33.7	22.93
	Sylvan Learning Systems	Bricks & mortar	46.1	9.75
	University of Phoenix Online	E-learning	110.5	20.86
	Vcampus Corporation	E-learning	−3.3	−54.10

Source: Knight (2006), adapted from Garrett & Maclean (2004).
* In US$s by millions.
**Profit as % of total annual revenue.

CHAPTER EIGHT

sub-degree or degree levels. It is interesting to note that the bricks and mortars are the most profitable, with 20 of the 23 showing profit, followed by those focused on IT training (four out of five are profitable). Only four of the 13 e-learning companies showed a profit in 2003. Unfortunately, no information is available on the size of the capital investment and how it has changed over the years. The home countries for these companies are provided but not the destination countries that are receiving the education offer.

A review of these companies' websites reveals that countries in every region of the world are receiving commercial crossborder education programs and services. The greatest numbers of receiving countries are located in the Asia-Pacific where the large demand for tertiary education cannot be met by domestic capacity and/or there is strong desire for foreign academic qualifications. Unfortunately, there are no reliable or comparable data on the number of students registered in programs offered by these companies or, for that by matter, most crossborder providers. Therefore, few national-level statistics exist on the percentage of tertiary-level students that are registered in course/programs offered by nondomestic providers, but the general sense is that it is a relatively small percentage, even though in densely populated countries, the absolute number may seem high (Knight, 2006).

This information illustrates that selling education and training courses/programs can be a profitable business and that there are students, households, and businesses able to pay the requisite fees for enrollment. An attractive profit margin is also encouraging an increase in the number of traditional higher education institutions and new commercial providers who are interested in offering fee-based education programs to students in other countries. What impact does this development have on financing the higher education sector in both sending and receiving countries?

The impact of crossborder education on public funding is complex. The implications differ for receiving or host countries and for sending countries; and according to the particular characteristics of a national system such as national policy objectives, mix of private/public funding, coverage rates, regulations, and socio/economic levels of students.

IMPLICATIONS FOR THE PUBLIC FINANCING OF HIGHER EDUCATION

The most important observation is that there are more questions than answers regarding the impact of crossborder education on national-level financing schemes and the funding of traditional public higher education institutions. Currently, the percentage of students enrolled in commercial crossborder programs is relatively small and thus, in reality, has had limited impact. The following discussion therefore focuses on potential issues and questions that need to be addressed for an individual country to maximize anticipated benefits and minimize potential risks.

Public Financing for Sending Countries

In many of the major sending countries (e.g., Australia, the United Kingdom, New Zealand, and the United States), the single most important impetus for growth in crossborder education has been the decrease in the amount of funding higher education institutions have received from the government. The need to seek alternative sources of funding has led many countries to engage in the business of international education, first by recruiting full-fee-paying students to home campuses and, more recently, through offering programs to foreign students in their home countries through diverse delivery modes. Efforts to generate revenue from crossborder education have been successful, especially for many institutions in Australia where funds generated from international education represent between 12 and 25% of annual income. Such undeniable success can, however, make institutions vulnerable to a downward turn in the international market. As a result, governments in, for example, Australia, Germany, New Zealand, and the United Kingdom are investing in major international marketing campaigns to brand and sell their domestic education programs and services abroad. It is interesting to note the contradiction in countries where public education funding for domestic higher education is decreasing but new investments are being made by other government departments (foreign relations or trade and commerce) to deliver/sell domestic education abroad.

Table 8.1 indicates that the United States and five countries in Asia–Pacific are home to the majority of private, for-profit companies selling education programs and services. The impact of their international operations on the home education country is complicated and, to date, an unexplored area of analysis. In some cases, there is no relationship as these companies are not part of the national higher education system and are considered "stateless" when delivering abroad. On the other hand, many of these companies also provide education domestically and therefore can have an impact on the domestic financing.

Public Financing for Receiving Countries

The debate on the impact of crossborder education on financing higher education in receiving countries is intense. The primary concern is that the presence of foreign providers will result in decreased public funding. To date, this fear is speculation only. There is no concrete evidence of a direct cause-and-effect relationship between an increased foreign presence and decreased domestic public funding. If, and when, foreign provision increases to cover a significant percentage of students, this situation may change—the reason for gathering systematic data and carefully monitoring this issue.

In the meantime, it is useful to look at some of the key factors and to consider possible scenarios. An important issue to address is the rationales and benefits that a receiving country expects from crossborder education programs provided through franchise, twinning, or distance operations or through the establishment of branch and independent institutions. In some cases, countries are looking for ways to increase access and capacity. Achieving this goal, however, requires clarity on national policy objectives so that capacity building is focused on national priorities and, second, so that appropriate regulations are in place to register and accredit all foreign programs and providers to ensure the quality and relevance of the program offer. In situations where these conditions are met and where a critical mass of students who can afford foreign tuition fees exists, there are different options to consider. One possible scenario could involve a decrease in domestic funding for higher education in light of the fact that students/households are contributing an increased percentage to overall funding of education and the public subsidy can therefore be lowered. Another scenario is that public funding levels could remain the same or even increase with the funds directed to other priorities such as infrastructure or research enhancement or improved conditions/training of higher education teaching and research staff.

In other situations, the primary rationale for importing crossborder education is to improve quality through competition with advanced foreign higher education institutions. This scenario is relevant to stabler and more mature higher education systems and could involve an increase in public funding in order to help domestic institutions improve teaching and research capacity and to compete with foreign providers. A second scenario could include the increase in education funding in order to provide financial incentives to high-quality foreign higher education institutions resulting in funds being directed to foreign providers, not domestic ones. A third possible scenario would be maintaining the status quo or even decreasing public funding, meaning that domestic providers may in fact be losing students to foreign providers and receiving less public funding. The size of the domestic private higher education sector could be a determining factor in this scenario as it may be that students paying fees to private domestic institutions are moving to foreign private providers and that public institutions are therefore not impacted in a major way.

These scenarios are based on higher education systems that are relatively well developed in terms of coverage rates and regulatory capacity. However, these characteristics do not prevail in many countries and therefore alternative scenarios need to be considered for these situations.

These four scenarios assume the existence of higher education systems that are relatively well developed in terms of coverage rates and regulatory capacity. However, this situation is not the case in many countries, and therefore alternative scenarios need to be considered. Many developed and developed countries have not yet developed the necessary regulatory capacity to register or accredit foreign academic programs and programs. In these cases, there is no assurance that incoming foreign education programs and services will (a) be of acceptable quality, (b) contribute to national policy objectives, (c) provide increased and equitable access, or (d) build/extend capacity in needed areas.

While there may be potential advantages in increased access (and human resource development) for those who can afford the requisite tuition fees, unplanned and unmonitored foreign provision can introduce elements of risk to the national education system. One of the potential risks is a decrease in public funding that provides short-term savings but results in long-term challenges. A key point to remember is that commercially oriented education providers—both traditional higher education institutions and new providers—will remain interested in delivering education programs and services as long as there is a return on their investment. Commercial crossborder education is driven by a for-profit rationale that distinguishes it from development cooperation and academic exchanges or from linkages motivated by academic, scientific, and social goals, not commercial gain.

In short, the hypothesis that public funding will decrease with the advent of crossborder education is not yet supported by concrete evidence; furthermore, such a hypothesis depends on many variables and characteristics of the receiving country. There is an urgent need for rigorous data collection on the volume and type of crossborder education provision and an analysis of the financial implications for both sending and receiving countries to determine the relationship of crossborder education to both domestic private and public financing.

Private and Public Partnerships

"Innovation" and "complexity" are two adjectives often used to describe new partnerships for the delivery of crossborder education. The collaboration between public and private providers, between for-profit and nonprofit providers, and now between domestic and foreign providers is creating some of the most interesting partnerships/networks and posing some of the greatest challenges. It is true that many of these new partnerships are facilitating more flexible and wider access to different types and levels of education and training. They may also be creating new models of how public and private institutions and companies can work together to create financially viable and accessible forms of both domestic and international academic programs.

However, with such innovations come new questions and concerns. Many of the issues relate to the quality of the education offer, recognition of the qualification, language of instruction, and relevance of the education to national contexts. Other more fundamental questions focus on the regulation of entities that involve public and private partners from different countries; the use of public financing in one country to deliver (sell) education in other jurisdictions including the opaque cross-subsidization of activities; and the determination of actual profit gained by public higher education institutions from crossborder activities.

NEW HIGHER EDUCATION FUNDING MODELS

It is clear that the knowledge society is generating an increased demand for higher education, new and alternative types of education providers, more flexible delivery methods, and a growing emphasis on knowledge creation. These trends are occurring in an environment of limited increase in public funding for higher education but greater accountability and stronger links between funding and performance. Growing numbers of students are now willing and able to pay for private education from both domestic and international providers. Consequently, new models are being developed to redirect and, in some cases, reduce public funds and also to put more emphasis on using private sources and student/household funds for financing higher education.

Around the world, reforms are being considered for financing higher education that involve a gradual shift from supply-driven public funding to more of a demand-driven market model. For instance, the proposed student voucher system channels more public funding through students than through the institutions, thus enhancing the system's demand-driven aspects. An alternative model is a system that includes funding programs of particular cultural, social, or scientific value that would not necessarily survive or thrive under a market model. One development could be education providers who obtain publicly funded contracts to deliver these special programs. (Jongbloed, 2004) These are only two of many alternative models, but they are worth noting due to their potential implications for financing cross-border education. It is already a fact that, in some countries, publicly financed student loans or scholarships can be used for public or private, domestic or foreign providers. In some cases, the loans can be applied to the costs of study abroad. This development raises the question whether the same conditions would apply in a student voucher system and, furthermore, whether a student could use the voucher to take an entire degree out of the country with a non-domestic provider.

If regulations permitted a student to use the voucher for a full degree with a foreign higher education institution or a new type of provider—either at home or abroad–there could be important implications for domestic institutions, both in terms of financial stability and in the programs they offer. Similar questions about consequences can be asked if foreign crossborder providers were to compete/ receive public subsidies or compete for contract programs tendered and supported with public funds.

One issue central to any funding model relates to the national regulations that determine what types of institutions—public, private, for-profit, nonprofit, secular, religious, domestic, foreign, domestically accredited, or foreign accredited—are eligible to receive government funding and support This is a complex question in light of the murky boundaries that differentiate one type of provider from another. However, one might assume that, as long as national regulations are in place and there is a national capacity to implement and enforce them, a country is able to determine which policies would maximize the benefits of foreign, commercial (or, for that matter, noncommercial) education and minimize any potential financial risks. This is the typical scenario, except that now there are new additional sets of regulations in the form of trade rules that must be taken into consideration.

IMPLICATIONS OF TRADE AGREEMENTS

Trade regulations now play a more important role in light of the fact that trade agreements include education services. For instance, education is now one of the 12 service sectors covered by the General Agreement on Trade in Services (GATS). This means that GATS rules such as "most favored nation" and national treatment articles apply to private commercial higher education. What does this mean? The most-favored nation rule requires equal and consistent treatment of all foreign trading partners. In essence, it means that allowing access to the domestic higher education sector for one country requires allowing the same access for all other 151 WTO members; conversely, denying market access to one country requires denying access to all members of the World Trade Organization.

The national treatment rule is potentially more troublesome. It requires that, once a foreign provider is given access to a particular sector, there should be no discrimination in treatment between the foreign and domestic providers. The implications for the higher education sector, of course, are significant since public financing and subsidies available to domestic students and private institutions would also have to be available to foreign institutions. It is important to note that each country determines its own limitations to a committed sector and that exemptions are allowed to certain rules. However, the purpose of GATS is to promote greater international trade in services, and it has a built-in agenda to remove barriers to trade with each round of negotiations. It is important that the higher education sector be informed about potential opportunities and risks that new trade rules pose for crossborder education. In particular, it is essential to monitor the impact of trade agreements on domestic national regulations regarding the access, registration, quality, and financing of crossborder education. Obviously, a condition that one country considers a fundamental aspect of national higher education policy may be perceived by a trade partner as a trade barrier to be removed or liberalized.

CONCLUDING REMARKS

In conclusion, it is fair to say that there are more questions than answers and that analyses of the impact of crossborder education on the public financing of higher education are rather complex but sorely needed. Key factors to consider for the receiving country are its social and economic conditions and the nature of its higher education system.

- What are its national policy objectives and priorities for the higher education sector?
- How can crossborder education contribute to them?
- What is the domestic capacity to meet the demand for higher education and what is the current coverage rate?
- What is the role of the government—as funder, provider, regulator, monitor?
- How regulated or deregulated (market-oriented) is the higher education sector?
- Are there tuition fees? If so, who determines them?
- Is public funding for higher education directed to the institutions, the students (voucher system), or to the programs based on national needs and priorities?
- Is the higher education sector a mixed system of for-profit and not-for-profit institutions?
- For publicly funded institutions, what is the mix of government, student/household, and private sources of income?
- What percentage of enrolled higher education students are paying tuition fees and service charges?
- What is the receiving country's position in terms of granting access to education through trade agreements? Is education seen as a public good/service or as a private good/service?
- If education is a public good/service can it be privately delivered?

CHAPTER EIGHT

These are but a few of the questions that need to be asked to determine what impact foreign providers—both traditional higher education institutions and commercial companies—will have on higher education in terms of financing the system.

In summary, global trends such as the increased demand for tertiary and continuing education, the role of ITCs in delivering education, the inability of public funding to keep up with increased costs and demand for higher education, and the treatment of education as a commodity/service to be internationally traded and regulated by trade agreements are all factors contributing to major reforms of higher education systems and especially to funding models. Crossborder education by traditional and new providers is both a response to these trends and a stimulus for change in the funding and regulation of higher education at the sector and institutional level. Whether crossborder education providers are viewed as competitors or collaborators, or as opportunities or risks, depends on a country's ability to develop appropriate policies and regulations to integrate foreign providers into a national higher education system which is capable of meeting national social, cultural, and economic goals.

Note: This chapter is based on two papers: J. Knight (2005), "The role of crossborder education in the debate on education as a public good and private commodity," Paper prepared for East West Centre; and J. Knight (2006), "Commercial crossborder education: Implications for financing higher education" (pp. 103–113), in GUNI, *Higher education in the world: The financing of universities* (London: Palgrave Macmillan).

RELATED REFERENCES

Bohm, A., Davis, D., Meares, D., & Pearce, D. (2002). *The global student mobility 2025 report: Forecasts of the global demand for international education.* Canberra: IDP Australia.

Garrett, R. (2004). *The global education index. Part 2: Public companies–relationships with non-profit higher education.* London: Observatory on Borderless Higher Education.

Garrett, R. (2005, November). *Global education index. Part 2: Public companies–relationships with non-profit higher education.* Report. London: Observatory on Borderless Higher Education.

Garrett, R., & MacLean, D. (2004). *The global education index. Part 1: Public companies–share price and financial results.* London: Observatory on Borderless Higher Education.

Jongbloed, B. (2004). *Funding higher education: Options, trade-offs and dilemmas.* Paper presented for Fulbright Brainstorms: New Trends in Higher Education. University of Twente, Netherlands: Center for Higher Education Policy Studies.

Knight, J. (2004). Crossborder education in a trade environment: Complexities and policy implications. In Association of African Universities (Ed.), *The implications of WTO/GATS for higher education in Africa.* Proceedings of the Accra Workshop on GATS. Accra, Ghana: Association of African Universities.

Knight, J. (2005, June). *New world of academic mobility: Programs and providers crossing borders.* Background report prepared for UNESCO Latin America Regional Seminar on Academic Mobility in a Trade Environment: Issues, Opportunities, Risks. Mexico City.

Knight, J. (2006). Commercial crossborder education: Implications for financing higher education. In *Higher education in the world: The financing of universities* (pp. 103–113). Global University Network for Innovation (GUNI) Report. London: Palgrave Macmillan.

Knight, J. (forthcoming). *The role of crossborder education in the debate on education as a public good and private commodity.* Paper prepared for East West Centre, 2007.

Larsen, K., Morris, R., & Martin, J. (2002). Trade in education services: Trends and issues. *World Economy, 25*(6).

Larsen, K., & Vincent-Lancrin, S. (2002). International trade in education services: Good or bad? *Higher Education and Management Policy, 14*(3).

Lee, M. (forthcoming). *Restructuring higher education: Public-private partnership*. Paper prepared for East West Centre.

Middlehurst, R., & Woodfield, S. (2003). *The role of transnational, private and for-profit provision in meeting global demand for tertiary education: Mapping, regulation and impact*. Paris: Commonwealth of Learning and UNESCO.

Newman, K., & Couturier, L. (2002). *Trading public good in the higher education market*. Report prepared for the Observatory on Borderless Higher Education. London: OBHE.

Organization for Economic and Community Development/World Bank. (2007). *Cross-border tertiary education: A way toward capacity development*. Paris: OECD/World Bank.

Organization for Economic and Community Development (OECD). (2002). The growth of cross-border education. In *Educational policy analysis*. Paris: Author.

Organization for Economic and Community Development (OECD). (2004). *Internationalization and trade of higher education: Challenges and opportunities*. Paris: Author.

Verbik, L., & Jokivirta, L. (2005). *National regulatory frameworks for transnational higher education: Models and trends, Parts 1–2*. Briefing Notes. London: OECD.

CHAPTER NINE

HIGHER EDUCATION IN A TRADE ENVIRONMENT:

An Analysis of the General Agreement on Trade in Services (GATS)

It is true that international academic mobility and education exchange have been a central feature of higher education for decades, if not centuries. Yet it is only during the last two decades that education has been thought of as a commodity or service to be traded commercially across borders. And only in the last several years have trade agreements clearly identified education provision as a lucrative trade sector. Beginning with the 21st century, international educators have needed to become more aware of the new opportunities and potential risks that trade liberalization can bring to higher education and, in particular, to the crossborder movement of students, researchers, professors, education programs, institutions, and providers.

This chapter introduces the purpose, structure, and major principles of the General Agreement of Trade in Services (GATS). An understanding of its basic framework helps to put its issues and implications for higher education (discussed in Chapter 10), into perspective. It is important to point out, first, that this overview of higher education in a trade environment is written from an educator's point of view, not from an economic or trade perspective, and second, that it emphasizes an international approach, meaning attention to implications for the higher education sector in both developed and developing countries.

GATS: A BASIC OVERVIEW

Structure and Purpose of GATS

The GATS is the first-ever set of multilateral rules covering international trade in services. Previous international trade agreements such as the General Agreement on Tariffs and Trade (GATT) covered trade in products, but never services. The GATS was negotiated in the Uruguay Round and the call for requests and offers came into effect in 1995. It is administered by the World Trade Organization (WTO), which as of the beginning of 2008, comprised 151 member countries. The World Trade Organization is the only global international organization dealing with the rules of trade between nations. At its heart are the WTO agreements, negotiated and signed by the majority of the world's trading nations. The GATS is one of these key agreements and is a legally enforceable set of rules as it is ratified by the parliament of each member country. The purposes of GATS are (a) to progressively and systematically promote freer trade in services by removing many of the existing barriers to trade, and (b) to ensure increased transparency of trade regulations.

The agreement has three parts. The first part is the framework which contains the general principles and rules such as National Treatment (NT) and Most Favored

Nation (MFN). The second part consists of the national schedules in which a country lists specific commitments on access to its domestic market by foreign providers. The third part consists of annexes that detail specific limitations for each sector; they are attached to the schedule of commitments. This chapter focuses on the first part which deals with key principles and rules.

The "Four Modes of Supply"

The GATS defines four ways in which a service can be traded, known as "modes of supply." These four modes of trade apply to all 12 service sectors in GATS, including education. Table 9.1 provides a generic definition for each mode, applies these definitions to the education sector, and comments on the relative size of the market.

Table 9.1. Modes of supply in GATS

Mode of Supply	Explanation	Examples in Higher Education	Size /Potential of market
1. Crossborder Supply	The provision of a service where the service crosses the border (excludes physical movement by the consumer)	Distance education E-learning Virtual universities	Currently a relatively small market, deemed to have great potential through the use of new ICTs and especially the internet but difficult to monitor quality
2. Consumption Abroad	Provision of the service involving the movement of the consumer to the country of the supplier	Students who go to another country to study	Currently represents the largest share of the global market for education services and is growing
3. Commercial Presence	The service provider establishes or has presence in commercial facilities in another country in order to render service	Local branch or satellite campuses. Twinning partnerships. Franchising arrangements with local institutions.	Increasing interest and strong potential for future growth. Most controversial as it appears to set international rules on foreign investment
4. Presence of Natural Persons	Persons traveling to another country on a temporary basis to provide service	Professors, teachers, researchers working abroad	Potentially a strong market given the emphasis on mobility of professionals

Source: Knight (2002, updated 2006).

Each of the 12 sectors (i.e., telecommunications, financial services, health, tourism, culture, etc.) is divided into subsectors. Trade in education is organized into five categories or subsectors of service. These categories are based on the United

Table 9.2. Classification system for education services

Category of Education Service	Education Activities Included in Each Category	Notes
Primary Education (CPC 921)	Preschool and other primary education services. Does not cover child-care services.	
Secondary Education (CPC 922)	General higher secondary. Technical and vocational secondary. Also covers technical and vocational services for handicapped.	
Higher Education (CPC 923)	Postsecondary technical and vocational education services. Other higher education services leading to university degree or equivalent.	Types of education (i.e., business, liberal arts, science) are not specified. Assumes that all postsecondary training and education programs are covered.
Adult Education (CPC 924)	Covers education for adults outside the regular education system.	Further delineation is needed.
Other Education (CPC 929)	Covers all other education services not elsewhere classified. Excludes education services related to recreation.	Needs clarification re coverage and differentiation from other categories. For example, are education and language-testing services, student recruitment services, quality assessment covered?

Source: Knight (2002).

Nations Provisional Central Product Classification (CPC) as described in Table 9.2 The four modes of supply apply to each of these categories.

Critics of this classification system believe that it does not reflect the contemporary reality that nontraditional and private providers exist and that alternate forms of delivery using new technologies are being used. However, countries are able to add their own qualifications or supplements to the United Nations CPC classification scheme and therefore, in principle, should not be limited by the scheme.

Principal Elements and Rules of GATS

The overall framework of GATS contains a number of general obligations applicable to all trade in services. These are called unconditional obligations and are often referred to as the "top-down rules," as they apply regardless of whether a country has made a specific commitment to sectors or not.

Each WTO member lists in its national schedules those services for which it wishes to provide access to foreign providers. In addition to choosing which service sector(s) will be committed, each country determines the extent of commitment by

CHAPTER NINE

Table 9.3. Key elements and rules

GATS Element/Rule	Explanation	Application
Coverage	All internationally traded services are covered in the 12 different service sectors (e.g., education, transportation, finance, tourism, health, culture, communication, construction).	Applies to all services with two exceptions: (a) service provided in the exercise of governmental authority, and (b) air traffic rights.
Measures	All laws, regulations, and practices from national, regional, or local government that may affect trade.	A generic term that applies to all sectors.
Unconditional Obligations *"Top Down"*	Four unconditional obligations exist in GATS: most favored nation, transparency, dispute settlement, and monopolies	They apply to all 12 service sectors regardless of whether a country has scheduled commitments or not.
Most Favored Nation (MFN) Treatment	Requires equal and consistent treatment of all foreign trading partners. Under GATS, if a country allows foreign competition in a sector, equal opportunities in that sector should be given to service providers from all WTO members. This condition also applies to mutual exclusion treatment. For instance, if a foreign provider establishes branch campus in Country A, then Country A must permit all WTO members the same opportunity/treatment. Or if Country A chooses to exclude Country B from providing a specific service, then all WTO members are excluded.	May apply even if the country has made no specific commitment to provide foreign access to its markets. Exemptions for a period of 10 years are permissible.
Transparency	Requires that member countries publish all measures that affect services, inform the WTO about changes, and respond to any request from other members re information about any changes.	Apples to all sectors and all countries.
Conditional Obligations *"Bottom Up"*	A number of conditional obligations are attached to national schedules: (a) national treatment, (b) market access	Applies only to commitments listed in national schedules. The degree and extent of obligation are determined by each country.
National Treatment	Requires equal treatment for foreign providers and domestic providers. Once a foreign provider has been allowed to supply a service in one's country, there should be no discrimination in treatment between the foreign and domestic providers.	Applies only where a country has made a specific commitment. Exemptions are allowed.

(Continued)

Market Access	Means the degree to which market access is granted to foreign providers in specified sectors. Market access may be subject to one or more of six types of limitations defined by GATS agreement.	Each country determines limitations on market access for each committed sector or whether to make a commitment at all.

Source: Knight (2002, updated 2006).

specifying the level of market access and the degree of national treatment it is prepared to guarantee. These conditions are known as the "bottom-up" aspects of GATS, as individual countries are making these decisions. The GATS is known as a "positive list" approach, meaning that countries specify which sectors are to be included in the schedule of commitments. This arrangement is different from other agreements, where all sectors are automatically included and each country must specify which sector is excluded. Table 9.3 lists the key elements of the GATS and provides brief explanatory notes. It is important to understand these basic rules.

BARRIERS

The purpose of GATS is to reduce or eliminate barriers to promote further trade. Liberalization of trade essentially means the removal of restrictions and barriers. It is important to note that some countries have established national policies and regulations to control the import of education and training services into their country and that exporting countries see these regulations as trade barriers that need to be removed. That said, it must be recognized that a key principle of GATS is acknowledging the need and right of member countries to apply regulations to meet national policy objectives.

While some barriers are applicable to all 12 service sectors, others may be mode or sector specific. The commonly identified barriers are those relating to Modes 1 and 3. Some of the generic barriers are:
- Lack of transparency in a government's regulatory policy and funding frameworks
- An unfair manner of administering a country's domestic laws and regulations
- Subsidies not being made known in a clear and transparent manner
- Economic needs tests
- Discriminatory taxes applied to foreign suppliers
- Delays in granting approvals and denials of explanation or information when approval is not granted

A number of barriers are specific to higher education services. The more important ones to which education and trade policymakers need to pay close attention are listed in Table 9.4

Of course, many of these barriers are not new or specific to the GATS, as they already impact the flow of education services across borders. However, the barriers

Table 9.4. Barriers to trade by mode of supply

Modes of Delivery	Barriers
1. Crossborder Supply Examples: Distance delivery (e-education), or virtual universities	Inappropriate restrictions on electronic transmission of course materials. Economic needs test on suppliers of these services. Lack of an opportunity to qualify as degree-granting institution. Required to use local partners. Denial of permission to enter into and exit from joint ventures with local or nonlocal partners on voluntary basis. Excessive fees/taxes imposed on licensing or royalty payments. New barriers, electronic or legal, for use of the internet to deliver education services. Restrictions on the use/import of educational materials.
2. Consumption Abroad Example: Students studying in another country	Visa requirements and costs. Foreign currency and exchange requirements. Recognition of prior qualifications from other countries. Quotas on numbers of international students in total and at a particular institution. Restrictions on employment while studying. Recognition of new qualifications by other countries.
3. Commercial Presence Examples: Branch or satellite campus, franchises, or twinning arrangements	Inability to obtain national licenses to grant a qualification Limit on direct investment by education providers (equity ceilings) Nationality requirements Restrictions on recruiting foreign teachers Government monopolies High subsidization of local institutions Difficulty to obtain authorization to establish facilities Economic needs test on suppliers of these services Prohibition of higher education, adult education, and training services offered by foreign entities Measure requiring the use of a local partner Difficulty to gain permission to enter into and exit from joint ventures with local or nonlocal partners on voluntary basis Tax treatment that discriminates against foreign suppliers Foreign partners are treated less favorably than other forms of business organization Excessive fees/taxes are imposed on licensing or royalty payments Rules for twinning arrangements
4. Presence of Natural Persons Examples: Teachers traveling to foreign country to teach	Immigration requirements Nationality or residence requirements Needs test Recognition of credentials Minimum requirements for local hiring high Personnel have difficulty obtaining authorization to enter and leave the country Quotas on number of temporary staff Repatriation of earnings is subject to excessively costly fees and/or taxes for currency conversion Employment rules Restrictions on use/import of educational materials to be used by foreign teacher/scholar

Source: Knight (2002).

are significant as they can be interpreted very differently by sending and receiving countries. For instance, importing countries see them as key elements of a public education system that need to be maintained while exporting countries that want increased market access can consider them as impediments to trade that need to be removed.

Finally, it should be mentioned that countries that have not made any formal commitments to trade in higher education services are currently in the process of easing some of the identified barriers. A good example of this development is the number of countries that are changing visa and employment requirements to attract more international students to study in their country. More of this is happening irrespective of the presence of the GATS.

In order to illustrate how these types of barriers apply to the education sector, Table 9.5 lists a sample of requests that one major country is making of those countries where increased market access is desired. To gain deeper market access, removal of the following specific barriers are requested.

One of the GATS principles is that countries can determine the degree of market access they will give to foreign providers. This is known as a "bottom up" rule, and

Table 9.5. Examples of one country's requests to remove trade barriers to education

Request to Remove Barrier	Targeted Country
Remove nationality requirements for certain executives and directors of educational institutions	Chinese Taiwan
Remove ownership limitations on joint ventures with local partners	Egypt, India, Mexico, Philippines, Thailand
Remove prohibition on joint ventures with local partners	El Salvador
Remove requirement that foreign entities teach only nonnational students	Turkey
Remove ban on education services provided by foreign companies and organization via satellite networks Remove requirements for foreign educational institutions to partner with Chinese universities Remove ban on for-profit operations in education and training services Relax other operational limits and restriction on geographic scope of activities	People's Republic of China
Recognize degrees issued by accredited institutions of higher education (including those issued by branch campuses of accredited institutions) Adopt a policy of transparency in government licensing and accrediting policy with respect to higher education and training	Israel, Japan
Remove burdensome requirements, including nontransparent needs tests, applicable to foreign universities operating or seeking to operate in South Africa	South Africa
Remove restrictions that the granting of degrees is limited to Greek institutions only	Greece
Remove requirement that foreign entities teach only nonnational students	Italy
Remove quantitative limitation of education institutions	Ireland
Adopt a policy of transparency in government licensing and accrediting policy with respect to higher education and training	Spain Sweden

Source: Knight (2006).

is seen as a certain kind of safeguard. However, the reality is that safeguards can be interpreted as barriers. Therefore, when one considers the GATS principle of progressive liberalization, one can question whether these so-called safeguards will, in fact, be able to withstand the pressure for liberalization in future rounds of negotiations.

RATIONALES AND BENEFITS OF INCREASED TRADE IN HIGHER EDUCATION

It is somewhat surprising and perhaps worrisome that very little has been written by educators or trade specialists on the rationales and benefits behind a country's interest in the import and/or export of education services. Besides the four negotiating proposals (the United States, Australia, New Zealand, and Japan), few statements have championed other benefits than increased economic, and perhaps political, benefits. It appears that rationales and benefits specific to education are taken for granted in the overall assumption that liberalized trade will increase a nation's economic prosperity. The analysis provided by Larsen and Vincent-Lancrin (2002) of the Center for Education, Research, and Innovation and the Organization for Economic and Community Development (CERI/OECD) is one of the few comprehensive studies on the implications of trade in education services. The authors conclude that, due to the complexity of the factors involved and because the issues vary substantially with the country, mode of delivery, and sector of education, it is difficult to make a definitive conclusion whether trade in education services is "good" or "bad." They suggest, however, that the impact will be on the lifelong learning market rather than the traditional-age higher education market.

More has definitely been written on why countries are cautious and guarded about the impact of trade, especially developing countries (Naidoo, 2007). For instance, the Minister of Education in South Africa (Ensor, 2003) states very clearly:

> It is important that we remain vigilant to ensure that increased trade in education does not undermine our national efforts to transform higher education and in particular to strengthen the public sector so that it can effectively participate in an increasingly globalizing environment. Trade considerations cannot be allowed to erode the public good agenda for higher education.

However, he also correctly warned against parochialism and narrow chauvinism and stressed the need for genuine international collaboration in education.

Overview of Rationales for Import/Export

An overview of rationales illustrates the different motivations that countries, actors, and education institutions/providers can bring to the dialogue on why there should more interest in trade in education. While there are different drivers and benefits for increased trade, self-interest is a common factor underlying them all. Self-interest appears to be the strongest motivator for trade, even if there can be benefits for all parties involved. India clearly articulates this motive by stating: "Commitments will be made in the best interests of the country. They have to be in the areas of the country's strengths and where there are strategic opportunities for exploitation through trade" (Powar, 2002, p. 8). Another concrete example of self-interest is reflected in the position taken by countries who are requesting greater liberalization of the education market in other countries than they themselves are willing to offer. The United States is a prime example of this situation.

There are a myriad of reasons why a country may be interested in importing higher education services and thus in making a commitment to market access in GATS. One of the most important and pressing rationales is the limited domestic capacity of a country to meet the growing demand for higher education; such a situation makes it attractive to look to private education providers either domestically or internationally to meet this unmet demand. Related to this situation is a country's limited ability to provide greater access to specific knowledge or skill-based education and training programs, which also becomes a motive for looking to imported training for these specialized areas. These two rationales are often linked to countries with small higher education systems or developing countries with systems that are still in the process of establishing their postsecondary systems.

Some countries believe that their domestic higher education sector can be upgraded and updated by importing prestigious and reputable foreign providers that will bring innovative management and pedagogical practices with them. It is believed that, by creating a competitive environment between domestic and foreign providers, the domestic higher education system will be improved and eventually lead to higher cost effectiveness. Another reason driving countries to engage in the commercial trade of higher education is strategic political alliances. In the knowledge society, the higher education sector has increased influence as a knowledge producer, transmitter, and trainer of knowledge workers. Thus, higher education is an important player in bilateral and multilateral political, economic, and scientific alliances. Furthermore, trade in education services can strengthen these strategic relationships. In other circumstances, countries anticipate that trade in educational services will lead to trade-tied aid development projects and funds. Lastly, the need to strengthen human resources capacity is a strong incentive for many developing countries to seek to import education and training providers through bilateral trade agreements or multilateral trade agreements such as GATS.

The primary reasons behind the export of higher education are equally diverse. The most pervasive rationale is income generation. Many countries and, more specifically, higher education institutions, see selling education services and programs abroad as a way to diversify sources of income and make up for decreasing or stagnant public funding and support. In countries experiencing a stable birth rate or an excess national capacity, an attractive option is to export excess supply on a commercial basis. Further, the potential to develop strategic political and economic alliances is as strong for exporting countries as it is for importing countries; and the education sector is being used as a conduit to access trade in other service sectors.

From a completely different perspective, it is interesting to see the effect that market recognition is having on the education sector. Both private and public higher education providers believe that international name recognition and branding bring major dividends in terms of attracting talented students, scholars, faculty, research projects, and membership in elite networks. Through twinning or franchise agreements, or through offshore study centers or branch campuses, higher education providers are able to export their education programs and services and build name recognition abroad–achievements that help both domestic and foreign enrollments, research, and more recently international rankings.

There are also academic rationales behind the trade in higher education. The export of programs in particular and the establishment of foreign teaching centers of branch campuses are seen as tools for the further internationalization of the domestic institution and also as way to introduce innovation in curriculum design and delivery and faculty development.

Thus, the reasons for crossborder education in general and commercial export in particular differ enormously. It is important to note that while self-interest may be the motivator for trade, it does not always figure largely in other forms of crossborder education. For instance, in academic exchanges and partnerships, "mutual interests" are usually central to the agreements. In terms of development projects, again there are "mutual interests" and often a greater emphasis on "others' interests."

CONTROVERSIAL ISSUES AND QUESTIONS

The GATS is described as a voluntary agreement because countries can decide which sectors they will agree to cover under GATS rules. This is done through the preparation of their national schedules of commitments and through the "request-offer" negotiation rounds. However, some aspects of the agreement call into question its voluntary nature, notably the built-in progressive liberalization agenda and other elements described in this section.

Which education services are covered or exempted in GATS? Probably the most controversial and critical issue related to the agreement is the meaning of Article 1.3. This article defines which services are covered or exempted. According to the WTO, the agreement is deemed to apply to all measures affecting services *except* "those services supplied in the exercise of governmental authority." But what does "exercise of governmental authority" mean? WTO officials maintain that education provided and funded by the government is exempted. However, the interpretation of what is funded by the government is unclear in many countries, due to the fact that both public and private institutions often receive public financing.

The agreement states that "in the exercise of governmental authority" means the service is provided on a "non-commercial basis" and "not in competition" with other service suppliers. This phrasing begs the follow-up question: What is meant by "non-commercial basis" and "not in competition"? These are the core issues at the heart of much of the debate about which services are covered.

Education analysts of GATS maintain that, due to the wide-open interpretation of "non-commercial" and "not in competition" terms, the public sector (or in other words, government service providers) may not, in fact, be exempt. The situation is especially complicated in countries where a significant amount of funding for public institutions comes from the private sector. Another complication is that a public education institution in an exporting country is often defined as private/ commercial when it crosses the border and delivers in the importing country. Therefore, one needs to question what "non-commercial" really means in terms of higher education trade.

The debate about what "not in competition" means is fueled by the fact that there do not appear to be any qualifications or limits on the term (Gottlieb & Pearson, 2001). For instance, if nongovernment providers (private nonprofit or commercial) are delivering services, are they deemed to be in competition with government providers? In this scenario, public providers may be defined as being "in competition" by the mere existence of nongovernmental providers. Does the method of delivery influence or limit the concept of "in competition"? Does the term cover situations where there is a similar mode of delivery; or for instance, does this term mean that public providers using traditional face-to-face classroom methods could be seen as competing with foreign for-profit e-learning providers?

Many unanswered questions need clarification. WTO officials emphasize that education is, to a large extent, a government function and that GATS does not seek to displace such public education systems nor the right of government to regulate and meet domestic policy objectives. Others express concern that the whole question of the protection of public services is very uncertain and potentially placed at risk by the narrow interpretation of what "governmental authority" means and a wide-open interpretation of what "not in competition" and "non-commercial basis" might mean. Clearly, the question about which higher and adult education services "exercised in governmental authority" are exempted from GATS needs to be front and center in the discussion between trade and education officials at national and international levels. Here are four key questions:

What is the impact on a country's ability to make its own national regulations?
Do GATS rules impact a nation's ability to determine and implement policy/ regulations for post-secondary education? Trade policy analysts are quick to alleviate any concern that the role of national government will change in terms of policy objectives and regulations; but the jury is still out on this issue until there are further clarification and development of Article 1.3, as discussed above, and Article 6.4, which addresses domestic regulations and a country's ability to set qualifications, quality standards, and licences.

Article 6.4 stipulates that "qualifications, requirements and procedures, technical standards and licensing are not more burdensome than necessary to ensure the quality of the service." The language is purposely vague, and there are no definitions for terms such as "more burdensome than necessary" or for "quality of services." This ambiguity leaves the higher education sector concerned about the potential impact of this statement on quality assurance and accreditation procedures. Direct questions to trade specialists do not yield answers more satisfactory than "it [the definition] is still being developed" and that the situation is in the "wait and see" status. However, these experts state strongly that it is certainly not the GATS's intention to limit government's role in the regulation of quality assurance of education or the professions. Article 6.4, part of which is often referred to as the "necessity test," merits close monitoring by the education sector because a country's ability to establish quality assurance and accreditation policy for domestic and foreign providers is central to the question of the government's role in determining domestic regulations.

What does the principle of progressive liberalization mean? The purpose of GATS is to promote and enforce the liberalization of trade in services. The process of progressive liberalization involves two aspects: (a) extending GATS coverage to more service sectors, and (b) decreasing the number and extent of measures which impede increased trade. Therefore, in spite of the right of each country to determine the extent of its commitments, with each new round of negotiations, countries are expected to add sectors or subsectors to their national schedules of commitments and to negotiate the further removal of limitations on market access and national treatment.

The intention of GATS is to facilitate and promote increasingly more opportunities for trade. Therefore, countries that are not interested in either the import or export of education services will most likely experience greater pressure to allow market access to foreign providers. GATS is a new instrument, and it is too soon to predict the reality or extent of these potential opportunities or risks.

What are the implications of negotiating across sectors? At the "request-offer" stage of the process, bilateral negotiations occur on market access and national treatment commitments. The key point at this step is that sectors for which access is sought do not have to correspond to those for which offers are made. For example, Country A may request of Country B greater access to transportation services. Country B can respond by requesting access to education services. It is up to each country to decide where it is willing to make concessions on foreign access to domestic markets. This situation applies to all sectors and may be of greatest concern to developing countries that have not made commitments to open up education services and might therefore consider their education service sector vulnerable to negotiating deals across sectors.

What other aspects of GATS need to be monitored? Other aspects of the GATS that education analysts need to monitor include subsidies, mechanisms for resolving disputes, and the treatment of monopolies–all of which are controversial and apply to all sectors. It must be remembered that GATS is still an untested agreement and that a certain amount of confusion exists on how to interpret the major rules and obligations. It took many years to iron out inconsistencies in the General Agreement on Tariffs and Trade (GATT) and the same will likely be true for GATS. While trade specialists and lawyers need to review the technical and legal aspects of the agreement, educators need to study how the agreement applies to and impacts education services.

HIGHER EDUCATION IN A TRADE ENVIRONMENT

NEGOTIATING PROPOSALS AND COMMITMENTS

To date, the education sector remains one of the least committed sectors. The reason is not entirely clear, but perhaps it can be attributed to the need for countries to strike a balance between pursuing domestic education priorities and exploring ways in which trade in education services can be further liberalized. The low commitment rate could also be linked to the fact that education in general has taken a very low priority in the major bilateral agreements; and rightly or wrongly, the same may be true for the GATS. In the early stages of negotiations, countries were encouraged to submit proposals to signal and highlight the nature of their commitments. Only four countries (the United States, New Zealand, Australia, and Japan) submitted a negotiating proposal outlining their interests and issues. It is revealing to analyze these proposals. Japan's proposal was strikingly different from the others as its statement highlighted quality assurance, recognition of credentials, and distance education as key issues that required further consideration.

Table 9.6 provides a comparative look at some of the key issues identified in three of the four countries. (Japan is not included due to unique aspects of its proposal). It is interesting to note that all of them acknowledge the role of government as a funder, regulator, and provider of education services. A comparison of the rationales and benefits of freer trade in education services reveals different perspectives and raises key issues.

Role of Government

It is clear that all proposals acknowledge the central role government plays in higher education. Perhaps the controversy about which public services are exempted from the GATS has prompted this explicit recognition of government's role. Some are comforted and appeased by these statements. Others are even more concerned about the potential erosion of government's role in providing higher education provision and setting domestic policy objectives.

In some countries, education is decentralized from the national level to provincial or state governmental bodies. Private education, though nominally under state authority, may not, in fact, be primarily governed or regulated by a government. These situations further illustrate the complexities involved in determining which services are exempted from GATS coverage and the very different impact GATS will have on individual countries.

Rationales and Benefits

The rationales which drive further liberalization differ from country to country. Australia stresses greater access for students, New Zealand points to economic and social benefits, and the United States focuses on opportunities for new knowledge and skills. Benefits are closely linked to rationales. Australia believes that the competition inherent in more trade will have flow-on benefits to students. New Zealand emphasizes that, in addition to generating revenue, it anticipates benefits at the

CHAPTER NINE

Table 9.6. Highlights of negotiation proposals

	Australia	*New Zealand*	*United States*
Role of Government	The government has a role in the financing, delivery, and regulation of higher education, either alone or in partnership with individuals, NGOs, and private education. Believes that governments must retain their sovereign right to determine domestic funding and regulatory policies/measures.	International trade in education services can supplement and support national education policy objectives (i.e., reduce the infrastructure commitments required of governments and so free resources to be concentrated on other aspects of education policy). Believes that the reduction of barriers does not equate to an erosion of core public education systems and standards.	Respects the principle that governments should retain the right to regulate to meet domestic policy objectives. Recognizes that in the education service sector, governments will continue to play important roles as suppliers of service. Recognizes that "education to a large extent is a government function and does not seek to displace public education systems. It seeks to supplement public education systems."
Rationale/ Purpose of Trade Liberalization	Means of providing individuals in all countries with access to wide range of education options.	Education has a role in economic and social development. In New Zealand, education exports are the fourth largest services sector export earner and 15th largest foreign exchange earner overall.	Intent is to help upgrade knowledge and skills through training and education, while respecting each country's role in prescribing and administering appropriate public education for its citizens.
Benefits of Trade Liberalization	Increased access to education in qualitative and quantitative terms that would otherwise not be available in country of origin. Competitive stimulus with flow-on benefits to all students. Most effective way to encourage internationalization and flow of students.	In addition to generating revenue for private and state sector education institutions and members' economies, there are benefits at the individual, institutional, and societal level through academic exchange, increased cross-cultural linkages, technological transfer, and increased access for Members.	These services constitute a growing, international business, supplementing the public education system and contributing to the global spread of the modern "knowledge economy." Benefits of this growth help to develop a more efficient work force, leading countries to an improved competitive position in the world economy.

(Continued)

Public/Private Mix	Least committed service sectors due to recognition of its "public good" element and the high degree of government involvement in its provision.	Private education coexists with public domain Private education and training will continue to supplement, not displace, public education systems.

Source: Knight (2002).

individual, institutional, and societal level through academic exchange, technological transfer, and cross-cultural linkages. The United States highlights the contribution to the global spread of the modern knowledge economy and improved competitiveness.

It is not a surprise that these three countries emphasize economic benefits; but it is noteworthy that social and academic value to individuals, institutions, and society are not totally overlooked. More work is needed to understand and analyze the perceived rationale and benefits as a clearer picture will emerge of what exporting countries expect from increased import and export in education. Of course, expectations can be seen in terms of desirable or undesirable results. A better understanding of anticipated outcomes will assist in developing policies to help achieve or prevent them. At the same time, it is equally important to be mindful of unintended negative consequences.

Public/Private Mix

These proposals both implicitly and explicitly recognize the public/private mix of higher and adult education provision. It is interesting that New Zealand suggests that education may be one of the least-committed service sectors due to recognition of its "public good" element and the high degree of government involvement in its provision. The United States more pointedly states that private education coexists with the public domain and will continue to supplement, not displace, public education systems. There are mixed reactions to this statement, and a great deal of uncertainty about how the GATS will affect the balance of a mixed system, especially given the individualized nature of mixed systems.

EDUCATION COMMITMENTS TO GATS

As of 2006, 47 countries (the European Union is counted as one country) have made a commitment to the education sector, with 38 countries making a commitment to liberalize access to the higher education subsector. (See Appendix.) At this point in the negotiations, the higher education subsector has the most commitments of the five education subsectors. In general, though, education is one of the three sectors (health, education, and culture) that are often referred to as the "sensitive" sectors and are seen to be undercommitted. In fact, there is an overall sense of disappointment in the progress made to date in the number of countries that have tabled offers, the degree of liberalization offered, and the number of sectors committed to.

CHAPTER NINE

The current round of negotiations, which is known as the Doha Round, was to have closed at the beginning of 2005 but major delays have been experienced, the proposed end has been extended several times, and as of early 2008 the final date is still uncertain. It is true that negotiations on the troublesome issues related to agriculture subsidies have been the major stumbling block to progress and closure of the Doha Round. But the unexpected low level of commitments has also been a deep concern; and therefore, much work has been done to develop new and alternative means of encouraging countries to improve their offers.

WTO-GATS and Developing Countries

Developing countries, which include the least developed countries (LDC), play an increasingly important role in the World Trade Organization because they now make up over three-quarters of WTO membership. There are no WTO definitions of developed or developing countries; members simply declare themselves as belonging to one of the categories. Developing countries are a collection of nations with very diverse views and concerns on different aspects of trade in services and, therefore, cannot be seen as a unified voice or force of influence. The same situation applies to developed countries as well.

It is recognized that developing countries (including LDCs) have particular needs and thus the GATS include articles, special provisions, and preferential treatments. For instance, Article XIX states that the process of liberalization is to take place with "due respect for national policy objectives and the level of development of individual Members, both overall and in individual sectors." Examples of preferential treatment includes extra time to fulfill their commitments, legal assistance, and training on technical aspects of agreements by different international bodies such as the United Nations Conference for Trade and Development (UNCTAD), the United Nations Development Program (UNDP) and the World Bank (Khor, 2005).

GATS was established during the Uruguay Round (1986–1995), and many developing countries believed that GATS favored developed countries. As a result, the Doha Round, established in 1995 received the name of the Development Round, indicating that it would pay more attention to and make further provisions for developing countries. There are very mixed and contentious views about whether this label is more rhetoric than reality. For instance, a key part of the "development package" is "aid for trade." However, there is a great deal of ambiguity about what is actually included in this package. There are ongoing deliberations about whether "aid for trade" assistance will be in the form of concessional grants or loans, whether it will come from new or old money, and what the criteria are. A group of developing countries has the perception that this "aid for trade" is nothing but a "trade-off ploy" or a sweetener to persuade developing countries to agree to certain concessions or changes being proposed by developed countries (Khor, 2005).

THE NEGOTIATION PROCESS

As previously explained, the "bottom-up nature" of GATS allows any country to choose whether it will make a commitment in any of the 12 sectors (made up of 160 subsectors), and what degree of liberalization or market access will be permitted. Restrictions and limits can be placed on any of the four "supply modes" in any sector. Furthermore, because negotiations are based on a bilateral request/offer system, any country is free to make a request of another; and in return, any country is free to decide whether or how to respond to the request. Thus, countries, and especially developing countries, are able to decide whether, how, when, and under what conditions they will participate in the GATS negotiations.

Given the particular conditions and needs of developing countries, additional clauses have been established in subsequent GATS-related documents stating that developing countries should be allowed to liberalize less than developed countries and to choose their own pace of liberalization. These clauses, designed to give greater flexibility to developing countries, are referred to as "special and differential treatment" measures and are seen as being "development friendly" (Khor, 2005).

To summarize, the combination of the "bottom-up nature" and the "special and different treatment" clauses are seen as ways to permit developing countries to control the extent of liberalization they grant to countries requesting improved market access. However, when the big picture of liberalization afforded through GATS is considered, there is both disappointment and concern by WTO members, especially developed countries, about the "slow" rate of progress being made in opening up trade in services, especially in developing countries.

NEW OPTIONS PROPOSED TO STRENGTHEN GATS COMMITMENTS

A number of developed countries (primarily the European Union, the United States, Japan, Korea, Hong Kong, Chinese Taipei, and Australia), frustrated by the lack of increased access to trade in services, have proposed a number of "complementary approaches" for negotiations. They include a variety of methods designed to push countries, especially developing countries, to commit to liberalization in a greater number of sectors and, more importantly, to deepen market access by removing more and more barriers to trade. Such steps are in line with the goal of progressive liberalization, but the options being suggested may be seen as a threat to the basic "bottom-up" nature and flexibilities built into the GATS framework. The proposed new approaches are:

- *Plurilateral Negotiations*: This involves a group of countries, with common interests in a specific sector, making a *joint approach* to a country for market access in specific sector(s). This is very different from the "bilateral approach" and puts increased pressure on a country to agree to the request, given the consequences of refusing a group of potentially important and powerful trading partners. On the other hand, it can also permit smaller and less developed countries to pool their expertise to influence the negotiation process.
- *Numerical Targets and Indicators*: This option is basically a formula approach which proposes that countries should include a minimum number of new or

improved commitments in an agreed-upon number of subsectors. The number or percentage of subsectors would differ for developed and developing countries. This proposal is perceived by many developed and developing countries as ignoring the fundamental principle that countries can choose which sectors to commit to. If targets are high, the education sector may be vulnerable, given the low number of commitments to date.
- *Qualitative Parameters for Modes of Supply*: This option suggests that specific types of barriers be removed for all commitments to a particular mode of delivery, irrespective of the subsector. For example, one could take the often-used restrictions related to limited foreign ownership in Mode 3 (commercial presence). The new approach would mean that any barriers related to foreign ownership for Mode 3 would be eliminated across all sectors/subsectors.

These are three examples of the new "complementary approaches" being used to bring additional pressure to the negotiating table. They are labeled as "plurilateral, sectoral, and modal" approaches. The position of many developing countries is that these options will significantly erode the flexibilities available to them to liberalize in sectors they choose and to the extent that they choose.

IMPLICATIONS FOR TRADE IN EDUCATION SERVICES?

As already indicated, education is one of the least committed sectors to date and may remain that way in relation to other, more important sectors such as financial services, transportation, or telecommunications. However, if and how these new complementary approaches are eventually implemented, it is likely that many countries will receive additional requests for access to their domestic education market and/or receive increased pressure to remove barriers and deepen the level of liberalization. For instance, in March 2006, five countries (New Zealand, Australia, Malaysia, Chinese Taipei, and the United States) made a plurilateral request for private education to 22 countries. Second, for countries that have already made a commitment to higher education, there may be increased pressure to remove restrictions or most favored nation (MFN) exceptions that were detailed in their schedules of commitments. Third, education may be seen as a useful "horse-trading" sector, meaning that commitments to education will be offered by receiving countries in order for them to gain access to other key sectors in the asking country.

It is important to emphasize that there will continue to be great speculation and controversy on these proposed changes to the GATS methods of negotiation. Developing countries are deeply involved in these discussions and are trying to ensure that the GATS articles and special provisions made for developing countries are still respected and observed. It is more important than ever that education policymakers develop a close and consultative relationship with the lead trade negotiators and GATS experts in their country. It is advisable that higher education leaders and policymakers provide their nation's trade negotiators with a solid analysis of the potential opportunities and benefits, and potential risks and disadvantages, related to trade in education services for their national higher education system.

Note: This chapter is based on reports prepared by J. Knight for four UNESCO Regional Meetings on "GATS and Higher Education" convened during 2004-2006 by the Forum on Higher Education, Research, and Knowledge; from papers prepared for Observatory on Borderless Higher Education (Knight, 2002, 2003) and Knight (2006), "Higher education crossing borders: A guide to the implications of GATS for crossborder education" (Paris: Commonwealth of Learning and UNESCO).

RELATED REFERENCES

AAU. Association of African Universities. (2004). *The implications of WTO/GATS for higher education in Africa*. Proceedings of the Accra Workshop on GATS, Accra, Ghana, including the Accra Declaration on GATS and the Internationalization of Higher Education in Africa, Education. Accra: Association of African Universities.

Education International and Public Services International (EI/PSI). (2004–2007). *Tradeducation News* [news bulletin published at irregular intervals]. Brussels: Education International and Public Services International.

Education International (EI)/Public Services International (PSI). (1999). *The WTO and the millennium round: What is at stake for public education?* Brussels, Belgium: Education International/Public Services International.

Ensor, L. (2003, March 6). *Business day 1st edition* [Newspaper published in South Africa].

Gottlieb, R., & Pearson, T. (2001). *GATS impact on education in Canada*. Legal opinion prepared for the Canadian Association of University Teachers. Ottawa, Canada.

Kachur, J. L. (2003). Whose intellectual property? Whose rights? GATS, TRIPS and education in Canada. *Globalization, Society and Education, 1*(3), 375–411.

Knight, J. (2002). *Trade in higher education services: The implications of GATS*. London: Observatory on Borderless Higher Education.

Knight, J. (2003). *GATS, trade and higher education–Perspective 2003: Where are we?* London: Observatory on Borderless Higher Education.

Knight, J. (2004). Crossborder education in a trade environment: Complexities and policy implications. In *The implications of WTO/GATS for higher education in Africa* (pp. 59–106). Proceedings of the Accra Workshop on GATS. Accra, Ghana: Association of African Universities.

Knight, J. (2006). *Higher education crossing borders: A guide to the implications of GATS for crossborder education*. Paris: Commonwealth of Learning and UNESCO.

Khor, M. (2005). *A development assessment of the current WTO negotiations*. A report of the Third World Network. Copy in my possession.

Larsen, K., Momii, K., & Vincent-Lancrin, S. (2004). *Cross-border higher education: An analysis of current trends, policy strategies and future scenarios*. London: Observatory on Borderless Higher Education.

Larsen, K., & Vincent-Lancrin, S. (2002). International trade in education services: Good or bad? *Higher Education and Management Policy, 14*(3).

Mohemedbhai, G. (2003). Globalization and its implications on universities in developing countries. In G. Breton & M. Lambert (Eds.), *Universities and globalization: Private linkages, public trust* (pp. 153–162). Paris: UNESCO/Université Laval, and Economica.

Naidoo, R. (2007). *Higher education as a global commodity: The perils and promises for developing countries*. London: Observatory of Borderless Higher Education.

Neilson, J. (2004). Trade agreements and recognition. In *Higher education: The crossborder challenge* (pp. 155–202). Paris: Organization for Economic and Community Development.

Organization for Economic and Community Development (OECD). (2004). *Internationalization and trade of higher education: Challenges and opportunities*. Paris: Author.

Organization for Economic and Community Development (OECD). (2002). *Indicators on internationalization and trade of post-secondary education*. OECD/CERI. Paper prepared for the OECD/U.S. Forum on Trade in Education Services, Washington, DC.

Powar, K. (2005). *Implications of WTO/GATS on higher education in India*. Paper presented in Seoul, Korea, at the UNESCO Regional Seminar on the Implications of WTO/GATS on Higher Education in Asia and the Pacific.

Power, K. (2002). *WTO, GATS, and higher education: An Indian perspective*. Paper prepared for Association of Commonwealth Universities, Perth, Australia.

Sauvé, P. (2002). Trade, education, and the GATS: What's in, what's out, what's all the fuss about? *Higher Education Management and Policy*, *14*(3).
Sehoole, C. T. (2004). Trade in education services: Reflections on the African and South African higher education system. *Journal of Studies in International Education*, *8*(3), 297–316.
WTO. World Trade Organization Secretariat. (1998). *Education services: Background note.* Geneva: Council for Trade in Services. S/C/W/49, 98–3691.
World Trade Organization Secretariat. (1999). *The general agreement on trade in services: Objectives, coverage, and disciplines.* Geneva: WTO.
Ziguras, C. (2003). The impact of GATS on transnational tertiary education: Comparing experiences of New Zealand, Australia, Singapore and Malaysia. *Australian Education Researcher*, *30*(3), 89–109.

APPENDIX

GATS Commitments to Education as of February 2006*						
Countries	Primary	Secondary	Higher	Adult	Other	Total
Albania	x	x	x	x		4
Armenia			x	x		2
Australia		x	x		x	3
Austria	x	x		x		3
Bulgaria	x	x		x		3
Cambodia			x	x	x	3
China	x	x	x	x	x	5
Chinese Taipei		x	x	x	x	4
Congo RP			x			1
Costa Rica	x	x	x			3
Croatia		x	x	x	x	4
Czech Republic	x	x	x	x	x	5
Estonia	x	x	x	x	x	5
European Community	x	x	x	x		4
FYR Macedonia	x	x	x	x	x	5
Gambia	x			x	x	3
Georgia	x	x	x	x		4
Ghana		x			x	2
Haiti				x		1
Hungary	x	x	x	x		4
Jamaica	x	x	x			3
Japan	x	x	x	x		4
Jordan	x	x	x	x	x	5
Kyrgyz Republic	x	x	x	x		4

Latvia	x	x	x	x		4
Lesotho	x	x	x	x	x	5
Liechtenstein	x	x	x	x		4
Lithuania	x	x	x	x		4
Mali				x		1
Mexico	x	x	x		x	4
Moldova	x	x	x	x	x	5
Nepal			x	x	x	3
New Zealand	x	x	x			3
Norway	x	x	x	x	x	5
Oman	x	x	x	x		4
Panama	x	x	x			3
Poland	x	x	x	x		4
Rwanda				x		1
Saudia Arabia	x	x	x	x	x	5
Sierra Leone	x	x	x	x	x	5
Slovak Republic	x	x	x	x	x	5
Slovenia		x	x	x		3
Switzerland	x	x	x	x		4
Thailand	x	x		x		3
Trinidad and Tobago			x		x	2
Turkey	x	x	x		x	4
USA				x	x	2
Total 47	**33**	**37**	**38**	**37**	**22**	**167**

Source: Knight (2006).
*The Doha negotions, which would presumably have resulted in changes, were slowed and suspended during 2007.

CHAPTER TEN

THE IMPACT OF GATS ON HIGHER EDUCATION POLICY AND PRACTICE

The higher education sector has become increasingly aware of and involved in thinking about trade policy and higher education, in particular the General Agreement on Trade in Services (GATS). In many ways, GATS has served as an important wake-up call. It has forced the education sector to carefully examine two separate but related issues. The first is the significant growth in crossborder education (both commercial and nonprofit) which is happening irrespective of trade agreements. The second issue is the impact of the GATS multilateral trade rules on domestic and crossborder higher education and the further liberalization or promotion of commercial trade in education services.

Many trade experts and educators note that the international mobility of students, teachers, education, and training programs has been happening for a very long time and therefore question why there is such interest in the prospect of expanding import/export of education services. The answer partially lies in the fact that, while crossborder education is an important aspect of the internationalization of higher education, it has not been subject to international trade rules and until recently has not really been described as commercial trade. The GATS, which clearly identifies education as a service sector to be liberalized, is relatively new territory for the education sector. This is why the debate within national and international education communities is necessary and welcomed. However, the discussions need to move from speculation toward informed analysis. The introduction of GATS serves as a catalyst for the education sector, first, to examine how trade rules may or may not influence higher education policy; and second, to determine whether the necessary national, regional, and international education frameworks are in place to deal with the implications of increased crossborder education, including commercial trade.

It is recognized that trade issues are closely related to the larger issues of the commercialization and commodification of crossborder education. The chapter therefore focuses on the complexities and challenges related to academic mobility in light of new trade agreements and rules. More attention is given to the delivery of education/training courses and programs across borders than to the movement of students to study in foreign countries. The intention of this chapter is to take a balanced approach in discussing the risks, benefits, and implications related to trade in education services through programs and providers moving across borders.

There is much discussion and debate over four rather controversial trends or "-izations" of higher education:
– Commercialization: buying and selling including commodification
– Privatization: private ownership and/or funding

CHAPTER TEN

- Marketization: allowing the market to determine supply and demand
- Liberalization: the removal of trade barriers and the promotion of trade.

Some would even add a fifth—globalization—and point to it as an underlying cause for the others. These trends or "-izations" are closely related to each other and are linked to the issues discussed in this section. The first group focuses on the implications of GATS for the role of government, financing, student access, and program offer. The second group of issues deals with the challenge for national governments, and other bodies, to develop new policies and regulations regarding the registration, quality assurance, and recognition of crossborder provision. The third group deals with a broader set of issues including culture, values, and brain drain/gain. The fourth group focuses on the implications for policy and practice at the institutional level.

GATS IMPLICATIONS FOR THE ROLE OF GOVERNMENT, ACCESS, FINANCING, AND PROGRAM OFFER

Role of Government

In most, if not all countries of the world, the government plays a critical role in regulating, funding, and monitoring the provision of higher education. This situation applies where education is more or less publicly funded and also where there is a mixed public/private higher education system. One has to ask whether trade liberalization will affect a mixed system differently than a public system and whether the role of government will change measurably? Inherent in these questions is the issue of just what services are covered by or exempted from GATS. There is an implicit understanding that public services will be exempted, but close scrutiny of Article 1.3 raises several related questions and concerns. (See discussion in Chapter 9.) Legal opinion and the general consensus in the higher education sector is that there is so much "wiggle room" in the definition that one should not count on government-funded and -mandated institutions being exempted from GATS rules unless a country so stipulates in its commitments. This point is an important one for education government officials to discuss with trade negotiators.

Student Access

Demographic changes, increasing number of graduates from secondary level education, lifelong learning, and changing human resource needs created by the knowledge economy are increasing the unmet demand for postsecondary education and training. Supporters of GATS and increased commercial crossborder education maintain that international trade will help countries satisfy this growing demand for further education and specifically increase student access. Crossborder commercial providers, who are primarily concerned with teaching (meaning limited attention is given to research and service), are targeting niche markets of these learners and responding to a clearly identified need. Therefore, GATS supporters believe that increased student access to education and training is one of the strong rationales and articulated benefits linked to trade liberalization. GATS critics question why trade rules are necessary when crossborder education is already occurring outside of a trade regime and can be regulated through education conventions and national education regulatory frameworks. So while there is general agreement on the need for greater student access, there remains concern that increased access will be available only to those who can afford it and much debate on how trade rules will impact the service providers and the student access.

Financing of Education

The fact that the growth rate in public funding is not keeping pace with the accelerated levels of private investment in higher education is a discernible trend in many developed and developing countries. This trend, plus the pervasive climate of stricter accountability for public support, is creating a more receptive environment for private and commercial providers of postsecondary education. As already noted, private provision of education in niche markets is increasing. These three factors are contributing to an expectation that there will be more private investment in education and more private providers in the future. When forces for increased liberalization of trade are added to this scenario, there is an expectation that private and commercial providers will be very active in the international education markets. According to Global Education Index, developed by Observatory on Borderless Higher Education, there are currently (March 2008) more than 50 companies listed on the stock exchange which provide education/training programs and services to support tertiary education, and most are doing so on an international scale. This does not include those companies that are not publicly listed.

The greatest fear among many education leaders is that while private investment in education rises, the public support may fall even more steeply. The role that trade plays in this scenario is that countries without the capacity or political will to invest in the physical and soft infrastructure for higher education will begin to rely more and more on foreign investors and crossborder education providers, and that this in turn, will lead to trade rules having a heavy influence on the use of the private investment and thereby policy for higher education. A review of the barriers to trade in education services show that measures relating to the commercial presence/foreign investment (mode 3) are in fact being targeted for removal. Of course, a huge proviso in this scenario is that the commercial crossborder education providers (including traditional institutions and new providers) will be able to make it economically worthwhile to deliver internationally, and if this is not the case then new questions will arise.

It is fair to say that there are more questions than answers about the impact of crossborder education on public financing of higher education. Key factors to consider are the social and economic conditions and the nature of the higher education system in the receiving country. What are the national policy objectives and priorities for the higher education sector and how can crossborder education contribute? What is the domestic capacity to meet the demand for higher education and what is the current coverage rate? What is the role of the government—funder, provider, regulator, monitor? How regulated or deregulated (market oriented) is the higher education sector? Are there tuition fees and if so who determines the fee? Is public funding for higher education directed to the institutions, the students (voucher system) or to the programs based on national needs and priorities? Is the higher education sector a mixed system of for-profit and not-for-profit institutions? For publicly funded institutions what is the mix of government, student/household and private sources of income? What percentage of enrolled higher education students is paying tuition fees and service charges? What is the position of the country in terms of granting access to education through trade agreements? Is education seen as a public good/service or a private good/service? If education is a public good/service can it be privately delivered? These are but a few of the questions that need to be asked in order to determine what impact foreign providers, both higher education institutions and commercial companies, will have on higher education in terms of financing the system.

Program Offer

The issue of commercialization has important implications for the diversification and differentiation of higher education institutions and providers and, more specifically, for the selection of academic programs and courses being offered. There are two key aspects to the issue of which courses are offered and by what type of providers. A market approach to higher education can lead to a situation where commercial or for-profit providers offer those courses that are in high market demand such as business, information technology, and communication programs. This means that some of the less popular, and often more costly programs, are the responsibility of public/nonprofit institutions. A result can be a differentiated menu of courses between profit and nonprofit, foreign and domestic providers based on discipline and profitability. Second, foreign for-profit providers will offer their programs as long as it is profitable for them to do so. This fact of educational life has long-term implications for national higher education planners and individual HEIs.

POLICIES FOR REGISTRATION, QUALITY ASSURANCE, AND RECOGNITION OF QUALIFICATIONS OF CROSSBORDER EDUCATION

Registration of Crossborder Providers in Receiving Country

A fundamental question is whether the institutions, companies, and organizations that are delivering award-based programs are registered, licensed, or recognized by the receiving country. The answer to this question varies. Many countries do not have regulatory systems in place to register out-of-country providers for several reasons, including lack of capacity or political will. If foreign providers are not registered or recognized, it is difficult to monitor their performance. Quite commonly, if an institution/provider is not registered as part of a national system, then regulatory frameworks for quality assurance or accreditation do not apply. This is the situation in many countries; and hence, foreign providers (both bona fide and rogue) do not have to comply with national regulations of the receiving countries.

The questions and factors at play in the registration or licensing of foreign providers are many. They include:
- Are different criteria or conditions applicable to those providers who are part of and recognized by a national education system in their home country than for those providers who are not?
- Does it make a difference if the provider is for-profit or nonprofit, private or public, an institution, or a company?
- What conditions apply if in fact the provider is a company that has no home-based presence and establishes institutions only in foreign countries?
- How does one monitor partnerships between local domestic institutions/companies and foreign ones?
- Is it possible to register a completely virtual provider?

Clearly, challenges are involved in trying to establish appropriate and effective national or regional regulatory systems for the registration of crossborder providers.

Often there are bilateral cultural/academic agreements in place to facilitate and monitor the foreign presence of education providers. However, the fact that education services are now part of bilateral and multilateral trade agreements introduces new regulations and questions. A key question facing national governments, as well as international organizations, is the extent to which the introduction of new national regulations to license or recognize crossborder providers will be interpreted as barriers to trade and therefore need to be modified to comply with new trade policies. All in all, the issue of regulating and licensing providers that deliver education across borders needs further attention by national education policy-makers.

Quality Assurance of Crossborder Education

First, it is important to acknowledge that the terms "accreditation" and "quality assurance" have different meanings and significance depending on the country, actor, or stakeholder using the term. This chapter uses "quality recognition" and "assurance" in a general sense that includes such review approaches as quality audit, evaluation, accreditation, and other review processes.

It must be noted that, in the last decade, increased importance has certainly been given to quality assurance at the institutional and national levels. New quality assurance mechanisms and national organizations have been developed in more than 60 countries in the last 12 years. New regional quality networks have also been established. The primary task of these groups has been quality recognition and the assurance of domestic higher education provision, primarily by public and private higher education institutions. However, the increase in crossborder education by institutions and new private commercial providers has introduced a new challenge (and gap) in the field of quality assurance. Historically, national quality assurance agencies have generally not focused their efforts on assessing the quality of imported and exported programs, with some notable exceptions. The question now facing the sector is how to deal with the increase in crossborder education by traditional HEIs and the new private commercial providers who are not normally part of nationally based quality assurance schemes.

It is also important to acknowledge that there is a great deal of crossborder mobility of students, teachers, and programs through noncommercial initiatives. Education activities that are part of development aid projects and international academic linkages and networks are good examples. Therefore, international trade in education services is not the only factor driving the urgency of addressing international quality recognition and assurance. At this point, it must be clarified that neither GATS or any other bilateral trade agreements claim to be establishing rules for quality assurance or accreditation. But increased trade in education is an important catalyst for more urgent attention being given to the creation of national-level systems to assure the quality for incoming and outgoing crossborder education.

As the discussion moves forward, it will be of strategic and substantive importance to recognize the roles and responsibilities of all the players involved in quality assurance, including individual institutions/providers, national quality assurance systems, nongovernment and independent accreditation bodies, and regional/international organizations, all of which contribute to ensuring the quality of crossborder education. Much is at risk if rogue providers or fraudulent qualifications become closely linked to crossborder education. It will be important to work in a collaborative and complementary fashion to build a system that ensures the quality and integrity of crossborder education and maintains the confidence of society in higher education.

It is timely that UNESCO and OECD (2005) have jointly developed a set of *Guidelines for Quality Provision in Crossborder Higher Education.* These guidelines address six stakeholder groups in higher education: governments, higher education institutions/providers, studentbodies, quality assurance and accreditation entities, academic recognition bodies, and professional associations. The purpose of the *Guidelines* is to encourage international cooperation and enhance the understanding of the importance of quality provision in crossborder higher education. The *Guidelines* aim to protect students and other stakeholders from low-quality higher education programs, accreditation and degree mills, and other disreputable providers. The *Guidelines* are not legally binding, but countries are encouraged to use them in the manner they find most appropriate given their national context. One of the steps toward assuring the quality of crossborder education is the development of national regulatory frameworks. To complement the *Guidelines,* UNESCO and the Asia Pacific Quality Network have prepared a *Toolkit on Regulating Quality Assurance in Cross-Border Education.* The *Toolkit* is designed to help receiving and sending countries understand the issues, models, and benefits of establishing a regulatory framework for crossborder education and provides practical information to do so.

In addition, several international/regional/national higher education organizations have produced declarations and position chapters on the issues related to quality crossborder education and GATS. These include the *Accra Declaration on GATS and the Internationalization of Higher Education in Africa* emanating from the Association of African Universities Workshop in 2004 on the "Implications of WTO/GATS for Higher Education in Africa." The International Association of Universities and national university associations have also prepared an international statement: *Sharing Quality Higher Education across Borders: A Statement on Behalf of Higher Education Institutions Worldwide (*http://www.unesco.org/iau/p_statements/index.html).

New Developments in Accreditation

The increased awareness of the need for quality assurance and/or accreditation has led to several new developments in accreditation, some of which are helping with the task of the domestic and international recognition of qualifications, but some of which are only hindering and complicating matters. First, it is important to acknowledge the efforts of many countries to establish criteria and procedures for quality assurance recognition systems and the approval of bona fide accreditors. At the same time, it is necessary to recognize the increase in self-appointed and rather self-serving accreditors, as well as accreditation mills that simply sell bogus accreditation labels.

Market forces are making the profile and reputation of an institution/provider and their courses more and more important. Major investments are being made in marketing and branding campaigns to get name recognition and to increase enrollments. Possessing some type of accreditation is part of the campaign, assuring prospective students that the programs/awards are of high standing. The desire for accreditation status is leading to a commercialization of quality assurance/accreditation as programs and providers strive to gain as many "accreditation" stars as possible to increase their competitiveness and perceived international legitimacy. The challenge is how to distinguish between bona fide and rogue accreditors, especially when neither the crossborder provider and accreditor is nationally based or recognized as part of a national higher education system.

At the same time, networks of institutions and self-appointed organizations are engaged in accrediting their members. These are positive developments when seen through the lens of trying to improve the quality of the academic offer. However, there is some concern that they are not totally objective in their assessments and may be more interested in generating income than in improving quality. While this caveat can apply to both crossborder and domestic provision, it is particularly worrisome for crossborder provision as such organizations often pay slight attention to national policy objectives and cultural orientation.

Another development that is worrisome is the growth in accreditation mills. These organizations are not recognized or legitimate bodies and they more or less "sell" accreditation status without any independent assessment. They are similar to degree mills that sell certificates and degrees with little or no course work. Different education stakeholders, especially students, employers, and the public, need to be aware of these accreditation (and degree) mills which are often no more than a web address and are therefore out of the jurisdiction of national regulatory systems.

CHAPTER TEN

Recognition of Qualifications

The credibility of higher education programs and qualifications is extremely important for students, their employers, the public at large, and, of course, for the academic community itself. It is critical that the qualifications awarded by crossborder providers are legitimate and will be recognized for employment or further studies both at home and abroad. This is a major challenge facing the national and international higher education sector in light of new crossborder providers and programs.

UNESCO has long acknowledged the need for an international system to facilitate and ensure the recognition of academic and professional qualifications. UNESCO established regional conventions on the recognition of qualifications more than 25 years ago; at present, these conventions have been ratified by more than 100 member states in Africa, Asia and the Pacific, the Arab States, Europe, and Latin America. They are unique, legally binding instruments dealing with crossborder, mutual recognition of qualifications. There is limited general awareness of these instruments except for the European regional convention, which in 1997 was updated jointly by UNESCO and the Council of Europe in the form of the Lisbon Convention. In 2001, the same two organizations established a Code of Good Practice for Transnational Education that is now a recognized part of the Lisbon Convention. At present, there is discussion on how these UNESCO conventions can be used as instruments to complement trade agreements and assure students, employers, and the public that there are systems in place to recognize academic and professional qualifications. Given the growth in academic mobility, the increased mobility of the labor force, and the fact that GATS is encouraging greater professional mobility, there is a clear and urgent need for national education policymakers to address this issue.

ISSUES RELATED TO VALUES, CULTURAL DIVERSITY,
AND BRAIN DRAIN/GAIN

Values Driving Higher Education

At the heart of the debate for many educators is the level of impact that increased commercial crossborder education and new trade policies will have on the purpose, role, and values of higher education. The growth in new commercial and private providers, the commodification of education, and the prospect of new trade policy frameworks are catalysts for stimulating serious reflection on the role, social commitment, and funding of public higher education institutions in society.

The trinity of teaching/learning, research, and service to society has traditionally guided the evolution of universities and their contribution to the social, cultural, human, scientific, and economic development of a nation. Is the combination of these roles still valid, or can they be disaggregated and rendered by different providers? Values that have traditionally underpinned public education—such as academic freedom, collegiality, and institutional autonomy—are being closely examined. Is education still considered to be a public good in the sense of contributing to the development of society and/or is it being perceived as a private good for consumption by individuals? Some believe that these traditional values and roles are even more relevant and important in today's environment; others suggest that there is a need for a shift away from these traditional values in light of globalization. And still others argue that, if higher education is to fulfill its role as a "public good," then it will need to move away from its traditional public-funding sources in favor of more market-based approaches. Once again, the existence of new trade rules covering education is an important catalyst demanding a rigorous review of the values fundamental to higher education and a nation's perception of how education meets national priorities and needs. Perhaps the issues of trade and the commercialization of higher education will eventually be fundamental elements that define and contrast different countries' values and approaches to the role and purpose of higher education.

Cultural Diversity and Acculturation

The impact of new forms and types of international academic mobility on the recognition and promotion of indigenous and diverse cultures is a subject that evokes strong positions and sentiments. Many believe that modern information and communication technologies and the movement of people, ideas, and culture across national boundaries are presenting new opportunities to promote one's culture to other countries and further chances for the fusion and hybridization of culture. Their position rests on the assumption that this flow of culture across borders is not new at all; only the speed has been accelerated. Others contend that these same forces are eroding national cultural identities and that, instead of creating new forms of cultures through hybridization, cultures are being homogenized (which, in most cases, is interpreted as being Westernized). Given that education has traditionally been seen as a vehicle of acculturation, these arguments are played out in terms of curriculum content, language of instruction (particularly the increase in English), and the teaching/learning process of exported/imported programs. Both perspectives have strong arguments. However, because commercial exports are often based on surplus capacity and the bottom profit line, it is important to ask whether efforts are made to customize programs to local needs and to make programs culturally appropriate and useful?

Will commercially traded education programs be any more or less culturally imperialistic or diversified than programs or curriculum that cross borders as part of development projects or academic exchange programs? There is no clear answer to this question yet. Many would argue that for-profit private providers will not be willing to invest the time and resources to ensure that courses respect cultural traditions and include relevant local content. Given that commercial providers are market driven there may be a demand from the students and employers for what is perceived to be "modern" (usually meaning "Western") education. The potential impact of crossborder programs and programs on cultural diversity requires policymakers to be alert and sensitive to these issues in their own cultural environment.

The Potential for Brain Drain/Gain

Brain power is an increasingly important issue for many countries due to the growing mobility of professional/skilled workers and the increased pressure for trade liberalization, especially in GATS Mode 4 (movement of persons). The increase in crossborder movement of scholars, experts, and teachers/professors is due in part to the increasing competition for human capital in the knowledge economy. Not only is there a trend toward higher education personnel moving from country to country, but they are also attracted to the corporate sector where benefits can be more attractive than in the education sector. The higher education sector is affected by this situation both positively and negatively depending on whether a country is experiencing a net brain drain or gain effect and the level of brain circulation. It is important to be aware of the long-term implications in terms of human resource capacity in specific fields at both the national and institutional levels. There are implications for education policies as well as for other sectors such as immigration, science and technology, trade, employment, and foreign relations. There are also direct links between foreign student recruitment/mobility (Mode 2) and the immigration needs for skilled labor of the recruiting country. Thus, the complex and increasingly interrelated dynamics between national policies for trade in education, migration policies, and nation building/human capacity-building efforts are areas worthy of serious investigation by education policymakers.

IMPLICATIONS FOR POLICY AND PRACTICE AT THE INSTITUTIONAL LEVEL

It would be incorrect to leave the impression that these issues do not have implications for individual providers and especially higher education institutions. Quality assurance starts with the provider that is delivering the program, whether domestically or internationally. Most HEIs have adequate quality assurance processes in place for domestic delivery, but these processes do not cover all aspects of delivering equivalent programs abroad. The challenges inherent in working cross-culturally—in a foreign regulatory environment and potentially with a partner—raise new issues. They include academic entry requirements, student examination and assessment procedures, work load, delivery modes, adaptation of the curriculum, quality assurance of teaching, academic and socio-cultural support for students, title and level of award, and others. Quality issues must be balanced with the financial investment and return to the source provider. Intellectual property ownership, choice of partners, division of responsibilities, academic and business risk assessments, and internal and external approval processes are only some of the issues on which HEIs need to be clear when they become engaged in crossborder education.

IN CONCLUSION: NEW REALITIES AND CHALLENGES

The purpose of this chapter is to make higher education policymakers and leaders more aware of the realities of higher education in an increasingly trade-oriented environment, in anticipation that an increased level of awareness and knowledge will lead to a closer examination of the role crossborder education plays in relation to one's country's priorities, resources, and goals for higher education. Higher education has new responsibilities and new challenges in a more globalized world—a world where the knowledge society, market economy, ICTS, and trade have increasing importance and influence.

Current Realities

International education, in all forms, is a phenomenon that has been occurring long before the advent of GATS. But new developments in crossborder education require a careful review of what national policies and regulations are needed to ensure that crossborder education—either outgoing or incoming—provides greater access to a quality education experience for learners, offers a bona fide qualification, and fits into the national-level policy framework for postsecondary education.

The introduction of bilateral and multilateral trade agreements that focus on services rather than on goods has been a wake-up call for many service sectors. The education sector is no exception. Who would have anticipated, even two decades ago, that education moving between countries for commercial reasons would be subject to trade regulations? But this is the current reality.

Has GATS been a catalyst for increased commercial higher education between countries? Many would contend that the opposite is true—that, in fact, one of the consequences of increased private for-profit education at national levels and the flow of students and education programs between countries has prompted the inclusion of education in trade agreements. But even so, most educators believe that trade rules are not necessary to regulate the movement of commercial education between countries. Education has been moving between countries through development cooperation, academic exchanges, and now commercial initiatives, for years; and the education sector has developed and can continue to create the appropriate policies and regulations. Yet today, bilateral, regional, and multilateral trade agreements exist. Their rules are applied to trade in higher education. This is a reality that must be faced and acted upon by the higher education sector. Some governments, HEIs and educators embrace this reality, while others are repelled by the notion that education is being treated as a tradable commodity. Both reactions exist, often within the same country or higher education institution.

Challenges Related to GATS and Higher Education

Dealing with the issues and implications of trade agreements is a relatively new policy area for the higher education sector. Similarly, trade negotiators have not had extensive experience with education services. This situation thus requires a closer collaboration and more intensive information exchange between trade negotiators and education policymakers than currently exists. Also, given that progressive liberalization is the ultimate goal of GATS, higher education leaders and policymakers need to be working in close consultation with trade negotiators to monitor current and future negotiations that include trade in education services.

As has been repeated many times, GATS is a new, untested, and evolving agreement. The interpretations of existing articles and obligations can change and new disciplines can be developed. The recent introduction of the "new complementary approaches" (see discussion in Chapter 9) is proof of this flexibility. Requests and offers are still being tabled. To date, there is little activity in higher education subsector, but current and future negotiations may put greater pressure on the use of education services as part of cross-sector trading—meaning that education may be "traded off" to permit market access in another sector or to meet a mandatory and predetermined number of commitments.

Further investigation into the types of barriers to trade in education services is necessary, for the removal/reduction of barriers is at the core of trade liberalization. What may be seen as barriers by a country wishing to access a foreign market can be seen as fundamental aspects of the regulatory system in the receiving country. It is important that the higher education sector be vigilant in assuring that domestic regulations representing policy priorities are not removed or watered down under pressure from exporting countries wanting access to domestic higher education markets through crossborder education or by the receiving country that wants more foreign commercial provision in the domestic market.

The focus of crossborder education and of GATS deliberations has been almost entirely on the teaching side of education and has not addressed implications for research. Research is an integral part of higher education, and further investigation is needed into the potential impact on applied research and especially privately contracted or funded research. Do public education institutions that are undertaking research and development activities have an unfair advantage over private organizations that do not usually receive public support for their activities? Could public subsidies be construed as a barrier to fair trade or be subject to removal under the condition that private foreign entities must be treated the same as national companies?

The rationales driving trade in education are complex. They differ if one is a receiving country or a sending country. For instance, receiving countries may be interested in increasing student access, creating a competitive environment between domestic and foreign providers to improve quality or provide education programs in areas where there is no domestic expertise. Sending countries often see crossborder education as a means of creating strategic alliances or generating alternative sources of income. Rationales are different for commercial crossborder education than for exchange partnerships or international development initiatives. Education policymakers need to be clear about the rationales that underpin national policies on crossborder education and ensure that the appropriate regulatory frameworks and strategies are in place to achieve the stated objectives.

It is the university sector, in the postsecondary education category, that has been most deeply involved in discussing GATS. The professional, technical, and vocational providers have been less vocal. It would be useful for national policymakers to have more information and discussion with the nonuniversity sector. The impact of trade rules on the regulations of the professions also merits further attention, especially given that higher education is often directly involved in the education, training, and possibly certification of the professions. To date there has been little discussion of issues related to the "other services" category. Increased trade in such education services as language testing or quality assessment and evaluation will have significant implications for higher education. They need to be kept on the radar screen. Finally, perhaps there is something to be learned from how other social service sectors, such as health and culture, have approached issues related to the inclusion of their services within the GATS regulations.

This chapter has focused on GATS, but TRIPS is another WTO agreement that merits careful monitoring. TRIPS stands for Trade Related Aspects of Intellectual Property Rights. Of particular interest to the higher education community are issues related to whether intellectual property rights will encourage or inhibit innovation and research, who owns the copyright of materials used in e-education, and how to protect indigenous knowledge.

Issues in Other Policy Domains

GATS and other regional/bilateral trade agreements are trying to facilitate increased mobility of professional and skilled workers on a temporary basis. Crossborder education, especially the movement of students, scholars, and professors will introduce new issues related to immigration policies in terms of visas, working permits, residency status, and even dual citizenship. What are the long-term implications for migration patterns and immigration status?

Crossborder education, including science/technology research and development, are seen as tools for strategic alliances between countries and institutions. In the past, there has been more emphasis on cultural, scientific, and political alliances; but given the increasing importance of commercial trade of education services, higher education is being perceived as a more important player for economic alliances as well. What role is emerging for higher education in bilateral and regional foreign policy development?

In the past, nation-building by investing in higher education through human resource development, institutional strengthening, and scholarship programs has been an important part of international development and technical assistance programs. In the last decade, these aid-oriented initiatives have given way to projects based on principles of partnership, exchange, and mutual benefits. Is the inclusion of education as a tradable service under the purview of trade agreements like GATS an indication of a shift away from aid and partnership initiatives toward commercial trade as a primary tool for developing higher education in developing and transition countries? What are the implications and consequences of the "aid to trade shift" and the existence of the "aid for trade" package in GATS?

The issues raised in this section highlight a number of critical areas for further investigation, analysis, and policy reform. Clearly, the list is more illustrative than comprehensive. Further attention needs to be given to these and other aspects of education which are potentially impacted by increased crossborder education and the presence of new trade regulations.

Maximizing Benefits and Minimizing Risks

The last two decades have seen significant growth in the mobility of programs and providers through physical and virtual modes of delivery. This development presents many new opportunities—for increased access to higher education, for strategic alliances between countries and regions, for the production and exchange of new knowledge, for the movement of graduates and professionals, for human resource and institutional capacity building, for income generation, for the improvement of academic quality, and for increased mutual understanding.

The list of potential benefits is long and varied. But so is the list of potential risks. Risks can include an increase in low-quality or rogue providers, a decrease in public funding if foreign providers are providing increased access, nonsustainable foreign provision of higher education if profit margins are low, foreign qualifications that are not recognized by domestic employers or for further study, elitism in terms of those who can afford crossborder education, overuse of English as language of instruction, and the failure to meet national higher education policy objectives. Risks and benefits vary between sending and receiving countries—and between developed and developing countries—for students, institutions, companies, and employers. In light of the rapid pace of crossborder growth and innovation, it is important that the higher education sector be informed and vigilant about the risks and benefits and, more importantly, about the need for appropriate policies and regulations to monitor current and future developments.

It is clear that the growth and changes in crossborder education are staggering. There are new types of providers, new methods of delivery, new learners, new partnerships, new financial arrangements, new types of awards, new policies, and new regulatory frameworks. This bewildering diversity presents new challenges for how crossborder education is conceptualized (and regulated). Using a trade frame-work to categorize crossborder activity is one approach; but given these new developments, some argue that a trade framework is too limited. Crossborder education occurs for a variety of reasons and under a diversity of arrangements—for example, through academic linkages and partnership programs, through development/aid types of projects and through commercial trade. The GATS trade mode framework covers only commercial trade types of activities. Therefore, it is urgent that the education sector begin to develop its own classification system and language to categorize crossborder education in a manner which includes all forms of mobility and all types of activities, not just the commercial ventures.

It is important that the wider international higher education community continues to work together on these issues to ensure: that educators' views and expertise come to bear on the developments in trade in education services; that the higher education sector continues to work toward national/regional and international education frameworks which address the quality assurance, accreditation, and recognition of qualifications for all types of crossborder education; that further work is done on investigating the implications of trade agreements on scholarly pursuits, research, and intellectual property; that trade is seen as only one subset of the larger phenomenon of crossborder education and internationalization; and that the impact of trade and commercial provision on the larger more philosophical questions related to the purpose, values, and role of higher education continue to be explored.

Note: This chapter is based on reports prepared for the four UNESCO Regional Meetings on "GATS and Higher Education" convened by the Forum on Higher Education, Research, and Knowledge (Knight, 2006) and from two reports prepared for the Observatory on Borderless Higher Education (Knight, 2002, 2003).

RELATED REFERENCES

Association of African Universities (AAU). (2004). The Accra declaration on GATS and the internationalization of higher education in Africa. In *The implication of WTO/GATS for higher education in Africa*. Accra: Author.
Breton, G., & Lambert, M. (Eds.). (2003). *Universities and globalization: Private linkages, public trust*. Paris: UNESCO, Université Laval, and Economica.
Jokivirta, L. (2005, November-December). *Higher education crossing borders in francophone Africa: Parts 1–2*. Briefing Notes. London: Observatory on Borderless Higher Education.
Knight, J. (2002, October). *Trade in higher education services: The implications of GATS*. Report. London: Observatory on Borderless Higher Education.
Knight, J. (2003, April). *GATS, trade, and higher education: Perspectives 2003. Where are we?* Report. London: Observatory on Borderless Higher Education.
Man-Sheng, Z., & Chun-Meng, S. (2003). Trends in international education services: Implications for China after entering WTO. *Education Research of Policy and Practice*, No. 2, 41–54.
McBurnie, G., & Ziguras, C. (2001). The regulation of transnational higher education in Southeast Asia: Case studies of Hong Kong, Malaysia, and Australia. *Higher Education*, 42(1), 84–105.
Middlehurst, R., & Woodfield, S. (2003). *The role of transnational, private and for-profit provision in meeting global demand for tertiary education: Mapping, regulation and impact*. Vancouver: Commonwealth of Learning and UNESCO.
Organization for Economic and Community Development (OECD). (2002). The growth of cross-border education. In *Educational policy analysis*. Paris: Author.
Organization for Economic and Community Development (OECD). (2004a). *Quality and recognition in higher education: The crossborder challenge*. Paris: Author.
Organization for Economic and Community Development (OECD). (2004b). *Internationalization and trade of higher education: Challenges and opportunities*. Paris: Author.
Powar, K. B. (2003). Indian higher education in a GATS-controlled regime: Looking for a pathway in the haze of uncertainty. *Higher Education Policy and Practices*, 1(2).
Singh, M. (2001) Re-inserting the "public good" into higher education transformation. *Kagisano: [Publication of the] Council on Higher Education, South Africa*, No. 1.
UNESCO. (2004). *Higher education in a globalized society*. Education Position Chapter ED-2004/WS/33. Paris: Author.
UNESCO/APQN. Asia Pacific Quality Network. (2006). *Toolkit: Regulating the quality of cross-border education*. Bangkok, Thailand: UNESCO.
UNESCO/OECD. (2005). *Guidelines for quality provision in crossborder higher education*. Paris: UNESCO/Organization for Economic and Community Development.
Uvalic-Trumbic, S. (2002). *Globalization and the market in higher education: Quality, accreditation and qualifications*. Paris: UNESCO and Economica.

CHAPTER TEN

Uvalic-Trumbic, S. (2004). UNESCO conventions on the recognition of qualifications: Regional frameworks in a global context. In *Quality and recognition in higher education: The cross-border challenge* (pp. 142–153). Paris: Organization for Economic and Community Development.

Verbik, L., & Jokivirta, L. (2005). *National regulatory frameworks for transnational higher education: Models and trends, Parts 1–2*. Briefing Notes. London: Observatory on Borderless Higher Education.

Van Damme, D. (2002). Trends and models in international quality assurance in higher education in relation to trade in education. *Higher Education Management and Policy, 14*(3).

Vincent-Lancrin, S. (2005). *Building capacity through cross-border tertiary education*. London: Observatory on Borderless Education.

Westerheijden, D. (2003). Accreditation in Western Europe: Adequate reactions to Bologna declaration and the general agreements on trade in services? *Journal of International Education, 7*(3), 277–302.

World Trade Organization Secretariat (WTO). (1998). *Education services: Background note, S/C/W/49, 98-3691*. Geneva: Council for Trade in Services.

World Trade Organization Secretariat (WTO). (1999). *The General Agreement in Trade in Services (GATS): Objectives, coverage, and disciplines*. Geneva: Author.

CHAPTER ELEVEN

INTERNATIONALIZATION AROUND THE WORLD:

*The Results of a Global Survey on the
International Dimension of Higher Education*

WHY A WORLDWIDE SURVEY?

Internationalization is fast becoming one of the most important and increasingly complex forces of higher education. The benefit of hindsight shows that the last decade has seen unprecedented growth in the international dimension of higher education and the next decade promises the same or an even greater rate of expansion. As discussed in previous chapters, internationalization means different things to different higher education institutions, university associations, governments, and nongovernmental agencies. These various perspectives reflect the fact that different rationales are driving higher education institutions to internationalize, bringing a wide range of anticipated benefits but also unintended outcomes. Higher education institutions in all regions of the world are addressing the international dimension of higher education in a way that reflects their values, priorities, opportunities, and available resources. Consequently, the internationalization of higher education is a hotbed of activity and a source of potential innovation leading to the development of new policies, programs, and practices at institutional, national, and international levels. levels.

The purpose of this chapter is to present and discuss some of the major findings from the 2005 worldwide survey on the internationalization of higher education conducted by the International Association of Universities. The results of the survey provide a reality test or a benchmark for some of the issues and trends discussed in the previous chapters.

COMMITMENT TO INTERNATIONALIZATION

The internationalization of higher education has been central to the work of the International Association of Universities (IAU) for many years. IAU's role has been to identify and monitor issues, trends, opportunities, and risks; to speak out to promote internationalization at various forums; to report on new developments and emerging challenges; and to provide information for its members and the higher education sector as a whole. To keep on top of this rapidly changing aspect of higher education, IAU has committed to undertake a worldwide internationalization survey of higher education institutions and other key actors at regular intervals.

The first IAU internationalization survey, conducted in 2003, polled IAU members only. The 2005 IAU Survey expanded to include a much larger group of higher education institutions around the world as well as national and regional university/rector associations. The objectives of the 2005 IAU survey were:

CHAPTER ELEVEN

- To identify key issues, trends, and new developments as perceived by higher education institutions and associations
- To gather information on the practices and priorities of internationalization at the institutional level
- To poll national and regional university/rector associations on their opinions, policies, and programs for internationalization
- To ensure that the voices of higher education institutions and university associations are heard regarding the rationales, benefits, risks, growth areas, and emerging challenges of internationalization
- To continue the collection of baseline data on internationalization (started in 2003) in order to monitor developments on a longitudinal basis.

SURVEY DESIGN

One of the important innovations in the 2005 IAU survey project was that three separate but related questionnaires were developed. The first was designed for higher education institutions (HEIs), the second for national-level university associations (NUAs), and the third for regional-level university associations (RUAs). Serious consideration was given to sending a survey to government education policymakers, but identifying the correct recipients in more than 120 countries complicated this task and the proposal was postponed for possible use in the future.

Each survey included questions relevant to the targeted recipients, but they all included a common set of questions to permit comparison among the three groups. Furthermore, questions from the 2003 survey were intentionally included in the 2005 survey to ensure that specific topics are monitored on a multi-year basis.

LEVELS AND TYPES OF ANALYSIS

The 2005 IAU survey was designed to allow for several types of data analysis and interpretation and thus provide more detailed and differentiated information on internationalization in the world.

The findings from the HEI respondents were analyzed according to four different sets of parameters. The first type of analysis was an aggregate level in order to see macro-level picture and trends. However, the large number of European respondents skews the aggregate level somewhat and makes the regional-level analysis more revealing and important. For the regional analysis, the host country of the higher education institutions was allocated to one of six regions; comparisons were then done among the regional groupings of higher education institutions. In order to determine whether there were significant differences between the higher education institutions' responses in developed and developing countries, all HEI responses were categorized according to the ranking of the host country on the Human Development Index (HDI). A high HDI ranking meant that the HEI was part of a developed country, while a low or medium HDI ranking indicated that the HEI was part of developing country. Finally, a comparison of the findings from questions common to the 2003 and 2005 IAU surveys was done. A country-level analysis of higher education institutions was not done, given the work involved in analyzing 95 different countries and the low number (and therefore non-representative nature) of the responses.

The National University Association data was analyzed on an aggregate level, recognizing the potential skewing effect from the large number of European respondents. Unfortunately, the response rate of 18 national university associations did not lend itself to a regional-level analysis. The findings from the questions common to the national university associations and to the higher education institutions were also compared.

RECIPIENTS AND RESPONDENTS

Higher Education Institutions

The total number of higher education institutions in the actual sample was 3,057. Of these, 526 higher education institutions completed and returned the questionnaire to IAU. This represents a response rate of 14.7% which, on the one hand, is disappointing given the effort involved but, on the other hand, is quite predictable and in line with expected response rates to international surveys. In 2003, 176 higher education institutions from 66 countries responded to the IAU survey. The numbers were lower due to the fact that only IAU members received the questionnaire. The 2005 survey, which collected replies from higher education institutions in 95 countries, is more international in scope and remains the largest internationalization survey project of its kind to date.

University Associations

A total of 102 national university associations received the questionnaire and 18 were returned. This is a surprisingly low return rate and raises the question about the level of importance these organizations attribute to internationalization. Furthermore, a high number of European national university associations responded, thus skewing the data to developed country perspectives. IAU continues to believe that the NUA opinions on internationalization are very important, and further efforts to harvest a greater return rate will be made for the next survey.

The Regional Rate of Responses

It is interesting to note that Africa, Europe, the Middle East, and the Asia Pacific had a similar ratio of recipients to responses—between 18 and 21%. (See Table 11.1) Latin America has the lowest percentage of responses at 9% followed by North America at 13%. When one looks at the numbers of regional responses as a percentage of the total received, a different picture emerges; Europe represents 52% of

CHAPTER ELEVEN

Table 11.1. Response rates of higher education institutions by region

Region	**Responses as % of Recipients by Region**	**Replies as % of Total Reponses**
Africa	20%	6%
Asia Pacific	18%	18%
Europe	20%	52%
Latin America and the Caribbean	9%	6%
Middle East	21%	4%
North America	13%	14%

the total responses. These response rates make regional-level analysis very important and perhaps more informative than the aggregated HEI analysis.

The full IAU report provides an in-depth analysis of the findings for all of the survey questions and examines their significance and implications for the higher education sector around the world. It is arguably the most up-to-date and extensive look at the internationalization of higher education institutions around the world and can be an important resource for higher education institutions, university associations, policymakers, and researchers. It is important that institutional perspectives and experiences are factored into the current discussions and debates about the international dimension of higher education.

THE PERCEIVED IMPORTANCE OF INTERNATIONALIZATION

The priority given to the international dimension is a question worthy of analysis from the institutional, national association, and government points of view. While there is a widespread perception that the scope and volume of internationalization has grown exponentially in the last decade, it is unwise to assume that its importance has increased at the same rate. There is not always a direct or causal relationship between the level of activity and the importance attributed to it. Factors such as politics and competing priorities have an influence. Nor is there always a correlation between a high level of articulated support and the availability of funding to facilitate implementation. Questions about the current priority attributed to internationalization merit close examination as information on the convergence/divergence between institutional and national levels of support is helpful in understanding the current and future role of the international dimension in the higher education sector.

Questions on the importance of internationalization were included in both the 2003 and 2005 IAU surveys. It is helpful to remember that the HEI perceptions are generally those of the senior administration and their views were solicited on the priority given to the international dimension by their own institution, their national university association, and their national government. The 2005 IAU survey also asked national university/rector associations for their opinions on the significance of internationalization at the same three levels. The differences between the HEI and NUA responses are revealing, as is the perception of the relatively low level of interest by national governments.

HEI Responses on the Importance of Internationalization

A clear majority (73%) of HEIs rank internationalization as a high priority. Interestingly, this finding is exactly the same as that of the 2003 IAU survey, indicating that no shift in the priority given to the international dimension of higher education has occurred during the two years between surveys. This is a welcome finding, confirming that the relatively high level of interest in the international dimension of higher education is being sustained in light of many competing priorities facing higher education institutions.

There is a marked difference among the level of importance given to internationalization by HEIs themselves (73%) and their perceptions of the lower importance given by NUAs (49%) and national governments bodies (46%). This difference is worth exploring to understand why HEIs believe that their national university associations are not giving the same degree of attention to the issues surrounding internationalization. Is it a natural and expected difference, given that institutions experience different realities in the everyday practice of internationalization than the issues that university/rector associations face at the national policy level? Or is the variance revealing a true area of disconnect between HEI and NUA priorities on the development of internationalization?

There is very little difference across the regions in how HEIs see the significance of internationalization. Latin America stands out as the only region where a very small number of HEIs (3%) indicated that internationalization commanded no priority at all. Yet the results reveal major differences among the regions in how HEIs versus NUAs and governments view the significance of internationalization. For instance, Europe (53%) and the Asia Pacific (54%) stand out as the two regions where HEIs believe that both NUAs and governments give high priority to internationalization, in contrast to lower percentages from the Middle East (29%) and Latin America (33%).

Overall, there are no major differences in priority levels when the results of the low/medium HDI countries are compared to the high-HDI countries. The one noteworthy finding is that HEIs in developing countries believe that NUAs (40%) give a much lower level of importance to internationalization than both the governments (47%) and the HEIs themselves (68%). This is a clear message for NUAs. The opposite is true for developed countries where NUAs (53%) give more importance to the international dimension than governments (45%) do, but certainly less than the HEIs (75%). Perhaps this counter-intuitive finding can be explained by the fact that the NUAs in developed countries are more numerous and better resourced than NUAs in developing countries. It is important to remember that these are the institutions' perceptions of the university associations. The next section provides information on how NUAs view the same issue.

CHAPTER ELEVEN

NUA Responses to the Importance of Internationalization

The NUAs were asked to rank the importance of internationalization for their member institutions, their own organization, and their national governments. Overall, NUAs believe that they attribute more significance (78%) to the international dimension of higher education than either their member institutions (67%) or governments (50%). It is fascinating to compare these results with those from the HEIs. There is agreement between HEIs and NUAs that the national government gives a lower priority to internationalization than either the HEIs or NUAs. But when HEIs and NUAs are ranking their own priorities, a major divergence occurs. Higher education institutions rank their own priority for internationalization as much higher than national university associations, but NUAs rank their own priority higher than that of HEIs. This is a major contradiction that merits further study to better understand the reasons behind it and also to find ways to build on what appears to be high level of support by both groups. Overall, it is a positive finding that the majority of NUAs and HEIs give high priority to the international dimension of higher education, but the discrepancy suggests that opportunities are lost for working on common issues of priority.

RATIONALES

The motivations driving internationalization are key to understanding all aspects of the international dimension of higher education. They help to explain why an institution or a country believes that internationalization is important, what strategies are used, which benefits are expected, and which risks are taken or feared. At a more fundamental level, rationales reflect the core values that a higher education system holds regarding the contribution that international, intercultural, and global elements make to the role of higher education in society. Rationales underpinning the process of internationalization have been changing in the last two decades. Much has been written about the shift from academic and social/cultural rationales to economic and political rationales. Furthermore, the increasing emphasis on international competition over international cooperation has been noted, and the reality of bilateral cooperation for the sake of unilateral competitiveness has been recognized.

In the 2003 IAU survey, respondents were asked to indicate their rationales through an open-ended question—that is, they were asked to identify the key reasons for internationalization and describe them in their own words. Interestingly, 2003 respondents often identified individual activities (such as student mobility) as a rationale rather than identifying a more generic purpose. Even so, the responses were categorized, ranked, and subsequently used to inform the options provided in the 2005 IAU survey. This measure ensured that the rationales listed in the 2005 survey were linked to those in the 2003 survey so that comparisons could be made and the rationales originally identified by HEIs were used. It was also important that a distinction be made between the reasons motivating an individual HEI and those driving the country as a whole. Therefore, in the 2005 IAU survey HEI and

A GLOBAL SURVEY ON HIGHER EDUCATION

Table 11.2. Rationales for internationalization

Institutional Level	*National Level*
1. Broaden and diversify source of faculty and students	1. Increase competitiveness (scientific, technological, economic)
2. Create international profile and reputation	2. Promote international solidarity and cooperation
3. Strengthen research and knowledge capacity and production	3. Develop strategic alliances (political, cultural, academic, trade)
4. Promote curriculum development and innovation	4. Strengthen export industry
5. Increase student and faculty international knowledge and intercultural understanding	5. Build country's human resource capacity
6. Contribute to academic quality	6. Further cultural awareness and understanding
7. Diversify income generation	7. Contribute to regional priorities and integration

NUA respondents were asked to rank the three most important rationales at the institutional level and at a national level from the options presented in Table 11.2.

Institutional-Level Rationales

No rationale stood out as the most important for internationalization at the institutional level. This diversity reflects the reality that there is no "one way" or "no right way" to internationalize and there is no "one size fits all" when it comes to why institutions are actively engaged in the internationalization process. No more than 50% of HEIs ranked the same rationale as most significant. This diversity of rationales has implications for national- and institutional-level policy and funding, as support needs to be spread across three or four key rationales. (See Figure 11.1.)

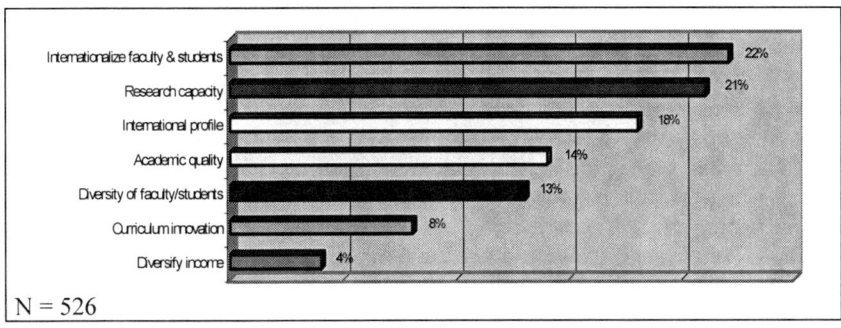

Figure 11.1: Ranking by HEIs of the most important rationale at the institutional level

Table 11.3. Regional ranking of rationales by HEIs at institutional level

Rationale at Institutional Level	Overall Ranking	Africa	Asia and Pacific	Europe	Latin America and Caribbean	Middle East	North America
Internationalize student and faculty	**22%**	18%	21%	21%	21%	15%	**35%**
Research capacity	**21%**	**33%**	20%	20%	28%	**33%**	14%
International profile	**18%**	16%	18%	**22%**	10%	12%	9%
Academic quality	**14%**	15%	10%	13%	**24%**	17%	12%
Diversity of faculty and students	**13%**	7%	18%	11%	8%	11%	**17%**
Curriculum innovation	**8%**	10%	7%	8%	9%	11%	8%
Income generation	**4%**	1%	6%	3%	0%	1%	5%

The two rationales that respondents identified as being most important at the institutional level were "to increase student and faculty international knowledge and intercultural understanding" and "to strengthen research knowledge capacity and production." Both rationales speak to the central mission of HEIs, which is teaching/learning and research. It appears that, overall, HEIs believe that internationalization should, first and foremost, be contributing to the core purpose and activities of their institutions. Of secondary importance is the motivation to have an international profile, which interestingly enough is seen to be a more important purpose of internationalization than improvement of academic quality.

It may come as a surprise—and even be counterintuitive to many—that only 4% of the respondents ranked "to diversify income" as the most important reason for internationalization. The current debate about the growth of commercial crossborder education and the role of higher education as a tradable commodity would lead many to question this low ranking. The explanation may lie in the fact that HEIs in 95 different countries responded to this survey and all were traditional institutions oriented to the trinity of teaching/learning, research, and service. Without doubt, there are HEIs, especially in Australia, New Zealand, the United States, and the United Kingdom, that see income generation as the number one reason for internationalization, but it is clear that they are a small though influential minority. This finding is an eloquent reminder that internationalization is still closely aligned to the primary functions of HEIs and is seen a means to an end, and not an end in itself.

Table 11.3 illustrates that HEIs in all regions of the world, except the Middle East, seek "to increase student and faculty international knowledge and intercultural understanding" as either the top or second-ranked rationale. In general, the findings

Table 11.4. Ranking of institutional rationales by HEIs according to HDI category

Rationale at Institutional Level	Overall Ranking	Low-Medium HDI Countries	High HDI Countries
Internationalize student and faculty	22%	18%	27%
Research capacity	21%	29%	17%
International profile	18%	15%	20%
Academic quality	14%	17%	11%
Diversity of faculty and students	13%	8%	14%
Curriculum innovation	8%	11%	7%
Income generation	4%	2%	4%

at the regional level seem to be in line with the perceived current interests and priorities at the regional level. For instance, the Middle East (33%), Africa (33%), and Latin America and the Caribbean (28%) all rank "to strengthen research and knowledge capacity and production" as their number one priority for internationalization. In contrast, European HEIs see 'to create international profile and reputation" as their number one priority, which is consistent with one of the goals of the Bologna Process. It is interesting to note that only North American HEIs have given second ranking to "to broaden and diversify sources of faculty and students." This attention may well reflect the need of HEIs in the United States and Canada to attract foreign faculty/scholars to their institutions to strengthen their competitive position in knowledge production.

Table 11.4 reveals some major differences between developing countries (medium-low HDI) and developed countries (high-HDI) regarding the most important rationale. A greater percent of developing countries (29%) rank "research" as their number one priority than developed countries (17%). This pattern may well reflect the limited capacity to develop research infrastructure (human, physical, technical) in developing countries. This limitation, in turn, would have policy implications for international development cooperation and academic exchange initiatives between developed and developing countries. It is noteworthy that developed countries rate an "international profile" higher in importance than developing "research capacity" or "academic quality." These rankings may reflect that developed countries see internationalization as providing a more competitive edge than developing countries, who rank research and academic quality higher than improving their international profile.

National University Associations (NUAs) were asked to rank the most important rationales for their member institutions. To "strengthen research and knowledge capacity and production" was clearly seen by NUAs as the most important rationale for their members followed by "to increase student and faculty international knowledge and intercultural understanding." It is interesting to compare the rankings of

NUAs and the HEIs. For instance, 32% of NUAs rank "research" as their number one priority compared to only 21% of HEIs. The other startling difference relates to the ranking to "promotion of curriculum development and innovations," which 8% of HEIs ranked as number one compared to 1% of NUAs. In terms of the priority given to "to diversify income generation," there was only a small difference between NUAs (6%) and HEIs (4%).

National-Level Rationales

Figure 11.2 shows that to "increase competitiveness—scientific, technological and economic" is the top-ranked rationale by HEIs at the national level. It is followed by "to develop strategic alliances—political, cultural, academic, trade"—which, in reality, is closely linked to the competitiveness rationale. It is revealing that to "promote international solidarity and cooperation" is ranked fourth. In fact, twice as many HEIs (28%) ranked "competitiveness" as the number one rationale as opposed to 14% of HEIs who ranked "cooperation" as the number one priority. This finding dramatically illustrates the shift in academic international relations over the last few decades from cooperation to competition. For many HEIs, in both developed and developing countries, the international orientation was grounded in development cooperation through scholarship programs and technical assistance/capacity building projects but this aspect of internationalization seems to be losing importance.

It is interesting to note that, in the current period of increased regionalization of higher education, only 7% of HEIs ranked as the top priority "regional priorities and integration." The same is true for the low response rate given to "cultural awareness and understanding," although it is slightly higher than regional priorities. Finally, contrary to the expectation of many, "to strengthen the education export industry" is also ranked by only 7% of HEIs as the most important national level rationale. Yet, it is worth noting that more HEIs perceived a higher priority at the national level to education exports/income generation (7%) than at the institutional level (4%).

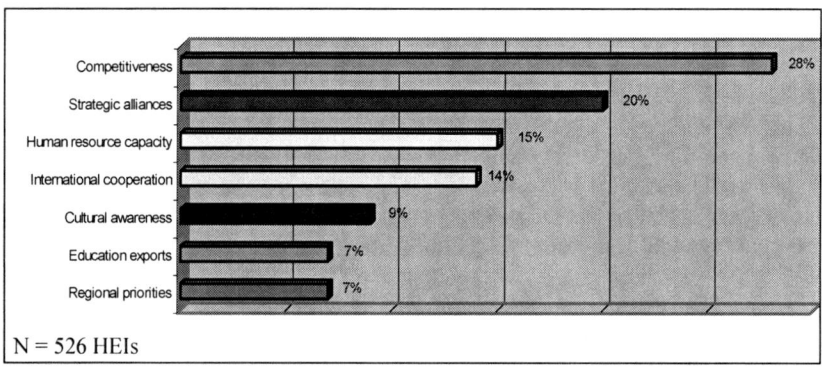

Figure 11.2. Ranking by HEIs of the most important rationale at the national level

From a regional perspective, it is interesting to see in Table11.5 that more HEIs in Europe (31%) and Latin America and the Caribbean (30%) rank "competitiveness" as the top rationale than in the Asia Pacific (26%) and North America (24%). The results from Latin America/Caribbean are somewhat surprising, raising the question whether this ranking may be more of a perception by the HEIs within the region than by HEIs outside the region. The opposite is true for Europe. New EU initiatives, coupled with the Bologna goal of "increased attractiveness" make it clear to HEIs around the world that European HEIs want to be seen as competitive (usually framed in terms of "attractiveness"), especially in relation to HEIs from the United States.

Internationalization as a tool to "build a country's human resource capacity" ranks as the first rationale by more institutions in the Middle East (32%) and Africa (22%). It may have been expected that more African HEIs would rank "human resource capacity" as their country's number one reason to internationalize, but the realities of brain drain and the political will to invest in human capital may have influenced the responses.

The Human Development Index (Table 11.6) level of analysis sheds some of the most interesting light on the perceived importance of national rationales by HEIs. It is striking that the difference is insignificant between developed and developing countries with respect to the ranking of "competitiveness" and "international cooperation and solidarity." This finding is contrary to the expectation that developing

Table 11.5. Regional ranking by HEIs of rationales at national level

Rationale at National Level	Overall Ranking	Africa	Asia and Pacific	Europe	Latin America and Caribbean	Middle East	North America
Increase competitiveness	28%	19%	26%	31%	30%	23%	24%
Strategic alliances	20%	20%	17%	21%	14%	20%	20%
Build human resource capacity	15%	22%	19%	12%	23%	32%	15%
International cooperation and solidarity	14%	18%	16%	14%	13%	14%	15%
Further cultural awareness and understanding	9%	6%	6%	8%	3%	4%	17%
Contribute to regional priorities and integration	7%	13%	6%	7%	14%	6%	4%
Strengthen education export industry	7%	2%	11%	7%	3%	1%	5%

CHAPTER ELEVEN

Table 11.6. Ranking of national rationales by HEIs according to HDI category

Rationale at National Level	Overall Ranking	Low-Medium HDI Countries	High HDI Ccountries
Competitiveness	28%	**25%**	**29%**
Strategic alliances	20%	16%	**21%**
Building human resource capacity	15%	**24%**	12%
International solidarity	14%	14%	15%
Further cultural awareness and understanding	9%	5%	10%
Contribute to regional priorities and integration	7%	11%	5%
Strengthen education export industry	7%	5%	8%

countries would rank international cooperation and solidarity higher. In fact, the ordinate rankings reveal that HEIs from developed countries rank international solidarity in third place while HEIs in developing countries rank it lower in fourth place. One explanation might be related to the fact that developing countries put much more emphasis on "building human resources capacity" and thus rank it second in importance while developed countries give it fourth place.

NUAs were asked to rank the same set of national level rationales. Their rankings did not differ in order of importance from the aggregate group of HEIs. The only notable difference as seen in Figure 11.3 is a higher level of agreement on competitiveness being the most important rationale among the NUAs with 44% of them ranking it as the top priority in contrast to 29% of the HEIs.

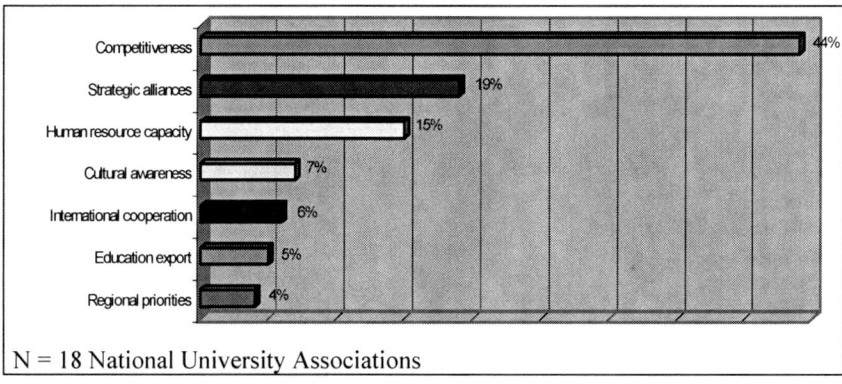

Figure 11.3. NUAs' ranking of most important rationales at the country level

This section has presented and analyzed the results of the survey with respect to the rationales that are driving internationalization at the institutional level and national level. It is important to remember that these are the opinions of the HEIs and the NUAs. Unfortunately, because representatives of national government departments were not surveyed, it is impossible to include their statements about the importance of rationales driving internationalization at the national level. To some degree, the NUAs' perceptions of national-level rationales can be seen as reflecting national priorities. But in reality, NUAs are there to represent the opinions of their members to national government representatives; thus, the key aspect in studying the NUAs' results is to see the similarities and differences between the NUAs and the HEIs.

A comparison with the 2003 IAU survey raises some questions about shifts in rationales. As explained, respondents to the 2003 survey included specific internationalization activities such as "increased mobility for students and teachers" as a rationale. Therefore, a direct line-by-line comparison is difficult, but it is revealing to do a more macro level of analysis. For instance, in 2003 "academic standards and quality" ranked very high in importance, surpassing the three top rationales in the 2005 survey: internationalizing faculty and students, conducting research, and improving the institution's international profile. This raises many questions about why the improvement of "academic quality" as a prime motivation for internationalization fell to fourth place over a two-year period. In 2003, income generation ranked least in importance, which mirrors the findings in 2005. Again, it is important to consider that, of the 66 countries participating in the 2003 survey and the 95 in the 2005 survey, the number of countries where HEIs would rank income generation as the top priority for internationalization is actually very small in number. It is interesting that, in both surveys, the impetus to diversify the source of faculty and students to make the campus more international and multicultural does not rank high in the overall standings for important rationales.

BENEFITS AND RISKS

The diversity of rationales for internationalization is matched by a similar variety of intended and unintended benefits and risks. Benefits are different from, but at the same time linked to, rationales, especially when strategies are carefully chosen to link goals with outcomes and benefits. But there are also major discrepancies between rationales and benefits resulting in unintended benefits and risks. This area merits further exploration.

From a list of nine benefits and a similar list of eight risks, respondents were asked to check those applicable to internationalization and then to rank the three most important ones. The lists of benefits and risks were developed from the answers to the same questions in the 2003 IAU survey. The lists of benefits and risks included in the 2005 IAU survey are included in Table 11.7.

In the 2005 IAU survey, HEIs and NUAs were asked if they thought there were important benefits and risks to internationalization. There is an overwhelming perception (96% of HEI respondents) that internationalization brings benefits to

Table 11.7. List of benefits and risks associated with internationalization

Benefits	**Risks**
More internationally oriented students and staff	Homogenization of curriculum
Improved academic quality	Loss of cultural or national identity
Increased revenue generation	Jeopardize quality of education
Opportunities for brain gain	Growing elitism in access to international education opportunities
Greater international understanding and solidarity	Overuse of English as a medium of instruction
Innovations in curriculum, teaching, and research	Commodification and commercialization of education programs
Foster "national and international citizenship"	Threat of brain drain
Greater diversity of education programs and qualifications	Increase in number of foreign "degree mills" and/or low quality providers
Strengthen research and knowledge production	

higher education, yet this perception is qualified by the report that 70% believe there are also risks associated with the international dimension of higher education. The purpose of this section is examine the benefits that HEIs and NUAs perceive as fundamental to the process of internationalization as well as the risks associated with it.

Analysis of Benefits

Figure 11.4 shows that "international staff and students" and "improved academic quality" are the two benefits seen as most important to HEIs around the world, while the three least important are "national and international citizenship," "revenue generation," and "brain gain."

A number of rationales and benefits were identical—which is not surprising given the obvious link between the two concepts. It is interesting to see in Table 11.8 the high degree of similarity in the ranking of five elements common to both rationales and benefits. Academic quality is one of the exceptions; it ranks fourth in importance as a rationale but second as a benefit. The consistency between "internationalize staff and students" as the number one rationale and benefit is a strong message of its importance, but it also indicates that HEIs are satisfied that the process of internationalization is serving the intending purpose. The same is true for the low ranking given to "income generation." It is not seen as a key rationale or as a primary benefit.

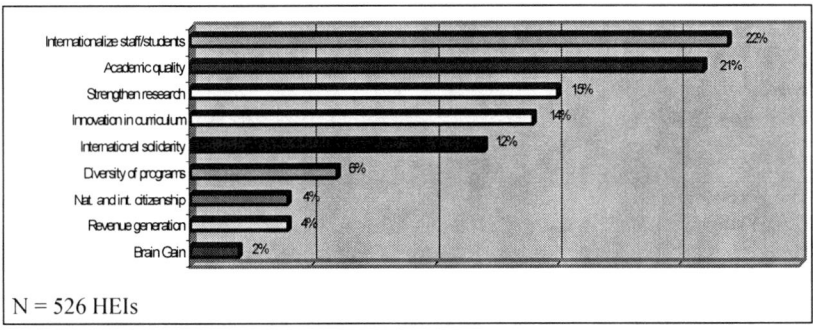

Figure 11.4. Aggregate HEIs ranking of most important benefits

It is difficult to speculate whether this degree of consistency between rationales and benefits will remain over the next few years. However, in the meantime it is good news for policymakers and funders as it demonstrates a strong link between articulated rationales or purposes and the actual benefits.

Regional differences in the perception of benefits are illustrated in Table 11.9. Of interest, is the high ranking given to "academic quality" in both Africa and Latin America/Caribbean. The benefit "to foster national and international citizenship" is generally ranked quite low, but it is noteworthy that substantially more HEIs in North America ranked it as an important benefit than in any other region of the world. "Revenue generation" also has an overall low ranking, but more HEIs in the Asia Pacific see it as both an important rationale and benefit. "Brain gain" ranks lowest for the majority of the regions, except the Middle East where it is ranked higher in importance than "national or international citizenship" and "revenue generation."

Table 11.8. Consistency between driving rationales and derived benefits

Rationale	Rank	Rank	Benefit
Internationalize staff and students	1	1	Internationalize staff and students
Improve research capacity	2	2	Improved academic quality
International profile	3	3	Strengthen research
Academic quality	4	4	Innovation in curriculum
Diversity of faculty and students	5	5	International solidarity
Curriculum innovation	6	6	Diversity of programs
Revenue generation	7	7	National and international citizenship
		8	Revenue generation
		9	Brain gain

CHAPTER ELEVEN

Table 11.9. Regional HEI ranking of most important benefits

Benefits of Internationalization	**Overall Ranking**	Africa	Asia and Pacific	Europe	Latin American and Caribbean	Middle East	North America
More internationally oriented students and staff	**22%**	10%	20%	24%	12%	12	25%
Improved academic quality	**21%**	29%	17%	22%	35%	20%	18%
Strengthen research and knowledge production	**15%**	8%	15%	14%	18%	19%	11%
Innovation in curriculum, teaching and research	**14%**	29%	12%	16%	14%	27%	12%
Greater international cooperation and solidarity	**12%**	13%	14%	10%	11%	8%	9%
Greater diversity of education programs and qualifications	**6%**	4%	8%	5%	5%	6%	6%
Foster "national and international citizenship"	**4%**	2%	5%	3%	2%	0%	13%
Increased revenue generation	**4%**	2%	8%	4%	0%	1%	4%
Brain gain	**2%**	3%	1%	2%	3%	7%	2%

Attention needs to be directed to the gap between developing countries and developed countries in terms of the importance they attribute to the benefit of "more internationally oriented students and staff." This rationale ranks first in importance for high-HDI countries but fourth for medium and low HDI countries. (See Table 11.10.) The developing countries put more emphasis on the benefits of "academic quality," "research," and "curriculum," which are fundamental elements of any HEI. One possible interpretation for the developing countries' rankings may be their assumption that these elements need to be firmly in place with a strong international dimension before it is possible to reap the benefits of more internationally oriented students and staff.

Interestingly enough, there is no difference in the rankings between the HDI categories with respect to "brain gain" as a primary benefit. One might have expected developed countries to see internationalization as bringing more benefits in terms of bright foreign students and promising faculty members or researchers. There are active campaigns in developed countries to attract the best and brightest to augment national brain power or to replace retiring faculty. On the other hand, there is a difference with respect to the benefit of "increased revenue generation," which is not surprisingly higher for developed countries.

A GLOBAL SURVEY ON HIGHER EDUCATION

Table 11.10. HDI ranking by HEIs of most important benefits

Benefits of Internationalization	Overall Ranking	Med-Low HDI Countries	High HDI Countries
More internationally oriented students and staff	22%	15%	28%
Improved academic quality	21%	25%	17%
Strengthen research and knowledge production	15%	17%	14%
Innovation in curriculum, teaching, and research	14%	16%	12%
Greater international cooperation and solidarity	12%	14%	10%
Greater diversity of education programs and qualifications	6%	7%	5%
Foster "national and international citizenship"	4%	2%	6%
Increased revenue generation	4%	2%	6%
Brain gain	2%	2%	2%

Once again, the NUAs' ranking of benefits differs significantly from that of the HEIs. (See Figure 11.5.) For instance, only 14% of NUAs believe that "internationalizing students/staff" is the most important benefit; in contrast, 22% of HEIs rank it first in importance. This difference merits further exploration. HEIs form the major constituency of NUAs; and a deeper understanding of why senior leaders in the HEIs see internationalization benefits so differently than senior leaders of NUAs is a finding that requires follow-up analysis. More NUAs (9%) see "revenue generation" as an important benefit than HEIs (4%).

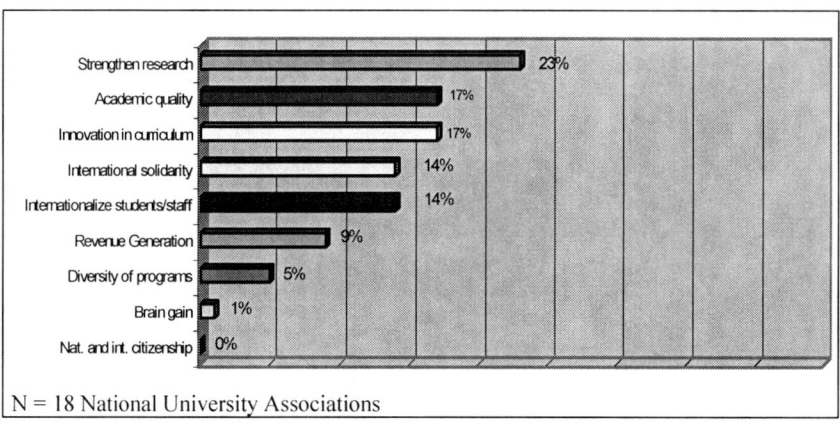

Figure 11.5. NUAs' ranking of most important benefits

CHAPTER ELEVEN

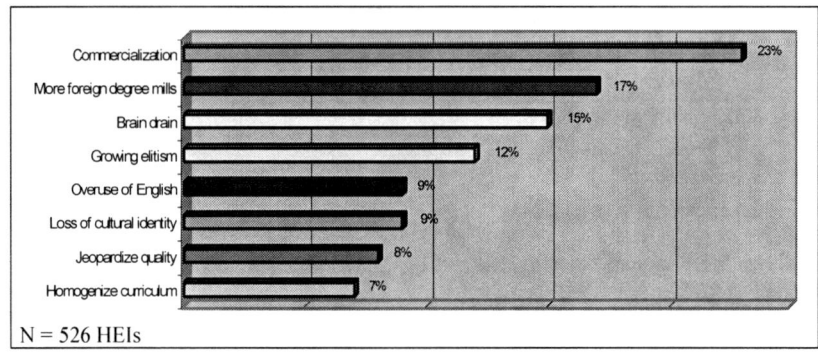

Figure 11.6. HEI aggregate ranking of most important risks

Analysis of Risks

As illustrated in Figure 11.6, "commercialization of higher education," "foreign degree mills," and the threat of "brain drain" rank as the three most imminent risks associated with internationalization, according to HEIs. Of notable interest is that the "overuse of English" is seen as a greater danger than putting quality at risk. It is difficult to do a direct comparison between the 2003 and 2005 surveys, as neither commercialization nor degree mills were included in the early survey. Nevertheless, in 2003 "brain drain" was ranked as the first risk and "cultural identity" as the second.

Worth noting is which regions of the world believe that internationalization does, in fact, come with major risks. Figure 11.7 shows that 81% of the responding HEIs in Africa, versus only 58% of the HEIs in North America identified the existence of risks. This difference is probably closely linked to the nature of risks. "Commercialization" and "brain drain" rank in the top three risks, and it seems likely that more African HEIs are vulnerable to these threats than HEIs in North America.

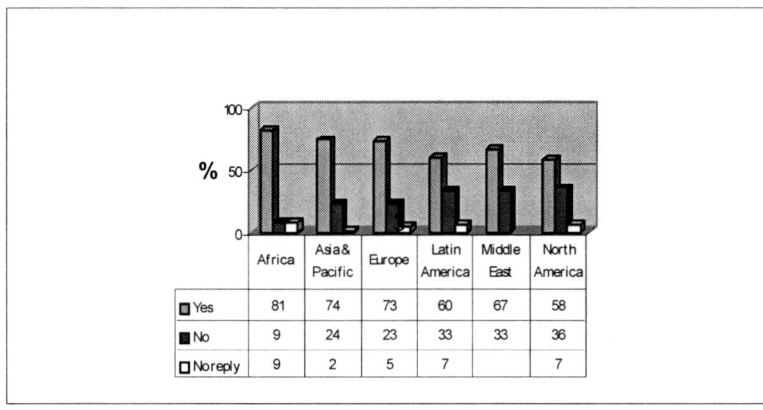

Figure 11.7. Regional ranking by HEIs of existence of risks

Table 11.11. Regional HEI ranking of most important risks

Risks of Internationalization	Overall Ranking	Africa	Asia/ Pacific	Europe	Latin American and Caribbean	Middle East	North America
Commodification and commercialization	**23%**	21%	26%	21%	16%	23%	24%
Increase in foreign degree mills	**17%**	17%	21%	14%	14%	11%	22%
Brain drain	**15%**	21%	9%	15%	22%	21%	10%
Elitism	**12%**	8%	12%	11%	17%	5%	18%
Overuse of English	**9%**	2%	4%	13%	3%	8%	8%
Loss of cultural identity	**9%**	12%	10%	7%	17%	32%	1%
Jeopardize quality	**8%**	7%	18%	8%	2%	0%	5%
Homogenization of curriculum	**7%**	0%	5%	9%	9%	1%	6%

Table 11.11 presents the regional analysis of the importance of risks. Latin America/Caribbean stand out as being somewhat different from the rest of the regions as respondents in those locales ranked "commodification and commercialization" lower in importance than "brain drain," "elitism," and "loss of cultural identity." This may be related to the fact that private education at the domestic level is a fundamental and long-term part of higher education provision; and to date, crossborder for-profit education is less prevalent there than in other regions of the world. In the 2003 IAU survey, Latin America/Caribbean ranked "cultural identity and awareness" as the greatest benefit of internationalization but, at the same time, at greatest peril. While the issue of culture has diminished in importance over the past two years, there is some consistency between the two surveys for Latin America/Caribbean.

For the Middle East, "loss of cultural identity" is definitely the number one risk. As the international dimension of higher education increases over the next three years in the Middle East, it will be enlightening to track the changes in risks and benefits and to determine whether the majority of growth in international relations is within the region or whether it is broader and includes other parts of the world.

Both developing and developed countries identified the "commodification and commercialization of higher education" as the number one risk. (See Table 11.12). This finding is revealing as the general opinion holds that developed countries are more active in buying and selling education across borders—yet still see this area as the greatest risk. It is not a surprise that "brain drain" is ranked as the second risk for developing countries but much lower for developed ones. Of particular interest is the diversity among the regions in their respective rankings of "loss of cultural identity."

Table 11.12. HDI ranking by HEIs of most important risks

Risks of Internationalization	**Overall Ranking**	*Med-Low HDI Countries*	*High HDI Countries*
Commodification and commercialization	**23%**	22%	24%
Increase in foreign "degree mills"	**17%**	13%	21%
Brain drain	**15%**	19%	11%
Elitism	**12%**	11%	13%
Overuse of English	**9%**	6%	12%
Loss of cultural identity	**9%**	17%	2%
Jeopardize quality	**8%**	5%	9%
Homogenization of curriculum	**7%**	7%	8%

INSTITUTIONAL POLICY/STRATEGY

Progress toward integrating the international dimension into a HEI and ensuring its sustainability is a key indicator of the status attributed to internationalization. In fact, the degree of implementation of an institution-wide policy/strategy can demonstrate whether the priority given to internationalization is rhetoric or reality. Thus, both the 2003 and 2005 IAU surveys asked HEIs questions related to the existence of a internationalization policy/strategy in their own institution. Finding words that have a similar meaning in over 100 countries is always a challenge when designing a questionnaire. The analysis of the 2003 IAU survey results showed that internationalization policy and strategy were the two most common terms to describe a plan for integrating an international dimension into the mission, vision, and functions of an institution. Based on this finding, both terms were used in the 2005 IAU survey.

It is encouraging, yet perhaps somewhat surprising, that 82% of the respondents have an internationalization policy in place at their institution. (See Figure 11.8). While this finding seems higher than expected, it may be explained by the fact that HEIs who responded to this survey were already predisposed toward internationalization and thus may have moved forward in developing such a strategy. It also reflects the maturation and priority given to internationalization. In the 2003 IAU survey, 63% of the respondents indicated that an internationalization policy/strategy was in place at their institution. Therefore, the two years between 2003 and 2005 saw an increase of 19% in the number of HEIs with an internationalization policy/strategy. Whether this is due to a larger and broader sample size or to the fact that

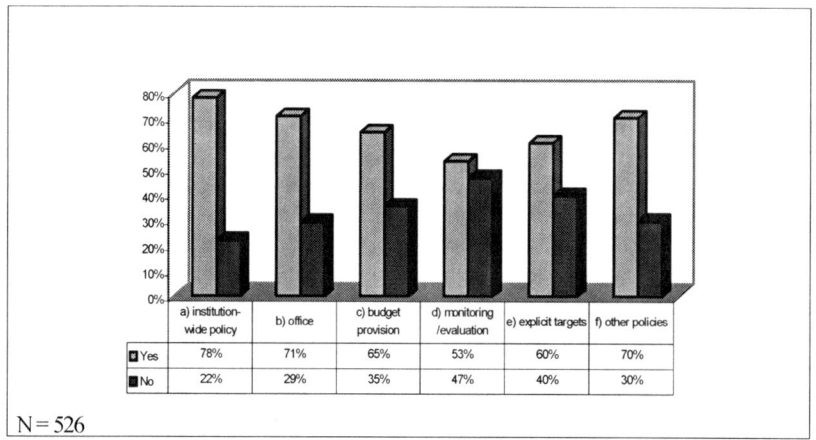

Figure 11.8. Implementation of policy/strategy.

more institutions are developing explicit internationalization plans, the jump is significant and therefore merits closer examination.

The regional analysis also presents some surprises. For instance, a larger number of North American HEIs (21%) indicated the absence of a policy/strategy than those in the Asia Pacific (9%), Europe (12%), Latin America (13%) and Africa (16%). While there is there no concrete information to explain this finding, one possible explanation is the rather high prevalence of a decentralized approach to university management in North America. It will be interesting to monitor changes over the next review period, especially with regard to the Middle East, which had a significantly lower number of HEIs without an internationalization strategy and also the highest "no reply" rate.

Implementing the Internationalization Policy/Strategy

To determine whether the policy/strategy was more than a "paper only" commitment to internationalization, HEIs were asked a series of questions related to the degree of implementation of the policy: (a) Is the policy/strategy institute-wide? (b) Is there an office that oversees the implementation? (c) Is there budgetary provision for implementation? (d) Is there a monitoring/evaluation framework to assess progress? (e) Does the strategy include explicit targets/benchmarks? (f) Is the international dimension included in other university policies/strategies/plans?

The majority (78%) of respondents report that their institutional policy covers the whole institution. This is an increase from the 66% of respondents in 2003 who indicated that the internationalization policy was institution wide. This finding illustrates a definite trend toward developing a policy that applies to all academic and related administrative departments. It was only a decade ago when the norm was that individual colleges, faculties, or departments developed a plan just for their own unit. One can assume that the development of an institution-wide policy has been a bottom-up process in some HEIs and a top-down process in others. Whatever the process used, it is remarkable that almost eight out of 10 HEIs responding to the survey have a comprehensive internationalization policy in place and, furthermore, that seven out of 10 have a designated office to oversee the implementation. The real question, of course, is whether the policy is more than a paper commitment and whether the office is sufficiently supported to be able to do a comprehensive implementation of the plan. Thus, the survey asked more specific questions about budget provision, monitoring, and evaluation frameworks. The percentage of HEIs with a budget dedicated to the implementation of the strategy is lower at 65%, but this figure is 14% higher than in 2003. This upward trend is another indication that HEIs are taking internationalization seriously. It is noteworthy that the results from both the 2005 and 2003 survey question about having an evaluation system in place show that only 53% are systematically monitoring the strengths, weaknesses, and progress of the policy/strategy implementation. The fact that there was absolutely no increase in this figure over the two-year span is telling, especially when compared to the increases noted for the other aspects of implementation.

A new factor, that of setting explicit targets to mark progress, was introduced into the 2005 survey. Sixty percent of the HEIs responded positively to this question. This is very curious given that only 53% indicated that they had an evaluation process established. It appears that some institutions have established benchmarks without having a more complete evaluation system in place. Finally, it is important to address the finding that 70% of the institutions had integrated an international element into other institutional-level policies. This is a key consideration in determining how pervasive, and eventually how sustainable, the international dimension is. Respondents were not asked to provide examples of the other policies, but the most common include research, student services, human resources, marketing, curriculum review, and sometimes faculty tenure and promotion.

At the regional level, the questions that yielded the greatest difference among regions included whether budgetary provision and a monitoring framework existed. Over 70% of HEIs in North America and the Asia Pacific have earmarked budget provisions for internationalization. It is somewhat surprising that only 63% of European respondents indicate the availability of funding, but perhaps this response is influenced by the fact that substantial funding of internationalization initiatives comes from sources external to the institution, notably the European Commission.

The Asia Pacific is the leader in terms of the number (68%) of HEIs that have established a monitoring framework—a sharp contrast to North America, the Middle East, and Africa where fewer than 43% of HEIs have an evaluation system in place. Europe is also surprisingly low, with only about half (53%) of HEIs reporting the existence of a framework to monitor implementation strategies. Those HEIs without such a framework may find that they are not achieving the results they expect and that their investment and interest in internationalization may not be sustainable in the medium to long term.

Obstacles to Implementing the Policy/Strategy

Putting the internationalization policy/strategy into practice presents many challenges to HEIs. It is common to hear about barriers and frustrations related to the implementation process. Based on the obstacles that HEIs identified in the 2003 IAU survey, nine different obstacles were included in the 2005 IAU survey and respondents were asked to rank the level of importance for each one. Table 11.13 presents the ordinate ranking from high (1) to low (6) of the importance of each obstacle.

Lack of faculty interest and involvement ranked as the most important obstacle. This is a significant and troublesome finding as faculty members are usually thought of as the "engine" for internationalization. In fact, it is striking to see that issues related to the staffing (interest, involvement, expertise, recognition) and leadership ranked higher than financial and material resources at the institutional and national levels. This finding has major implications for human resource development policies in HEIs in terms of hiring, promotion, tenure, professional development, and recognition.

Table 11.13. Obstacles to implementing internationalization

Obstacles	Ordinate Ranking
Lack of faculty interest and involvement	1
Administrative inertia or bureaucratic difficulties	2
Limited experience and expertise of staff to implement internationalization plan.	2
Lack of policy/strategy to guide the process	3
International work not recognized for promotion or tenure	3
Little recognition or interest in internationalization by senior leaders	4
Absence of financial and material resources and support at institutional level	4
Competing priorities for time and resources in the institution	5
Lack of financial support from the national level	6

One point of confusion is the high ranking attributed to the "lack of policy/ strategy to guide the process." It seems to contradict the finding that 78% percent of HEIs responding to the survey had a strategy/policy in place and were making progress in the implementation in terms of having an office and budgetary provision to guide the process. It is difficult to provide an explanation for this apparent contradiction, especially when the same person completed both questions. One possible interpretation is that, while a policy/strategy does exist, it may be too generic—and perhaps even more of a marketing tool—to be an effective plan or guide for what can be a rather complicated internationalization process. This proposed explanation is speculation only. The next survey, to be conducted in 2008, will try to shed some light on this finding.

CHAPTER ELEVEN

ELEMENTS OF AN INTERNATIONALIZATION STRATEGY

The 2005 IAU survey included a list of 17 different internationalization elements that would likely be part of an institutional internationalization policy/strategy. (See Table 14.) Respondents were asked to indicate which of the elements were part of their policy/strategy and which elements their HEI was actively involved in. The results of the aggregated analysis show that there was a high level of convergence between these two aspects, indicating that the institutional policies are directly linked to, and most probably influence, the major internationalization activities engaged in by the institution. This is yet another indication that the policy/strategies are more than only a "paper commitment" or reality.

The ranking from most frequently used strategy (1) to least frequent (17) shows that "international institutional agreements/networks" is the most common element, followed by "outgoing mobility opportunities for students" and "international research collaboration." In fact, the top five most common elements are fairly consistent with observers' perceptions of the current practice of internationalization. What is not expected is the low ranking given to distance education, since it was identified as one of the fastest-growing aspects of internationalization in the 2003 IAU survey. Crossborder mobility of programs (twinning, franchising, articulation) and the establishment of branch campuses were the least common elements. This pattern would not be the case in some countries which are very active in exporting education, such as Australia, the United States, the United Kingdom, and New Zealand. Yet when the results of 95 different countries are taken into account, it is confirmed that these are not priority internationalization activities or an important part of the institutional policy/strategy.

This same list of internationalization elements or activities has been used in several survey questions to compare and contrast the importance, rate of growth, and existence of a policy related to each of the elements. (See Table 11.14.)

GROWTH AREAS AND GEOGRAPHIC PRIORITIES

There is no doubt that higher education is undergoing significant changes both domestically and internationally in terms of access, financing, mode of delivery, quality, providers, accreditation, and its role in society. The international dimension is influenced by all these changes and is itself an agent of change. The purpose of this section is to focus on areas of change that HEIs are both experiencing and anticipating in the international dimension of higher education. To ensure some consistency in the analysis between the current state of affairs in HEIs and the anticipated changes, respondents were asked to rank the same list of internationalization elements used in the discussion on institutional policy.

Growth Areas

Survey recipients were asked which aspects of internationalization are expanding most quickly in their institution and also at the national level in their country. The growth areas were exactly the same as the elements of the institutional policy/ strategy. Both the HEI and NUA surveys included this question to allow comparison of the different perspectives. Table 11.14 summarizes all the data related to this question. The HEI information is broken down into institutional and national levels, then further divided into aggregated level of analysis and HDI category. In a completely separate column are the aggregated data for the NUAs.

The convergence of all levels of analysis is remarkable. It is fair to say that there is consensus that the three areas of current and expected growth are: (a) international institutional agreements/networks, (b) outgoing mobility opportunities for students, and (c) international research collaboration. The recruitment of fee-paying students

Table 11.14. Most common elements of internationalization policy/strategy

Element of Internationalization Policy/Strategy	Ordinate Ranking of Most Common Element
International institutional agreements/networks	1
Outgoing mobility opportunities for students	2
International research collaboration	3
Outgoing mobility opportunities for faculty/staff	4
Visiting international scholars	5
International/intercultural dimension of curriculum	6
Area studies, foreign language, international-focused courses	7
International development projects	8
Recruitment of fee-paying foreign students	9
Joint/double/dual degrees	10
Recruitment of foreign faculty/researchers	11
International/intercultural extracurricular activities	12
Recruitment of non-fee-paying foreign students	13
Liaison with community-based cultural and international groups	14
Distance education	15
Delivery of education programs abroad	16
Establishment of branch campuses abroad	17

CHAPTER ELEVEN

is ranked as the fourth or fifth priority except at the national level for developing countries where it is ranked eighth in importance, coming after outgoing mobility opportunities for staff and development projects.

The areas of growth where there is the greatest divergence are (a) international development projects, (b) recruitment of non-fee-paying foreign students, and (c) visiting international scholars. It is no surprise that developing country HEIs might rank international development projects higher (4) at the national level than developed country HEIs (6), but it is unexpected that NUAs rank them at 11 out 17. In light of the decrease in funding for higher education development projects, perhaps the NUAs assessment is more realistic.

The difference between the rankings of developed and developing countries for the growth of "recruitment of non-fee-paying foreign students" merits close attention. Developing countries rank this area of growth at the institutional level much higher (8) than developing countries (13), and the same pattern holds at the national level. This finding relates to increasing competition to recruit the best and the brightest of students. The competition for students often costs HEIs large sums of money in the form of scholarships and bursaries to cover tuition and living costs, a directly opposite effect from recruiting students for income-generation purposes. Institutions in developing countries are normally not able to afford these costs unless they appropriate development funds; and if that is the case, the support is usually allocated for domestic students, not foreign ones. Therefore, this aspect of internationalization is one that can disadvantage developing countries, as they are often not in a position to subsidize the costs of recruiting international students.

This same line of reasoning is true for "visiting international scholars." Once again, developed country HEIs rank it higher than HEIs in developing countries, as the former are able to self-finance these activities. It will be interesting to monitor this aspect of internationalization in the future, as the North-South and South-South networks among HEIs are expanding rapidly and they often include a student and staff mobility component.

Another growth area worthy of examination is the "delivery of education programs abroad." NUAs ranked this area as sixth in future growth, but HEIs in general ranked it much lower at 14. This discrepancy between NUAs and HEIs (from both developed and developing) countries is striking. Is it a case where the NUAs are not reflecting the realities or the perspectives of their member institutions?

Finally, it is telling that all responding HEIs see "the establishment of branch campuses abroad" as the one of the three areas least likely to grow. Once again, the NUAs rank it higher at 12. This finding is further evidence that the growth of satellite campuses abroad is not a widespread phenomenon among the 95 countries participating in this survey. Rather, it is an area of growth for a selected group of HEIs in a small number of countries including Australia, the United Kingdom, the United States, India, and to a lesser extent New Zealand, China, Canada, and a few western European countries like Germany and France. (See Table 11.15.)

Table 11.15. Growth areas of internationalization by ordinate ranking of importance

Area of Growth	HEIs						NUAs
	Institutional Level			National Level			
	Total	HDI Med-low	HDI High	Total	HDI Med-low	HDI High	Total
International institutional agreements/networks	1	1	2	3	1	3	2
Outgoing mobility opportunities for students	2	3	1	2	3	1	3
International research collaboration	3	2	3	1	2	2	1
Recruitment of fee-paying foreign students	4	5	4	4	8	4	4
International/intercultural dimension of curriculum	5	6	5	6	9	5	5
Outgoing mobility opportunities for faculty/staff	6	4	6	7	5	8	9
Joint/double/dual degrees	7	9	7	8	7	9	8
International development Projects	8	8	9	5	4	6	11
Recruitment of non-fee-paying foreign students	9	13	8	9	14	7	7
Visiting international scholars	10	7	10	10	6	13	14
Area studies, foreign language, international focused courses	11	11	11	13	11	14	13
Distance education	12	10	14	12	10	11	10
Recruitment of foreign faculty/researchers	13	12	12	14	12	12	15
Delivery of education programs abroad	14	17	13	11	16	10	6
International/intercultural extracurricular activities	15	14	15	16	15	16	16
Establishment of branch campuses abroad	16	16	16	15	17	15	12
Liaison with community-based cultural and international groups	17	15	15	17	13	17	17

From a regional perspective as illustrated in Table 11.15, it is fascinating that the European HEIs have identified "outgoing opportunities of faculty/staff" as the number one area of growth. None of the other regions placed this topic in their top three. The second interesting finding is that the Middle East is the only region that has identified the international/intercultural dimension of curriculum as the third most important area of growth. Finally, the Asia Pacific region stands out in ranking "recruitment of fee-paying foreign students" as the second most important growth area. This placement is consistent with the fact that more HEIs in the Asia Pacific

CHAPTER ELEVEN

Table 11.16. Growth of internationalization at the institutional level by region

Growth of Internationalization Elements at the Institutional Level	Overall Ranking	Africa	Asia/ Pacific	Europe	Latin America and Caribbean	Middle East	North America
International institutional agreements/ networks	1	1	1	3	1	1	2
Outgoing mobility opportunities for students	2	3		2	3		1
International research collaboration	3	2	3		2	2	3
Recruitment of fee-paying foreign students	4		2				
International/ intercultural dimension of curriculum	5					3	
Outgoing mobility opportunities for faculty/staff	6			1			

region ranked income generation as the most important rationale than in any other region. (See Table 11.16).

Geographic Priorities

Geographic priorities are an important aspect of internationalization in terms of both on-campus and crossborder activities. The 2003 and 2005 respondents were asked to indicate the top three geographic regions for internationalization activities. It is revealing to study the significant changes in geographic priorities during the last two years.

Europe is seen as the most attractive, or perhaps most important, region of the world in terms of international education activities and studies, as 37% of HEIs ranked it in first place. It is true that this finding could be highly influenced by the large number of respondents from Europe; however, the regional-level analysis also provides supports. Overall, the Asia Pacific was ranked second at 24%, followed by North America at 19%. It may come as a surprise to the United States that North America was seen as the third-favored region for internationalization activities. There is much speculation on the reasons behind this ranking, including the positive benefits of the Bologna Process in increasing the attractiveness of Europe and the negative impact of terrorism and security measures in the United States. The United States is highlighted in this case because it is clearly the most important country in North America in terms of recruiting foreign students and scholars and for its international image.

The analysis of geographic priorities is more intriguing and revealing when examined at the regional level. (See Table 11.17.) The first observation is that Europe is the only region that ranked as first or second across all six regions. One may ask whether this high ranking results from the European Commission's policies and funded programs which are aimed at increasing the international recognition and participation of the European higher education sector. The importance attributed to Europe is significantly different from North America. North America appeared only once in the top two rankings and, even then, was tied with Europe for second place by the HEIs in the Asia Pacific.

Of particular interest is the fact that four of the six regions ranked their own region as their top priority, evidence of the importance being given to the current trend of regionalization. Cooperation, collaboration, and competition with HEIs in one's own region seems to be a growing worldwide phenomenon, with the exception of North America. The first priority for North America is tied between Europe and the Asia Pacific followed by Latin America. International activities among the three countries of North America ranked in fourth place.

A comparison of the 2005 regional results with 2003 shows some shifts in priorities. Most noteworthy is that Europe has moved its second-place geographical priority from North America in 2003 to the Asia Pacific in 2005. The significance and sustainability of this shift is yet to be fully understood. Perhaps it is a signal of increasing competitiveness between Europe and North America in terms of international alliances in other parts of the world—especially the Asia Pacific.

There have also been key changes in Latin America priorities. North America fell from a first ranking in 2003 to third in 2005, while Europe remained in second place over the two years. However, the biggest change in Latin America was the importance that HEIs gave to their own region as it jumped from number three in 2003 to first place in 2005. One can question whether many of the efforts to develop a Latin American community of higher education are now being recognized and having an impact on the importance of intraregional cooperation.

Both Africa and the Middle East ranked very low for all regions except their own. In the case of Africa, it must be asked whether it shows that this continent is not seen as a viable partner in international education alliances and is losing ground because of the low importance being given to international development cooperation/projects. One is hopeful that this trend will be turned around with the renewed international efforts to support Africa and ensure that it is not the forgotten continent. Yet the question remains: Even if the scope and volume of activities increase, will Africa still have a low priority in relation to other more developed regions of the world?

The Middle East is a different story. The international participation and image of the Middle East are growing by leaps and bounds. It is happening at the HEI level and also for government and nongovernmental education bodies. The fact that the

CHAPTER ELEVEN

Table 11.17. Regional-level HEI geographic priorities

Geographic Priority Attributed to	*Overall Ranking*	*Africa*	*Asia/ Pacific*	*Europe*	*Latin America and Caribbean*	*Middle East*	*North America*
Europe	37%	28%	23%	44%	33%	33%	26%
Asia Pacific	24%	7%	44%	22%	3%	10%	26%
North America	19%	13%	23%	18%	27%	20%	12%
Latin America	9%	10%	2%	6%	37%	7%	17%
Africa	7%	39%	2%	6%	0%	8%	9%
Middle East	5%	3%	6%	3%	0%	27%	10%

Middle East is ranked low in importance hides the increase in the amount of new international collaboration and cooperation.

CROSS-CUTTING ANALYSIS AND THEMES

The purpose of this section is to look at the issues that emerged from a cross-cutting analysis of key findings. This type of analysis provides rich insights into connections and disconnections among rationales, benefits, risks, policies, funding, and the growth of several key aspects of internationalization. More importantly, such analysis raises new questions about the opportunities and challenges that higher education practitioners, professionals, policymakers, and researchers need to address as the process of internationalization evolves and responds to societal changes and the forces of globalization.

Quality

The issue of quality appeared in many of the survey questions and is one of the most interesting topics to examine as there are several findings which give mixed messages. In terms of the overall rankings of institutional level rationales, "contributing to academic quality" was ranked fourth out of seven by HEIs and fifth by NUAs. These rankings are markedly lower than the importance given to "quality" as a means of improving internationalization in the 2003 IAU survey. Even more curiously, "quality" ranked below "to create an international profile and reputation," which occupied third place. The growing importance of the international dimension for domestic and global branding has been noticeable in the last few years but it is a surprise that, overall, "profile" has now surpassed "quality" as a motivator for internationalization at the institutional level. This new prominence is particularly meaningful when the importance of "profile" is linked with "competitiveness," which respondents ranked as the top rationale at the national level. Does it mean that quality is less important than profile and branding for national competitiveness? Obviously, profile and quality are closely connected, but this finding raises new questions. It must be noted that the Middle East and Latin America are exceptions; both regions ranked quality higher than profile as the leading reason to internationalize.

The survey findings demonstrate a strong convergence between rationales and benefits. This news is welcome, as it suggests a close connection between outcomes and motivations/expectations. But this finding does not necessarily apply to quality. HEI respondents indicated that "improvement in quality" was the second most important benefit of internationalization, placing it even higher than "research." This is strong evidence supporting the belief that the international dimension can contribute to the quality of higher education. Yet quality ranked seventh as a rationale. It is interesting to speculate why quality is perceived as a benefit but not as a rationale and to ask whether it is possible to sustain this benefit without articulating it as a goal and putting the appropriate strategies in place.

From a regional perspective, Africa and Latin America ranked quality as the number one benefit. In fact, the low-HDI countries ranked quality as the top benefit, and high-HDI countries ranked it in second place. Clearly, internationalization is perceived as making an important contribution to improving the quality of higher education, especially for developing countries, even if quality is not a key driver and even if quality assurance systems are not in place. Quality is a critical but vulnerable part of internationalization. The question and challenge of how internationalization can contribute to quality without being vigilant about its own process of quality assurance needs to be addressed.

Overall, the 2005 HEI respondents ranked "jeopardize quality of education" as a low-risk factor—seventh out of eight in terms of priority. The Asia Pacific was the only region to rank it higher (third place), perhaps because HEIs in the Asia Pacific reported the highest level of incoming and outgoing academic programs. Developed countries saw the threat to quality as a higher risk than developing countries. This finding is somewhat unexpected, given the controversy surrounding the potential for low-quality programs being imported into developing countries.

The second greatest risk identified by HEIs was the growing presence of "foreign degree mills" or, in other words, organizations that grant fake qualifications. This finding is closely connected to the quality of crossborder education and coincides with the finding that national quality assurance agencies are reported to be one of the most important national-level actors for internationalization. This trend signals a major shift toward increased recognition being given to quality assurance and accreditation at the national level but not necessarily at the institutional level.

One of the most puzzling findings is the high number of HEIs that believe a national quality assurance system exists in their country to monitor the quality of incoming and outgoing programs. The perception is real but the reality is different, as only a handful of countries have established a quality assurance or evaluation system focusing on crossborder education. A possible explanation is that respondents have assumed without checking that, if a national quality assurance agency exists, it must cover international as well as domestic education. This assumption is false, but it may explain why both HEIs and NUAs ranked internationalization's potential to "jeopardize quality of education" as low.

Finally, it is worth noting that only about half of the HEIs that had an internationalization strategy/policy had an evaluation system in place to monitor its implementation. This finding raises questions about the quality control of both domestic and crossborder internationalization initiatives at the institutional level.

In short, when the findings of the survey are collectively analyzed, they raise many new questions and concerns about the rationales, benefits, risks, and role of quality and quality assurance with respect to the internationalization work of HEIs. The question must be asked: Is quality an invisible or underrated problem of internationalization, ready to implode in the near future?

Competitiveness, Cooperation/Competition

There is a great deal of speculation and debate about internationalization and its role in furthering national or institutional competitiveness and promoting international competition or cooperation. Participation in development-related projects, along with various bilateral exchange programs, have historically been an important element of the international work of many HEIs and a symbol of international cooperation and solidarity. The survey therefore included several questions which addressed these issues both directly and indirectly.

The respondents signaled loudly and clearly that, at the national level, the number one rationale (first of seven options) was "competitiveness." More HEIs in Europe and Latin America/Caribbean chose "competitiveness" as the top driver; but altogether, both developing and developed countries ranked it as number one. Competitiveness is linked to, but different from, competition per se. HEIs use a number of different strategies to contribute to national competitiveness, and competition is certainly one of them—but so is cooperation. Networks at the national (and international) levels are good examples of a cooperative strategy for competitive purposes. Inherent in the design of most networks is an element of cooperation so that the collection of HEIs can accomplish what one individual institution cannot. This dynamic should not imply that the primary goal of all networks is to increase competitiveness. Many networks are involved in joint curricula design, exchange of students/faculty, or collaborative research initiatives. But at the same time, many networks are being developed to gain competitive advantage in recruiting international students, winning research contracts, or achieving high international or regional rankings. More respondents to the 2005 IAU survey reported that competitiveness (scientific, technological, or economic) at the national level was the number one rationale which in turn impacts the institution's priorities and activities and their role in contributing to national competitiveness.

"To promote international solidarity and cooperation" has historically been seen as a driving force for international education and thus was listed as another possible rationale at the national level. Overall, HEIs ranked it fourth out of seven—definetely less important than the number one rationale of increased competitiveness. Interestingly, there was little difference between the developing and developed country responses or among the responses of the six regions; they all ranked competitiveness higher than cooperation. The responses from the NUAs were similar; 44% ranked "competitiveness" as their number one motivation versus only 6% who ranked "international solidarity and cooperation" as the top rationale. This finding is concrete evidence of the diminishing role of internationalization as a tool for international solidarity and cooperation, a value that has characterized international academic work of universities for several decades.

Development projects have traditionally been seen as a strategy for such projects of international cooperation and solidarity and were therefore included as one of the 17 elements of internationalization. In terms of anticipated growth, HEIs ranked development work eighth at the institutional level and fifth at the national level. However, NUAs provided a different perspective as they ranked it 11th out of 17 in terms of anticipated future growth. It appears that development projects are not perceived as a high priority in coming years.

Individually and collectively, these findings demonstrate a major shift in emphasis in the internationalization of higher education over the last two decades. Many would attribute this shift to the growing importance of political and economic drivers and the concept of competitiveness at the national level, apparently replacing more social- and academic-oriented values and motivations at the institutional level. This area is one of the most interesting and critical to monitor on a long-term basis, as a gradual and discernible shift seems to be developing. Perhaps a divergence is growing between national-level rationales and those of the individual institutions as discussed in the next section on income generation and the commercialization of higher education.

Income-Generation and Commercialization

Commercialization is one of the current issues attracting the most discussion and controversy in the higher education sector. It is closely linked to the privatization, marketization, and commodification of education, and the larger question of whether education is a public good or private commodity. The 2005 IAU survey introduced several questions related to this issue, but unfortunately, the 2003 survey did not, so comparisons or analysis of trends are not yet possible.

"To diversify income generation" was included as one of seven rationales at the institutional level and "to strengthen the education export industry" was one of seven at the national level. HEIs ranked both these rationales seventh—dead last. This counterintuitive response may raise questions about whether the HEIs were giving "socially desirable" responses. Perhaps, a more accurate explanation may rest on the fact that HEIs from 95 countries responded to this survey, 58 from developing and 37 from developed countries. When all of the responses are tallied, income generation is still not seen as a primary reason to internationalize. Nor is it seen as a primary benefit, being ranked eighth out of nine in terms of benefits. There seems to be little evidence at present that internationalization is seen as a profit-making enterprise for most HEIs. This is not to deny that it is a top priority for some HEIs, but they do not predominate and are limited to probably eight or 10 countries out of 95.

Some regional differences merit further examination. For instance, the Asia Pacific and North America stand out as being the most predisposed to the profit motive, as 6% and 5% of HEIs in those respective regions indicated that income-generation was the main reason to internationalize. In contrast, 3% of European HEIs rated income-generation as a main rationale, 2% for African and Middle East HEIs, and 0.0% percent for Latin America. Overall, very small numbers of HEIs are promoting income-generation as the number one reason to internationalize. In terms of benefits, more HEIs (8%) in the Asia Pacific again placed income-generation as the primary benefit. No country-level analysis has been done, but it is speculated that HEIs in Australia and New Zealand (and perhaps Malaysia and China) are those assigning a high importance to income generation and growing the export industry as both rationale and benefit.

There are differences between developed and developing countries, albeit the numbers are again very small. With regard to rationales, twice as many HEIs in developed countries (4%) than developing countries (2%) put income-generation as its number one rationale. The same is true for benefits, with 6% from high-HDI countries and only 2% from low/medium-HDI countries ranking income-generation benefits in first place. Despite the small numbers, the trend is noteworthy, since even these small numbers probably would not have existed five or 10 years ago. Is it the thin edge of the wedge? It is premature to label these figures as a worldwide trend, but the phenomenon is certainly worthy of close monitoring over the next few years.

"The commercialization and commodification of education" was ranked by both HEIs and NUAs as number one in a list of eight potential risks. There was no appreciable difference between high- and low-HDI countries. The most intriguing finding was that the largest number of HEIs that listed commercialization as the greatest risk came from the Asia Pacific. It is interesting to speculate if this is because of or in spite of the fact that more HEIs in the Asia Pacific reported income generation as the primary reason for and benefit of internationalization. Latin America and the Middle East are the only regions that did not rank "commercialization" as the most important risk. For the Middle East it ranked second after the "loss of cultural identity," and in Latin America it ranked sixth.

In spite of these low rankings on the priority of income generation and the threat of commercialization, HEIs ranked the recruitment of fee-paying students in fourth place for growth areas, and recruiting non-fee-paying students in 11th place. This seems contradictory and shows a major disconnection between the perception of risk and the priorities for growth. Is charging tuition fees to foreign students not a form of commercialization or selling education? It is hard to find a credible explanation for this discrepancy, except that HEIs do not see the recruitment of fee-paying students as an income-generation activity in the same way that they regard the establishment of branch campuses and program franchising as income-generating initiatives. The regional-level analysis for growth shows that HEIs in the Asia Pacific have ranked the recruitment of fee-paying students as a second priority at the institutional level and the first priority at the national level while commercialization and commodification are seen as the greatest risk. In contrast, HEIs in the Middle East have ranked it the least important area of growth.

Another sign of the inconsistency between fee-paying students and the low priority given to income-generation activities is the high number of HEIs that reported the existence of national policies and funding mechanisms for student recruitment. For instance, more HEIs indicated a national policy and the availability of funding for fee-paying students than for non-fee-paying students. National policymakers are evidently sending a message to their HEIs about the importance of recruiting fee-paying students over non-fee-paying students.

Human Capacity Building

The aggregate findings from both the 2003 and 2005 IAU surveys show that the principal reason driving internationalization at the institutional level is "to increase student and faculty international knowledge and intercultural understanding." This emphasis places the focus on human capacity front and center. But there are telling regional differences. HEIs in the Asia Pacific and North America rank this rationale in first place, Europe and Africa in second, and Latin America and the Middle East third. The analysis between developed and developing countries also reveals a divergence as HEIs in high-HDI countries rank this rationale as number one, closely followed by research; but the low/medium-HDI countries overwhelmingly rank "to strengthen research" first and "to increase the international knowledge of student/faculty" as second. National priorities and the level of maturation of the higher education system are key factors influencing these differences. They merit closer examination in the future.

On the topic of human capacity, survey respondents were asked to rank eight rationales at the national level, one of which was "to build the country's human resource capacity." Overall, HEIs ranked this rationale in third place after "increasing competitiveness" and "building strategic alliances." Again there are interesting differences among the regions and between developed/developing countries. Both Africa and the Middle East rank "human resource capacity" as the top priority, while the Asia Pacific and Latin America rank it as number two, and Europe and North America as number three. These differences are not a surprise, but they point out different priorities and expectations which need to be addressed when forging bilateral/multilateral networks and strategic alliances. The different rankings raise the possibilities of conflicting expectations between countries/regions and may help to explain why most regions give first preference to intraregional collaboration, not interregional cooperation.

The relationship between "to internationalize students and faculty" as a rationale and benefit is worthy of further analysis. At the aggregate level, HEIs ranked "developing a more internationalized students and faculty" as the number one benefit and rationale. In terms of the variance between countries by HDI level, it is interesting to note that developed countries ranked this benefit as the most important benefit but developing countries ranked it in fourth place. This shift points to a disconnect between developing countries' stated priority to develop "human capacity" through internationalization and its actual priority as indicated by their lower ranking of it in terms of perceived benefits. It is important to pursue the discrepancy between what developing countries state as driving rationales and their perception of the actual benefits gained through internationalization.

The theme of brain gain/drain is linked to the topic of human resource capacity. Brain gain was one of nine institutional benefits to be ranked; and overall, it placed last. Clearly it is not perceived to be an important benefit by HEIs in developed or developing countries. Nor is it reported as a means to increase human capacity. But perhaps this placement is inevitable given the priority assigned to national competitiveness and the need for bright students and scholars to contribute to a country's cutting-edge research and knowledge production. It will be fascinating to monitor this issue and see if current recruitment strategies that are closely linked to immigration policies in some countries will be seen and reported by HEIs as brain gain strategies, rationales, or benefits. An important question to ask is whether recruitment strategies are a diplomatic and acceptable label for brain-gain activities and whether internationalization is inadvertently or deliberately facilitating this trend.

On the other hand, brain drain was included as one of eight risks and was ranked in third place. Obviously, it is a threat that needs attention. Regional differences in the perception of brain drain risks are enlightening. Africa and Latin America ranked brain drain as the number one risk, which is not a surprise. What is unexpected is that European HEIs rank it number two. It would be interesting to know if the threat of brain drain is seen as intraregional or as external to the European Union. Mobility is one of the cornerstones of the Bologna Process, but does the fostering of mobility create vulnerability to brain drain?

Cultural Identity and Awareness

In the 2003 IAU survey, the risk of "loss of cultural identity" was ranked high by several regions, especially by Latin America. The results of the 2005 IAU survey did not corroborate the 2003 findings. Overall, "loss of cultural identity" ranked low (in sixth place) as did the related issue of "overuse of English." Yet some significant regional differences need to be taken into account. HEIs in the Middle East ranked "loss of cultural identity" as the number one risk, Latin American HEIs ranked it second, and Europe and North America put it last. The difference between low- and high-HDI country responses is also striking. Only 2% of high-HDI countries listed it as a major risk compared to 17% of developing countries. This divergence in opinion is extremely important to monitor, as cultural identity is likely to become a more controversial and critical issue in coming years.

"To further cultural awareness and understanding" was one of the seven national rationales ranked by HEIs. Overall, it placed low at five, but it is intriguing that North America ranked it third in importance and the Asia Pacific ranked it last. The difference between high- and low/medium-HDI countries raises many questions because twice as many HEIs in developing countries ranked it higher than their counterparts in developing countries. It is fair to say that the numbers of HEIs who ranked "cultural awareness" as a rationale or benefit, and the "loss of cultural identity" as a risk are very few, but the divergence between regions and developed/ developing countries is an important finding for future investigation.

The issue of language is closely tied to the question of culture. The "overuse of English" ranked fourth out of seven as a national risk. Thus, it is regarded as a medium-level risk; but when this finding is combined with the related finding that English is the number one preferred language for learning, additional weight can be added to the risk. Both surveys show that English is growing in popularity as a language of instruction and as a foreign language to be learned. Therefore, it is interesting to speculate whether more HEIs will see it as an increasingly important risk.

Research

The responses to a number of different questions in the 2005 IAU survey point to the central role of research in the process of internationalization. For instance, HEIs ranked it a very close second (21%) as the leading rationale, while "to internationalize students and faculty" was rated first, but only by one percentage point (22%). The regional analysis shows that more HEIs in Africa and the Middle East ranked it higher as a reason to internationalize than those in other regions, especially in North America. HEIs ranked research as a benefit third in importance, and NUAs attributed even more weight to it by identifying it as the top benefit of internationalization. These findings substantiate the claim of its critical importance.

Respondents were asked to indicate which elements of internationalization were most important in terms of future growth at the institutional and national levels. Out of 17 elements, research ranked in third place at the institutional level and in first place at the national level. This is a strong endorsement of the central role that research will continue to play in internationalization. At the institutional level, developing countries actually rated it higher than developed countries. This perception may influence development cooperation work in the future.

In response to questions about the existence of national policies and funding for international initiatives, 55% of HEIs reported that both a policy and funding were in place in their country for international research. In fact, research ranked second after student mobility in terms of the frequency of being recognized by both policy and funding. This finding is further testimony to the critical role attributed to research. One of the most unexpected findings in the 2005 IAU survey related to the rating of national actors involved in the promotion and support for internationalization activities. NUAs reported that their departments of science and technology were the most important actors, followed by the departments of education. Assuming that science and technology are supporting international research, this finding provides further evidence of the significance of research and knowledge production for internationalization initiatives.

CHAPTER ELEVEN

Student and Faculty Mobility

The survey findings reinforce the perception that student mobility is currently one of the most popular and best supported internationalization activities for HEIs and that it will continue on this trajectory. Overall, it ranks second (out of 17), for future growth at both the institutional and national levels. This convergence between institutional- and national-level priorities is rare and bodes well for the continued support and growth of outgoing student mobility opportunities. The results from the HDI-level analysis, however, show that, while mobility holds first place for growth in developed countries, it ranks third in developing countries. This difference is often due to financial and language limitations.

Faculty mobility does not enjoy the same priority. As an area of growth, it was ranked sixth (out of 17) at the institutional level and seventh at the national level. Europe stood out as being very different from the other regions; European HEIs ranked faculty mobility as the number one growth area at the institutional level. Middle East HEIs placed faculty mobility in third place at the national level.

The existence of national policies and funding programs is critical; and once again, the findings show that 61% of the HEIs reported national policies to guide student mobility, and 78% reported the availability of some financial support. While it is somewhat disconcerting to see that funding is often available without the guidance of policies, it demonstrates the broad level of support for this internationalization activity. Overall, student mobility ranked higher than faculty mobility in terms of availability of funding and the existence of an internationalization policy.

A system to recognize and facilitate the transfer of credits certainly supports student mobility. Seventy-seven percent of the responding HEIs reported that a credit system was in place in their country, but unfortunately there are no data on its transferability out of the country. It comes as no surprise that 91% of the European HEIs responded positively to the question on the presence of a credit system. This finding is eloquent testimony to the widespread awareness and use of the European credit transfer system, implemented more than 15 years ago through the Erasmus program.

Recognition of qualifications is another factor related to student mobility. Over half of the respondents (54%) reported no problems in analyzing foreign degrees, but 41% did have difficulties. (The remaining 5% did not respond.) There is room for improvement here, but apparently transferring academic credit and recognizing qualifications are not major blocks to student mobility for many countries.

New Forms of Mobility

Student and professor mobility have been hallmarks of international education for centuries. Bilateral/multilateral agreements and development cooperation projects are other traditional forms of international education collaboration. The past 20 years, however, have seen a gradual increase in new forms of academic mobility, including crossborder programs, double degrees, distance education, and satellite campuses. It is no longer just the students who are moving. Traditional public/private universities and new companies are now delivering foreign education programs to students in their own countries using a variety of delivery modes. The 2005 survey included these new delivery arrangements in the list of major internationalization elements, and respondents were asked to indicate the presence of national policies and funding mechanisms to support them and the level of priority they had for future growth. New forms of international collaboration—which include distance education, satellite campuses, satellite program delivery, and double degrees—are generally seen to be lower priorities than networks, outgoing student mobility, recruitment of students and visiting scholars. To date, these forms have not been incorporated into institutional policies/strategies. It is interesting that double degree programs seem to be the most promising new form of collaboration and are ranked even higher than visiting scholars and the recruitment of non-fee-paying international students.

There is a fair degree of consistency between HEIs and NUAs responses for growth at the national level. The two notable exceptions are crossborder program delivery where NUAs are much more optimistic about new developments and the recruiting of foreign scholars to which HEIs give greater priority. Of particular interest is the high importance attributed to networks and the relatively low ranking given to distance education, especially in comparison to the 2003 IAU survey findings.

Curriculum and Campus-Based Activities

A number of factors related to campus-based or "internationalization at home" activities were included in the 2005 IAU survey. The "international/intercultural dimension of curriculum," "research collaboration," and "area and foreign language studies" are three examples of "internationalization at home" elements, even though they also have relevance to "internationalization abroad." There is convincing evidence for the high importance of "international research collaboration," medium-level support for "curriculum," and low priority given to growth of "area studies, extra-curricular activities" and "liaison with local cultural groups." One could argue that these findings indicate that generally more importance is attached to cross-border mobility than to campus-based activities. This finding is true but rather porous as these two aspects of internationalization are very interdependent. Still, it is informative to take a comparative look at the priorities and growth prospects of internationalization abroad and at home.

An analysis of benefits reveals that "innovation in curriculum" is ranked fourth out of eight overall. From a regional perspective, it is noteworthy that HEIs from Africa and the Middle East ranked curriculum in first place as the most important benefit of internationalization. The "homogenization of curriculum" was not seen as a major threat; both developed and developing countries ranked it as a very low risk.

Regional Priorities

One of the responses to globalization has been increased activity, networking, and integration at the regional level. This finding applies to many sectors, including education. Therefore, "to contribute to regional priorities and integration" was included as a rationale at the national level. Overall, HEIs ranked this reason in last place as did the NUAs. Without a doubt, regional interests appear to be a low priority as a motivation for internationalization. Yet interestingly, regional-level actors were ranked higher in importance than international government and nongovernmental actors, but lower than bilateral ones.

When HEIs ranked their geographic priorities, all regions except North America indicated that collaboration within their own region was number one priority. This raises some interesting questions about why intraregional cooperation is so important. Is it because of distance, language, cultural, political, and historical reasons? Second, why is furthering regional interests not considered an important reason or outcome of the international dimension of higher education when it is for several other sectors?

It is intriguing to look at the results from Latin America as it appears that HEIs in that region have a different view of regional interests. Respondents from Latin America ranked "regional priorities and integration" as the third most important rationale driving internationalization at the national level. They also ranked "loss of cultural identity" as a high risk in both the 2003 and 2005 IAU surveys. Regional issues, connections, and culture appear to play a more important role for internationalization in Latin America than in other parts of the world, including Europe where there is a strong focus on Europeanization.

ISSUES TO BE ADDRESSED

Respondents were asked to express in their own words what they thought were aspects of internationalization that required further attention. The response to this open-ended question was overwhelming both in volume and diversity. A review of the identified issues illustrates the enormous breadth and depth of concerns and challenges facing the very complex process of internationalization. It is impossible to list all of the points raised, but the following sections include those aspects that were mentioned most frequently or that were particularly interesting. It must be added that a list oversimplifies the multi-faceted nature of these issues, but the list's primary purpose is to show the full range of concerns that were raised. The issues that transcended the six regions and were most frequently mentioned include:

- Providing quality assurance and accreditation systems at the national level for domestic and international education
- Defining the role of government in terms of the development and coordination of a national internationalization strategy
- Increasing external funding sources for student mobility, development projects, and research
- Developing curriculum with an international and intercultural dimension
- Devising better systems for the recognition of qualifications
- Finding solutions to visa issues for international students

- Providing financial support for research collaboration
- Dealing with institutional implications from increased student and faculty mobility.

A number of new points were raised and/or existing issues were given a renewed emphasis:

- The establishment and accreditation of double degree programs
- The need for regional credit transfer system
- More foreign language teaching
- Prevention of brain drain
- Training institutional personnel to work on the international dimension
- Incentive programs to keep or attract foreign nationals
- The security of students studying abroad
- Intercultural training for students and faculty
- Appropriate marketing strategies to increase the institution's international profile
- Recognition of international work in faculty promotion and tenure schemes
- The use and evaluation of distance education program delivery
- Loss of national language and cultural identity.

The issues that are emerging in relation to new aspects of internationalization include:

- Immigration problems related to recruiting new faculty, researchers, and graduate students
- The removal of trade barriers to allow greater access to new education markets
- How to find appropriate international partner institutions and criteria for selection
- Linking international education to national immigration, economic development, and trade plans
- Financial and risk analysis of crossborder program delivery
- The registration and quality assurance of new types of private education providers
- Issues of intellectual copyright for joint research and curriculum development
- Labor licenses for foreign faculty
- Income generation from exporting education programs and training.

Unexpected questions addressed the following points:

- The promotion and export of such Bologna Process reforms as three cycles
- The development of experts to deal with legal issues of crossborder and commercial education
- The commercial export of program curriculum (but not the teaching)

Issues at a more macro or conceptual level include:

- The impact of internationalization on university autonomy

CHAPTER ELEVEN

- Preserving the "public good" approach in international education
- Keeping a balance between cultural diversity and local values/norms
- Appraising the benefits and risks of international accreditation practices
- The impact of crossborder education delivery on affordability and access.

In summary, the findings from the 2005 IAU survey paint a relatively positive picture in terms of the sustained importance attributed to internationalization and the increase in the number of HEIs that have moved from an ad hoc approach to internationalization activities toward greater planning. The picture is less encouraging at the national level. In the open-ended questions, respondents from all regions reported that national governments are giving inadequate attention to international education and do not play the role that they should in terms of setting national policy and providing funding to facilitate international research, mobility, and development projects, and to ensure that appropriate quality assurance and accreditation systems are in place for the crossborder delivery of programs. Respondents also pointed to lost opportunities for improved national profile and competitiveness due to the lack of coordination at the national level in terms of the different actors, programs, and policies that address international education.

While the benefits of internationalization are many and varied, so are the risks. The growing commercialization of higher education, the increase in foreign degree mills, and the threat of brain drain were identified as three serious risks associated with internationalization. HEIs around the world report a continuing growth in institutional networks, student mobility, and research as forms of international collaboration; but the recruitment of fee-paying students continues to gain importance and double degrees are rising in popularity. The shift from international co-operation to national competitiveness as a motive for internationalization was dramatically confirmed as respondents placed increased cooperation and solidarity in fourth place out of seven rationales and ranked competitiveness as number one. The increased interest in and use of international education as a tool for strategic alliances (economic, political, technological) was also confirmed. To the surprise of many, income generation was ranked very low as a rationale or benefit of internationalization. Finally, the shift in geographic priorities from the 2003 IAU survey was revealing as Europe moved to top place, followed by the Asia Pacific in second, and North America in third. All in all, the survey findings provide useful information and insights on how the internationalization process is evolving and, more importantly, on how it can contribute to the development of individuals, institutions, countries, and society at large.

Note: This chapter has been excerpted from *Internationalization of Higher Education: New Directions, New Challenges,* The 2005 IAU Global Survey Report (Paris: International Association of Universities). The complete report is available from the International Association of Universities http://www.unesco.org/ iau/internationalization/index.html.

INDEX

A

Abroad. *See* crossborder.
Academic Co-operation Association (ACA), 55, 63
Academic exchange. *See* partnerships.
Academic freedom, 13
Academic mobility. *See* mobility.
Academic quality. *See* quality.
Academic rationales. *See* rationales.
access
 and commercial education, 142
 and crossborder programs, 81, 110, 133, 173, 228
 and GATS, 144–145, 172–173
 demand for, 14, 110, 145, 157, 182
 equity of, 14
accountability, 42, 143, 173. *See also* quality assessment/assurance.
Accra Declaration on GATS and the Internationalization of Higher Education, 176
accreditation
 and commercial providers, 124, 176
 and crossborder education, 12, 14–16, 28, 36, 84, 130, 142, 175, 228
 and quality, 41
 commercialization of, 125–126
 diversity of, 125–126
 monitoring of, 114, 124–134. *See also* quality assurance.
accreditation mills, 15, 102, 125, 177. *See also* providers *and* degree mills.
accreditation registry, need for, 125–126
ACE. *See* American Council on Education.
AUF. *See* Association of Francophone Universities.
administration. *See* institution-level.
admissions, 36, 56
Advtech, 139
affiliation. *See* partnerships.
Africa
 and higher education internationalization, 87, 114, 189–190, 194, 197, 207, 214
 perceptions of risks/benefits, 201–202, 204–205, 222
 ranking of, 214–216
 rationales and priorities, 197, 207, 217, 220–223, 225

African Association of Universities, 11
African Leadership Forum (AFL), 114
African Union, 11
Africanization, 7
Aga Khan Foundation, 11, 114
aid to trade. *See* development.
Al-Abram Canadian University, 116
Al-Azhar Al-Sharif University, 113
Albania, 168
Alliant International University, 114, 116
alternative providers. *See* providers.
ambiguity, of GATS regulations, 159–160, 164–165, 172
American Council on Education, 87
American University, 112
APEC. *See* Asia Pacific Economic Council.
Apollo Group, 8, 11, 97, 116, 138–139
Apollo International, 115
"approach," differentiated from "definition," 31
 levels of, 31–33
APQN. *See* Asia Pacific Quality Network.
Aptec, 8, 11, 101, 118, 138–139
Arab Open University, 105
area studies. *See* curriculum.
Argentina, 117
Armenia, 168
articulation agreements, 24, 56, 94, 100, 128
 defined, 105
Arum, S., 20
Asia Pacific
 and crossborder education, 113–114, 118, 130, 139, 189–191, 207
 demand for education, 137, 140
 perceptions of risks/benefits, 201–202, 204–205, 217, 220–221
 ranking of, 214–216
 rationales of, 197
Asia Pacific Economic Council, 5
Asia Pacific Network for Quality Assurance, 11, 128
Asia Pacific Quality Network, 128
 toolkit of, 176
Asian Development Bank, 11
assessment. *See* quality *and* students.
Association of African Universities Workshop, 176
Association of Canadian Universities and Colleges, 116

229

INDEX

Association of Commonwealth Universities (ACU), 11
Association of Francophone Universities, 11
Association of Universities and Colleges of Canada, 87, 89
"at home internationalization, ix, 22–24, 33, 35. *See also* crossborder.
attractiveness. *See* competitiveness.
AUCC. *See* Association of Universities and Colleges of Canada.
audit. *See* quality.
austerity. *See* funding.
Australia
　branch campuses, 212
　commercial programs, 43, 88, 139, 141, 194, 220
　crossborder higher education, 85–86, 97, 111–114, 117–119, 210
　data collection, 90
　public funding, 140–141
　quality assurance, 128–129
　terminology preferences, 87
　trade requests, 156, 161–163, 165–166, 168
Australian Universities Quality Agency, 128
Australian Vice-Chancellors Committee, 53, 86, 90
Austria, 168
autonomy. *See* governance.
AVCC. Australian Vice-Chancellors Committee.
AVCC Offshore Programs of Australian Universities, 119
Award. *See* qualifications.

B

Bahrain, 97, 112
Baldridge Awards, 126
barriers. *See* trade.
Belgium, 112–113
benchmarking
　and internationalization, 24, 28, 49, 52, 57, 59, 64, 100, 131, 208
　defined, 59
　tracking measures, 52
benefits/risks, of crossborder education, 184, 199–206. *See also* named regions.
best practices. *See* benchmarking.
bilateral agreements. *See* partnerships *and* exchanges.
Boeing Company, 112
Bologna Process, 7, 195, 197, 214, 222, 227

Bologna University, 117
Bond University, 114
borderless education, 19, 81, 84–85, 87, 89. *See also* crossborder education.
"borderless" issues, 9
bottom up rules. *See* GATS.
BPP Holdings, 139
brain drain/gain, 12, 15–16, 26, 81, 108, 133, 180, 197, 200–205, 222, 227–228. *See also* capacity.
branch campus, ix, 24, 33, 83, 94, 99, 112, 128, 141, 150, 155, 158, 211–213, 220
　defined, 105. *See also* delivery.
branding, 15, 28, 43, 125, 141, 157–158, 177, 216–217. *See also* reputation.
Brazil, 97
"Breaking News" (bulletins), 112
bricks and mortar institutions. *See* traditional institutions.
British Council, 53
British University, 112
Bulgaria, 114, 168
bursaries. *See* scholarships.
business programs, 174
Business of Borderless Education, 89

C

Cambodia, 168
Canada, 97, 112, 116, 139, 195, 212
Canadian Bureau for International Education, 53
Canadian Institute of Business and Technology, 116
capacity
　and education, 142, 157
　as rationale, 24, 99, 108
　building, 27, 95, 99, 109, 141, 180, 184
　human resources, 26, 31, 34, 172, 183, 193, 196–197, 208, 221–222
Caparo Group, 114
Capital Alliance Group, 139
Career Education Corporation, 116, 139
Caribbean, 190, 194, 197. *See also* Latin America.
Carnegie Foundation, 11
Carnegie Mellon University, 97, 106, 114
CBIE. *See* Canadian Bureau for International Education.
Center for Education, Research, and Innovation, 85, 109, 156
Centra Software, 139

230

INDEX

Centro Escolar University, 139
CERI. *See* Center for Education, Research, and Innovation.
CHEA. *See* Council for Higher Education Accreditation.
Chicago University of Graduate School in Business, 113
Chile, 97, 106, 117
China, and crossborder education, 43, 97, 113, 115–116, 118, 130–131, 155, 168, 212, 220
Chinese Service Centre for Scholarly Exchange, 130
Chinese Taipei, and trade requests, 165–166, 168
CIDA, 11
citizenship. *See* cooperation *and* immigration.
Click2Learn, 139
climate change, 14
"Code of Conduct for CrossBorder/Transnational Delivery of Higher Education Programs," 86
"Code of Ethical Practice in International Education," 53
"Code of Ethical Practice in the Offshore Provision of Education and the Educational Services by Higher Australian Higher Education Institutions," 86, 127
"Code of Ethical Practice in the Provision of Education to International Students by Australian Universities," 53
"Code of Good Practice in the Provision of Transnational Education," 86, 89, 126–127, 178
"Code of Practice for Overseas Education Institutions Operating in Mauritius," 86, 127
"Code of Practice on Transnational Education," 83
codes of practice, 52–53, 83, 86, 89, 126–127, 129
collaboration. *See* partnerships.
Columbia University, 97
commercial providers, 8, 13, 16, 24, 29, 31, 35, 101–102, 104, 137–146, 173–174, 227
and GATS, 150, 155
in China, 130–131
quality, 14, 138
profit motive, 26–27, 109, 138–140, 143, 179, 181
publicly traded, 137–138, 173
traditional institutions as, 140–142
traditional values, 172, 178
types of, 137–140

commercialization of crossborder higher education, 9, 13–14, 16, 29–30, 87, 94–95, 98, 101, 120, 124, 133, 171–172, 174, 179, 228
and quality assurance, 15, 177
as priority, 219–221
risks, 133, 200, 204–205, 220. *See also* market *and* trade.
commodification. *See* commercialization.
communication. *See* information and communication.
community outreach. *See* culture groups.
comparative education, as term, 19
competitiveness, 26, 28, 31, 43, 111
and quality, 42
as rationale/priority, 193, 196–198, 216–219, 228
differentiated from competition, 218
regional, 215–216. *See also* cooperation.
Concorde Career Colleges, 139
conferences/seminars, international. *See* partnerships.
conflicts, 29
Congo RP, and GATS, 168
constituencies. *See* stakeholders.
consultancy. *See* external services.
consulting, 100
consumer movement. *See* stakeholders.
consumption abroad, defined, 150, 154
contract education. *See* commercial providers.
cooperation, 215
as priority, 226
as rationale, 197–198, 201, 202, 218–219
as term, 82, 196
examples of, 225. *See also* partnerships.
copyright. *See* intellectual property.
Corinthian Colleges, 139
Cornell University, 97, 112
corporate sector. *See* commercial providers *and* funding.
corporate universities, 8, 101
cost-sharing. *See* fee-paying.
Costa Rica, 97, 117, 168
Council for Higher Education Accreditation, 87, 89, 129–130
Council of Europe, 83–84, 86, 126–127
Council of Europe Convention on the Recognition of Qualifications, 89
coverage rate. *See* access.
CPC. *See* United Nations Provisional Central Product Classification.
credentials. *See* qualifications.

231

INDEX

credit transfer, 224, 227
crime, 14, 30. *See also* security.
Croatia, 168
crossborder education, 12, 19, 33, 51, 81–82, 86, 217
   and GATS, 88, 150
   as rationale, 197–198, 219–220
   defined/described, xi, 19, 23–24, 81–95, 98, 104, 111–119, 137
   delivery guidelines, 36, 53
   examples of, 112–116
   growth of, 171, 213
   mobility, 81, 98, 99, 101, 104–108, 110–112, 115, 117, 120
   risks/benefits of, 228. *See also* quality.
"Crossborder Guidelines," 87
culture, and diversity, 13, 16, 21–23, 29, 79, 81, 179–180, 193, 196, 199, 228
   and identity, 25, 200, 222–223, 227. *See also* homogenization, capacity, *and* curriculum.
cultural understanding, as rationale, 26–27, 31, 57, 107–109, 125, 194–196, 200, 221. *See also* capacity.
culture groups, outreach to, 22–23, 211, 213, 225
curriculum, 36, 94, 99
   as rationale/priority, 158, 193, 195–196
   delivery of, 22
   internationalization of, xi, 6, 14, 16, 22–23, 30, 57, 68–70, 109, 179–180, 208, 211, 213–214, 225–227
   joint development of, 30, 81, 100
   risks/benefits to, 200, 204–205
   tracking measures, 52
CVCP, 89
cyber islands, 114
Czech Republic, 116, 168

D

DAAD British Council, 11
Dar Al Faisal University, 112
data collection, 82, 90–94, 117–119
De Montfort University, 114
De Paul University, 97
De Wit, Hans, 20
degree mills, 101, 125, 128, 176–177, 200, 204, 217, 228
degrees, joint/double/dual, 23–24, 68, 94, 99, 105, 113–115, 119, 128, 211, 213, 224–225, 227–228. *See also* recognition.

delivery
   and assessment, 55, 91
   as mobility, 225
   modes of, 22, 24, 33, 83, 133, 137, 180, 184
demand, for higher education, 8–9, 12, 26, 81, 97, 118, 120, 130, 137, 145, 172–173. *See also* access.
demographics, 14
Department of Education, Science, and Technology (Australia), 90, 118
DEST. *See* Department of Education, Science, and Technology.
destination countries. *See* receiving countries.
developed/developing countries, and internationalization, 93, 195, 211–213
   rationales/priorities, 197, 220–221, 223–224
   risks/benefits, 203–206, 217–218
   self-assignment to, 100. *See also* International Association of Universities, surveys.
development aid, 12, 24, 27, 36, 51, 71, 101, 126, 157–158, 176, 182–184
   evaluation of, 52, 71
   projects, 71, 82, 133, 179, 195–196, 211–213, 218–219, 224
   trends in, 12, 98, 137, 187–188. *See also* partnerships.
DeVry (educational company), 101, 116, 139
diaspora. *See* brain drain.
Digital Think, 139
direct teaching. *See* face-to-face teaching.
distance education, ix, 12, 24, 33, 83–84, 88, 89, 106, 131, 137, 150, 161, 210–211, 213, 224–225, 227
   Hong Kong, 131
   and Japan, 161. *See also* delivery.
diversity. *See* culture, funding, programs, staff, *and* students.
Docent (company), 139
Doha Round, 164
double degrees. *See* degrees.
dual citizenship. *See* immigration *and* mobility.
Dubai Health Care City, 97
Dublin Business School, 116
Duke University, 115

E

Ecole Polytechnique de Montreal, 116
Ecole Superiure du Commerce Exterier de Paris, 115

Ecollege, 139
economy. *See* funding *and* partnerships.
"education cities," 107, 138
Education City, 112
Education Management Corporation, 139
Egypt, 112–113, 116, 155
Einstein, Albert, 43
e-learning. *See* distance education.
El Salvador, 155
elitism, 95, 133, 184, 200, 204–205
employment. *See* labor market.
Endicott College, 116
English, as language of instruction, 8, 13, 95, 133, 179, 184, 204–205, 222–223
entry requirements, 180
environment, 9, 30
Epic Group, 139
equity ceiling, 154
ERASMUS, 5, 224
Estonia, 168
ethnic groups. *See* culture groups.
EU-ASEAN, 5
EU-Latin America, 5
Euro University, 112
Europe
 and internationalization, 87, 114–115, 139, 188–191, 194, 207, 214
 ranking of, 214–216
 rationales/policies, 197, 220–221, 224, 226
 risks/benefits, 204–205, 222
 regional cooperation, 226
European Commission, 5, 11
European Community/Union, 5, 7, 16, 165, 168, 222
European University Association, 11
evaluation, 39, 41, 43–45, 48, 49, 51–54, 56, 175. *See also* quality assessment *and* peer review.
EVCI Career Colleges, 139
exchanges, 100, 179, 182, 195, 218. *See also* students.
exempt services, 158–159
export of education. *See* crossborder education.
exporting country. *See* sending country.
external services, 71
extracurricular activities
 and internationalization, 3, 22–23, 34, 68, 211, 213, 225

F

"face." *See* self-assessment.
face-to-face education, 33, 81, 100, 105, 131
faculty/staff
 diversity as rationale, 195, 199, 201
 internationalization of, 29, 36, 59, 67, 70–71, 113, 227
 recruitment of, 71, 154, 157, 213
 tenure and promotion, 208
 tracking measures for, 52. *See also* mobility.
Far Eastern National University, 115, 139
fee-paying students, 9, 26, 138, 143, 145
 recruitment of, 28, 57, 108, 141, 174, 211, 213–214, 220–221, 228
field work, 99–100. *See also* research.
financing. *See* funding.
Florida State University, 117
for-profit education, 3, 24, 28, 104, 107, 138
Ford Foundation, 11
foreign language studies, 23, 51, 71, 213, 225, 227. *See also* English.
foreign relations/policy, 35, 141, 180
foreign students. *See* students.
foundations. *See* funding.
France, 97, 113, 115, 212
franchising, ix, 24, 26, 33, 83, 94, 99, 100, 108, 113, 141, 150, 157, 220
 defined, 105
 evaluation of, 128
 examples of, 112, 115. *See also* delivery.
FSBM Holdings, 139
Fudan University, 113
funding
 and crossborder education, 36, 51, 67–68, 81, 85, 209, 228
 and foreign aid, 57, 94
 and GATS, 145, 158
 and student mobility, 224
 demand-driven, 144
 models of, 8–9, 100, 141–145, 179, 226
 private, 9, 12, 15–16
 public, 8–9, 13, 29, 42, 94–95, 140–145, 172–174, 184
 trends in, 103, 138, 157, 178. *See also* research *and* scholarships.
fusion, of culture, 179
FYR Macedonia, and GATS education commitment, 168

233

INDEX

G

Gambia, 168
Garratt's Limited, 139
GATE. *See* Global Alliance for Transnational Education.
GATS. *See* General Agreement on Trade in Services.
GATT. *See* General Agreement on Trade and Tariffs.
General Agreement on Trade and Tariffs, 149, 160
General Agreement on Trade in Services (1994), 149, 161, 166, 171–185
  ambiguity of, 159–160, 164–165, 172
  analysis of, 150–151, 158–163, 180
  and education, x, 13, 27, 88–90, 108, 144, 149–169, 176, 181–182
  and mobility, 107, 127, 171–185
  bottom-up rules, 152–153, 155–156, 165
  classifications, 151
  exempt services, 172
  negotiations, 163–166, 182
  structure and purpose, 149–150
  unconditional obligations ("top down"), 151–153. *See also* trade.
Georgetown University School of Foreign Service, 97, 112
Georgia, 168
German Technische Universitat Munchen, 113
German University, 112
Germany, 113, 212
Ghana, 168
Gilion Hotel School, 115
  Global Alliance for Transnational Education, 53–54, 64, 83–84, 89
  "global education," as term, 19. *See also* crossborder education.
  global warming, 9
Global Education Index, 102, 115, 129, 173
Global Higher Education Index, 138–139
globalization, and education, 4–6, 30, 42, 172, 179
  defined, x, 1–2, 4–5, 21–22, 82–83
governance. *See* institution level.
government. *See* national level.
Greece, 115, 155
Green, D., 40–41
Guidelines for Quality Provision in Crossborder Higher Education, 85–86, 89, 127–132, 176
Gulf University of Science and Technology, 115

H

Haiti, 168
Hanoi University of Technology, 113
Hartford Holdings, 139
Harvard University, 97
Harvey, L., 40–41
HDI. *See* Human Development Index.
health issues, 9, 14, 30
Health Stream, 139
Henley Management College, 114
Heriot-Watt University, 112
Hibernia College, 106
"Higher Education in a More Globalized World," 85
Higher School of Economics, 115
Ho Chi Minh City National University, 113
home countries. *See* sending countries.
homogenization, 13, 16, 179, 200, 204–206, 225
Hong Kong, 43, 90, 131–132, 165
Horizon Education & Technologies, 139
host countries. *See* receiving countries.
human capital. *See* brain drain.
human resources, 16, 26, 108, 120, 180, 222. *See also* capacity.
human rights, 9
Human Development Index, 195, 197. *See also* developed/developing countries.
Hungary, 168
hybridization, 13, 16, 179. *See also* homogenization.

I

IAU. *See* International Association of Universities.
IBM, 116
ICT. *See* information and communication technologies.
IDP Australia, 81, 109
IMHE. *See* Institutional Management of Higher Education.
immigration, and crossborder education, 9, 15–17, 36, 95
  and skilled workers, 109, 157
  and student recruitment, 26, 108, 227
  policy, 85, 154, 180, 183
"Implications of WTO/GATS for Higher Education in Africa," 176
importing country. *See* receiving country.

income generation, 25, 26, 29–32, 95, 108, 111, 157, 184
  and internationalization, 31, 32, 109, 182, 193, 194, 196, 199, 200, 212
  as rationale/priority, 29–30, 108–109, 157, 193–196, 199, 219–221, 228
independent campuses. *See* institutions *and* branch.
India, and branch campuses, 212
  and crossborder higher education, 97, 112, 114–116, 118, 139, 157
  and GATS, 155
Informatics Holdings, 139
information and communication technologies, 3–7, 9, 13, 29, 179
institutions, and internationalization, 19, 27–33, 64–80, 213–214
  governance, 6, 12–13, 34
  independent, 24, 94, 105, 141, 228
  policies/strategies, 33–36
  quality assurance, 56, 180
Internationalization, strategies/process of, 33–35. *See also* national, provider, regional, *and* reputation.
Institutional Management of Higher Education, 55, 63
intellectual property, 81, 90, 105, 180, 183, 185, 227
intercultural knowledge. *See* culture.
international agreements. *See* partnerships.
International Association of Universities, 11, 18, 87, 89, 176–177, 187
  2003 survey, 187, 199, 199, 206, 208, 214–215, 219, 221–222, 228
  2005 survey, x, 87, 187–228
International College of IT and Management, 113
international cooperation. *See* cooperation.
international development. *See* development.
International Institute of Information Technology, 115
International Policy and Development Unit of the Ministry of Education (New Zealand), 90, 118
International Standards Organization. *See* ISO.
international students. *See* students.
international understanding. *See* culture.
International University (Vietnam), 11, 113, 114, 116
International Virtual University, 106
internationalization. *See also* crossborder education, curriculum, culture, *and* mobility.
  as sustainable policy, 32, 52, 133, 206–210
  benchmarks of, 52, 59, 208
  competencies in, 3, 16–17, 29, 32
  defined/described, ix-xi, 1–8, 19–24, 40, 41, 44, 46, 53, 64, 82–83, 120, 124, 207–208, 210–211
  importance of, 190–192
  obstacles to, 209–210
  risks/benefits of, 199–206
  strategies, xi, 33, 39–40, 60, 64
  surveys, 187–228. *See also* crossborder education, curriculum, culture, *and* mobility.
"Internationalization and Trade in Higher Education: Opportunities and Challenges," 109
"Internationalization Cycle," phases of, 39, 45
Internationalization Quality Review, 52–55, 63–65, 79
  as strategic planning tool, 56, 78–79
  guidelines, 43, 52, 63, 77–80
  methodology, 75–80
  peer review phase of, 70–77
  self-assessment phase of, 52, 65
  timing of, 75, 78–79
internships, 23, 50, 69, 94, 99–100. *See also* curriculum.
Inti Universal Holdings, 139
IQRP. *See* Internationalization Quality Review Process.
Iran, 97, 112
Ireland, 97, 112, 116, 139, 155
ISO 9000+, 52, 55–57, 64
Israel, 112, 155
IT. *See* information and communication technologies.
Italy, 97, 117, 155
ITT Educational Services, 139

J

JAICA (Japan), 11
Jamaica, 168
Japan, and GATS, 5, 145, 155–156, 165, 168
Japan Foundation, 11
Jinan University, 97, 113
Johns Hopkins University, 97
joint degrees. *See* degrees.
joint ownership/ventures. *See* partnerships.
Jones International University, 11, 54
Jordan, 97, 168

INDEX

K

Kaplan (educational company), 116
Kazakhstan, 97
Kenya, 114
Kingdom University, 97
KK Modi Group, 116
"knowledge center," 114
knowledge economy/society, 1, 5, 6, 12, 14–15, 26, 108, 29, 36, 42, 95, 97, 120, 133, 143, 157, 162, 163, 172, 180–181
knowledge generation, as rationale for internationalization, 193–195
"knowledge parks," 107, 138
knowledge production, 6, 25, 30–31, 194–195, 200, 202, 203. See also research *and* partnerships.
"Knowledge Village," crossborder higher education in, 97
Korea, 115, 165
Kuwait, 115
Kyrgyz Republic, 168

L

labor market, 20, 25, 29, 110
language of instruction, 13, 85, 95, 110, 133, 179, 184, 223. See also English.
language, of report-writing, 72
language testing, 28, 151, 183. See also foreign language.
Larsen, K., 9, 101, 156
Latin America (and Caribbean), and crossborder education, 87, 105, 116–117, 126, 178, 189–191, 194, 195, 197, 201, 205, 207, 214–218, 220–222, 226
   policies, 207
   rationales/priorities of, 197, 216–222, 228
   risks/benefits, 200–205, 214, 216–220, 222, 225, 228
Latvia, and GATS education commitment, 169
Laureate Education, 97, 115–116
legal expertise, 227
Les Roches (training center), 115
Lesotho, 169
liberalization. See trade barriers.
licensing, 36, 81, 90, 101–103, 123, 124, 137, 154, 159, 174, 175. See also regulation *and* providers.
Liechtenstein, 169
lifelong learning, 1, 4, 6, 9, 12, 14, 156, 172
links. See partnership.

Lisbon Convention, 126, 178
Lithuania, 169
loans. See students.
London School of Economics, 115

M

Malaysia, 5, 43, 90, 106, 113, 115, 118, 131, 139, 166, 220
Malaysian Qualifications Authority, 131
Mali, 169
manufacturing, standards of, 55–56, 58, 126
market access, 153, 160. See also General Agreement on Trade in Services.
market approach/model, 19, 21, 24, 42, 144, 146, 176, 179, 208
market economy, 6, 12, 97, 181
marketing campaigns, 111, 141. See also branding *and* commercialization.
Mauritius, 114
Mauritius Tertiary Education Commission, 127
McKinnon, K. R., 59
McMaster University, 116
merger/acquisition, 94, 99, 106
Mexico, 97, 106, 116, 155, 169
Microsoft, 116
Middle East, and internationalization, 112, 189–190, 195, 207, 213, 215–217, 220–221
   rationale/policy, 197, 202, 217, 221, 223, 226
   risks/benefits, 200, 204–205, 220, 222
Middlesex University, 115
mission statements, 36
mobility, academic, 3, 16, 81, 85, 86
   defined, 82
   and crossborder higher education, 12, 25, 94, 97–120, 226
   of faculty/staff, 5, 15–16, 25, 28, 34, 49–51, 55, 76, 83, 105, 211, 213–214, 224
   of professionals, 184
   of programs/projects, ix, 8, 23–24, 81, 84, 86, 94, 99–100, 104, 124, 137, 171–180, 182–184, 210
   of providers, ix, 23–24, 81, 86, 94, 124, 138, 184
   of students, ix, 6–7, 23–24, 26, 57, 81, 99, 108, 150, 193, 211, 213–214, 223–224, 227–228
modal negotiating approach, 165–166
Modern College of Business and Science, 115
modes of supply, 150–151. See also delivery.
Modi Apollo International Institute, 116
Moldova, 169
Monash University, 106, 114

monitoring, 39–60, 124–125, 141, 172. *See also* regulations.
monopolies, 160
Moscow International Slavonic Institute, 114
Moscow State University of Industry, 114
most favored nation rule, 144–145, 149, 152, 166
Motorola corporate university, 8, 11, 101, 138
movement. *See* mobility.
multilateral. *See* partnerships.
multinationalization. *See* crossborder.

N

NAFTA. *See* North American Free Trade Association.
name recognition. *See* branding.
nation building, 16, 27, 31, 108, 113. *See also* capacity.
National Indian Institute of Technology, 118
national level
   and crossborder education, 19, 24, 33, 173, 183, 217, 228
   and GATS, 149
   as stakeholders, 128, 176
   policies, 32, 35–36, 42, 105, 124, 129, 144–145, 153, 162, 164, 172, 178–181, 183–184, 187, 228. *See also* regulations.
National University Association, 189, 191–192, 195–196, 198–199, 203, 211–212, 216, 219–220, 223, 226
National University of Singapore, 113
necessity test, of GATS, 160
Nepal, 169
Netherlands, 97, 113, 115
Netherlands Business School (Universitiet Nijenrode), 97, 114
networks. *See* partnerships.
New England Association of Schools and Colleges, 86
New Horizons Worldwide, 139
New Zealand
   and crossborder higher education, 90, 117–119, 132, 140–141, 194, 212, 220
   and GATS, 156, 161, 163, 166, 168
New Zealand Qualifications Authority, 132
New Zealand Vice Chancellors Committee, 132
niche markets, 172
Nigeria, 97, 114
NIIT, 139
nongovernment organizations, 86–88, 107
nonprofits. *See* providers.

North America. *See also* United States *and* Canada.
   and internationalization, 87, 115–116, 189–190, 207, 214–216
   ranking, 214–216
   rationales, 197
   risks/benefits, 200, 204–205, 220, 222
North American Free Trade Association, 5
Northface University/Northface Learning, Inc., 116
Norway, 169
NUA. *See* National University Association.
NUFFIC, 11

O

OBHE. *See* Observatory of Borderless Higher Education.
objectives. *See* national-level policies.
Observatory for Borderless Higher Education, 87–88, 112, 115, 119, 138
OECD. *See* Organization for Economic and Community Development.
offshore. *See* crossborder education *and* students.
Oman, 115, 169
online delivery. *See* e-learning *and* distance education.
Organization for Economic and Community Development, 63, 156
outcomes-based approach, 42

P

Pakistan, 97, 114
Panama, 97, 117, 169
partnerships, data collection on, 90
   and mobility, 30, 105, 107, 176
   and quality assessment/assurance, 42, 52, 124–125, 158
   and research, 26, 57, 138
   in crossborder education, 24, 30–31, 36, 68, 70, 86, 98, 100–101, 107, 109, 111–119, 125–127, 130, 138, 143, 158, 175, 180, 211, 228
   models/examples of, 34, 81, 85, 104, 112–113, 118, 133, 154, 157, 175
   trends in, 30, 97, 98, 112, 120, 155. *See also* mobility.
Pearson (educational company), 8, 11, 101
peer review, 65, 72–80
Peoples Republic of China. *See* China.
performance indicator. *See* tracking measure.

INDEX

Philippines, 115, 139, 155
Phoenix University, 97, 116
planning, 36, 47, 67
PLATO Learning, 139
plurilateral negotiating approach, 165–166
Poland, 112, 169
policies. *See* institution-level, national-level, partnerships, rationales, *and* named regions.
presence of natural persons. *See* GATS.
Primeserv, 139
Prince Sultan Private University, 112
"Principles for Transnational Education," 54
"Principles of Good Practice for the Educational Programs for Non-US Nationals," 86, 127
private funding. *See* funding.
privatization, 42, 171
professional associations. *See* stakeholders.
professional development, 24, 100
professors. *See* faculty.
profile. *See* reputation.
profit motive, 174–175, 179–180, 184. *See also* providers *and* rationales.
profit. *See* providers.
programs. *See also* curriculum *and* commercialization.
 approaches to, 31
 diversity of, 200, 202–203
 quality assessment/assurance, 42
Programme on Institutional Management of Higher Education. *See* Institutional Management of Higher Education.
programs. *See* curriculum.
promotion and tenure, 227. *See also* faculty.
providers, 20, 22, 84, 111. *See also* commercial, rogue, *and* stateless.
 data collection, 90–93
 defined, 98
 GATS status of, 158, 183
 internationalization strategies, 33–35
 mobility, 82, 90, 98–100, 105–106
 nonprofits, 3, 24
 quality, 42, 81, 101
 types of, 12, 90, 95, 102–104, 133, 183
PRT. *See* peer review.
public good, education as, 13, 16, 145, 156, 174, 178–179, 219, 228
public/private education, mix of, 103, 162–163, 172, 174
publishers, as providers, 138–140
Puerto Rico, 97
Purdue University, 115

Q

QAA. Quality Assurance Agency for Higher Education.
Qatar, 112
Qatar Education City, 97
qualification. *See also* providers *and* recognition.
 diversity of, 107, 133, 200
 fraudulent, 176
 in China, 130
quality, academic, 39, 184, 194–195
 as rationale, 43, 193, 199, 216–217
 and internationalization, 67, 83–85
 benefit/risks of, 184, 200–205
 defined, 40–41, 175
 terminology of, 41, 66
quality assurance/accreditation, 12, 14, 16, 36, 39, 41–43, 73–80, 110–111, 131, 217–218, 226
 agencies, as stakeholders, 5, 127, 176
 and codes of practice, 86, 127
 in receiving countries, 124, 133–134, 166
 need for, 41–43, 92, 120, 124, 125, 131–133
 of providers, 81, 90, 107, 138, 174, 180, 227
 trends, 175–177, 180
"quality review fatigue" syndrome, 78–79
Quality Assurance Agency for Higher Education, 129
"Quality Assurance Code of Practice: Collaborative Provisions," 86, 127

R

Raffles LaSalle, 113, 115, 118, 139
rankings, 42, 158
rationales, types of, 16, 20–21, 24–31, 33, 35–36, 67, 76, 107–111, 156–157, 172–173, 182–183, 192–199. *See also* named regions *and* countries.
receiving countries, 140–143, 145, 158, 182. *See also* partnerships.
recognition, data collection on, 92
 defined, 104
 of degree/qualification, 12, 15, 17, 81, 95, 99–100, 104, 107, 111, 120, 126–127, 138, 155, 161, 178, 180, 184, 224–226
 of providers, 104, 124–125, 143, 178. *See also* qualification *and* regulation.
recognition agencies, as stakeholders, 127, 176
recruitment. *See also* immigration, students, *and* faculty.

regionalism, 10–12, 17, 111–117, 214. *See also* surveys.
regionalization, 4, 5, 7, 12, 19, 196
regions, benefits/risks of internationalization, 201–202, 204, 220–223
  rationales/priorities, 124, 175, 188–189, 193, 196–198, 218, 223, 226
registration, of providers, 107, 138, 174. *See also* providers.
regulation, and crossborder education, 36, 145, 172, 174, 180
  by receiving countries, 128, 130, 133–134
  for sending countries, 128, 132–133
regulations, 128, 132, 172
"Regulations on Chinese and Foreign Cooperation in Running Schools," 130
repatriation of earnings, 107, 138, 154
"Report on Transnational Education and Regulations," 89
reputation, institutional, 15, 28–29, 109, 111, 125, 177, 193, 195, 216
research, 36, 94, 99, 100
  and internationalization, 22–24, 34, 35, 69–70, 82, 85, 93, 193–194, 200–203, 208, 211, 213–214, 223, 225
  and partnerships, 34, 215, 227
  and trade agreements, 182–183, 185
  as priority, 195–196, 199, 224
  funding, 223, 228
  not by new providers, 101, 138
  tracking measures for, 52
residency status. *See* immigration *and* mobility.
review. *See* peer review *and* quality assessment.
risk management, 180, 227
risks. *See* benefits *and* named regions.
RMIT University, 113
rogue providers, 95, 100–102, 120, 124, 132–133, 176, 184.
Russia, 114–115
Russian-Indian Center for Advanced Computer Research, 115
Rwanda, 169

S

sabbaticals, 36, 94, 100. *See also* faculty.
safety. *See* security.
SAT. *See* self-assessment.
satellite campus, 26, 100, 108, 150, 154, 224–225
Saudia Arabia, 112, 169
scholars. *See* faculty.
scholarships, 100, 144, 196, 212. *See also* human resources.
science and technology. *See* research.
sector, education. *See* national.
sectoral negotiating approach, 166
security, 9, 14, 110, 215, 227
SEG International, 118, 139
Sejong University, 115
self-assessment, 52, 76–77, 80
  in IQRP, 64–65, 72–78. *See also* peer review.
self-interest, as rationale, 156–158. *See also* commercial providers.
sending countries, 140, 157–158, 176, 182. *See also* partnerships.
Serebra Learning Corporation, 139
service sectors, 152
Shanghai Jiao Tong University, 113
"Sharing Quality Higher Education across Borders," 89
Sharing Quality Higher Education across Borders: A Statement on Behalf of Higher Education Institutions Worldwide, 87, 177
SIDA (Sweden), 11
Sierra Leone, 169
Singapore, 5, 90, 113, 115, 118, 139
SkillSoft Corporation, 139
Slovak Republic, 169
Slovenia, 169
social/cultural. *See* cultural understanding.
software and consultancy firms, as providers, 138–140
solidarity. *See* cooperation.
South Africa, 87, 90, 106, 114, 139, 155–156
South African Ministry of Education, 86
Spain, 97, 155
staff. *See* faculty.
stakeholders, and internationalization, 10, 20–21, 42, 89, 107, 127, 176–177
Stamford College/Holdings, 118, 139
stand-alone institutions. *See* institutions.
Stanford University, 113, 115
stateless providers, 90, 104, 124–125, 130, 132, 141, 175, 178
statistics. *See* data.
Stevens Institute of Technology, 112
Stockholm School of Economics, 115
strategies, as rationale/priority, 26, 30, 108, 193, 196–198, 221, 228
  of internationalization, 31–34, 79, 133, 157, 182–184, 206–210
Strayer Education, 139

239

INDEX

students, as stakeholders, 42, 127, 176
   assessment of, 180
   diversity of, 13, 195, 199, 221
   data on, 140, 154
   exchanges, 69–70, 94
   foreign, 31, 51, 56, 68, 94, 213
   funding, 36, 182
   international opportunities for, 29, 50, 69–70, 94, 210
   recruitment of, 16, 36, 57, 69, 83, 86, 108–109, 129, 151, 180, 211–212, 218. *See also* fee-paying students, scholarships, *and* commercial providers.
study abroad, 36, 49–50, 56, 69–70, 82, 99–100, 150
study centers, 106, 158
supply-driven funding, 143
supply modes. *See* GATS.
surveys (2003, 2005), 187–228. *See also* International Association of Universities.
Sweden, 155
Swinburne University of Technology, 113
Switzerland, 97, 115, 169
SWOT (strengths, weaknesses, opportunities, and threats), 76
Sylvan Learning Systems. *See* Laureate Education.
Syracuse University, 115

T

Tata Infotech, 139
tax laws, 107
teaching/learning process. *See* curriculum *and* research.
teaching/testing centers, 94
technical assistance, 24, 100, 183, 196. *See also* development.
Technical Institute of Monterrey, 117
Technische Universiteit Eindhoven, 113
technology, impact on crossborder higher education, 95
"technology zones," 107, 138
terminology of internationalization, ix, x–xi, 1–3, 66, 82, 87, 93, 107
terrorism. *See* security.
Tertiary Education Commission, 86
Texas A&M, 106, 112, 116
Thai-German Graduate School of Engineering, 113
Thailand, 97, 113, 115, 118, 155, 169
Thales (company), 112

Thomson (Canada), 8, 11, 101
Toolkit on Regulating Quality Assurance in Cross-Border Education, 128, 176
top down rules. *See* GATS.
Total Quality Management, 64
Toyota corporate university, 8, 101, 138
tracking measures, 39, 41, 43, 44–47, 52, 60
tradable commodity, education as, x, 13, 26, 88
trade agreements. *See also* General Agreement on Trade in Services *and* commercial providers.
   and crossborder education, 12–13, 14, 33, 81, 85, 95, 141, 145, 158, 175–185
   and good practice codes, 178
   barriers, 124, 141, 145, 153–155, 172–173, 175, 182, 227
trade liberalization, 6, 12
trade negotiators, 181–182
trade regulations, 124, 126, 144149
"Trade Related Aspects of Intellectual Property Rights," 183
traditional institutions, 138, 140, 178–179, 194
training centers, 115
transnational education, and GATS, 86, 88
   defined, 20, 82, 91,104. *See also* crossborder education.
"Transnational Education Quality Framework," 129
transparency, as GATS goal, 152–153, 155
Trinidad and Tobago, 169
TRIPS. *See* Trade Related Aspects of Intellectual Property Rights.
Troy State University, 106, 113
tuition fees, 212. *See also* fee-paying students.
Turkey, 155, 169
twinning agreements, ix, 24, 33, 83, 94, 99, 100, 105, 115, 128, 141, 150, 154,158. *See also* delivery modes.

U

U.K. *See* United Kingdom.
UK Open University, 115
UK Quality Assurance Agency, 86
UKCOSA. *See* United Kingdom Council for Overseas Student Affairs.
UMAP. *See* University Mobility Program of Asia Pacific.
UNDP. *See* United Nations Development Program.
UNESCO
   and crossborder higher education, 11, 83–85, 89, 112, 127–128, 178

conventions, 17, 126–127, 178
guidelines, 87, 176
toolkit of, 176
UNESCO/CEPES, 86, 127
UNESCO/OECD, 89. *See also* Organization for Economic and Community Development.
UNICEF, 11
United Arab Emirates, 97, 112
United Kingdom, 43, 87, 112, 117–119, 129, 140–141, 194, 210, 212
United Kingdom Council for Overseas Student Affairs, 53
United Kingdom Higher Education , 90, 118
United Nations Conference for Trade and Development, 164
United Nations Development Program, 164
United Nations Provisional Central Product Classification, 151
United States, and branch campuses, 212
and crossborder higher education, 112–113, 116, 139, 140–141, 194, 210
and trade requests, 156–157, 161–163, 165–166, 169
quality assurance/accreditation in, 129–130
United States Department of Education, 129
United States Distance Education Association, 54
"universe," root of "university," 123
Universidad del Valle de Mexico, 116
Universidad Europa de Madrid, 115
Universidad Interamericana, 116–117
Universitas, 11, 113
Université du Quebec, 116
Université Francaise d'Egypte, 112
Universitiet Nijenrode. *See* Netherlands Business School.
University Mobility Program of Asia Pacific, 5
University of Arizona, 112
University of Hanover, 112
University of Hawaii, 113
University of Hué, 113
University of Indianapolis/University of Indianapolis Athens, 106, 116

University of Missouri, St. Louis, 115
University of New South Wales, 113
University of Northern Virginia, 116
University of Oslo Center for Medical Studies, 115
University of Phoenix Online, 139
University of Southern Queensland, 115
University of the Incarnate Word, 116
University of Westminster (UK), 97
Uruguay Round, 149, 164
USAID, and higher education, 11
Uzbekistan, 97

V

validation. *See* recognition arrangements.
values. *See* public good *and* tradition.
Van de Water, J., 20
Van der Wende, M., 20
Vcampus Corporation, 139
Vietnam, 113, 115
Vincent-Lancrin, S., 156
virtual provider. *See* distance education.
virtual universities, 100, 104, 138, 150, 154
visas, 154, 155, 226. *See also* immigration *and* mobility.
visiting scholars, 211–213
vouchers, 144–145, 174

W

Washington Post, 116
Western International University, 116
Westernization, 13, 179
Woodhouse, D., 41
working permits. *See* immigration *and* mobility.
World Bank, 11, 164
World Trade Organization, 11, 88, 144–145, 149, 151–152, 158
and "Trade Related Aspects of Intellectual Property Rights," 183

Printed in the United States
210085BV00003B/1-6/P